D0728737

THE CHANGING TERRAIN OF RACE AND ETHNICITY

The Changing Terrain of Race and Ethnicity

Edited by

Maria Krysan and Amanda E. Lewis

Russell Sage Foundation ❧ New York

The Russell Sage Foundation

The Russell Sage Foundation, one of the oldest of America's general purpose foundations, was established in 1907 by Mrs. Margaret Olivia Sage for "the improvement of social and living conditions in the United States." The Foundation seeks to fulfill this mandate by fostering the development and dissemination of knowledge about the country's political, social, and economic problems. While the Foundation endeavors to assure the accuracy and objectivity of each book it publishes, the conclusions and interpretations in Russell Sage Foundation publications are those of the authors and not of the Foundation, its Trustees, or its staff. Publication by Russell Sage, therefore, does not imply Foundation endorsement.

BOARD OF TRUSTEES
Robert E. Denham, Chair

Alan S. Blinder	Jennifer L. Hochschild	Cora B. Marrett
Christine K. Cassel	Timothy A. Hultquist	Eugene Smolensky
Thomas D. Cook	Kathleen Hall Jamieson	Eric Wanner
John A. Ferejohn	Melvin Konner	Mary C. Waters
Larry V. Hedges		

Library of Congress Cataloging-in-Publication Data
The changing terrain of race and ethnicity / edited by Maria Krysan and Amanda E. Lewis.
p. cm.
Papers presented at a conference held at the University of Illinois at Chicago in 2001.
Includes bibliographical references and index.
ISBN 10: 0-87154-491-1 (cloth)
ISBN 13: 978-0-87154-491-9 (cloth)
ISBN 10: 0-87154-492-X (paper)
ISBN 13: 978-0-87154-492-6 (paper)
   1. United States—Race relations—Congresses. 2. United States—Ethnic relations—Congresses. 3. Racism—United States—Congresses. 4. Ethnicity—United States—Congresses. 5. Minorities—United States—Social conditions—Congresses. 6. United States—Social conditions—1980—Congresses. I. Krysan, Maria. II. Lewis, Amanda E., 1970–

E184.A1C444 2004
305.8'00973—dc22

2004050849

Copyright © 2004 by Russell Sage Foundation. All rights reserved. First paperback edition 2006. Printed in the United States of America. No part of this publication may be reproduced, stored in a retrieval system, or transmitted in any form or by any means, electronic, mechanical, photocopying, recording, or otherwise, without the prior written permission of the publisher.

Reproduction by the United States Government in whole or in part is permitted for any purpose.

The paper used in this publication meets the minimum requirements of American National Standard for Information Sciences—Permanence of Paper for Printed Library Materials. ANSI Z39.48-1992.

Text design by Genna Patacsil.

RUSSELL SAGE FOUNDATION
112 East 64th Street, New York, New York 10021
10 9 8 7 6 5 4 3 2 1

To W. E. B. DuBois for setting the standard for careful and engaged work on racial dynamics in the United States

CONTENTS

Contributors

MARIA KRYSAN is associate professor of sociology at the University of Illinois at Chicago and fellow at its Institute for Research on Race and Public Policy.

AMANDA E. LEWIS is associate professor of sociology and African American studies and fellow at the Institute for Research on Race and Public Policy at the University of Illinois at Chicago.

LAWRENCE D. BOBO is Martin Luther King Jr. Centennial Professor of Sociology and director of the Center for Comparative Studies in Race and Ethnicity and Program in African and African American Studies at Stanford University.

EDUARDO BONILLA-SILVA is research professor of sociology at Duke University.

SHARON M. COLLINS is associate professor of sociology at the University of Illinois at Chicago.

KORIE EDWARDS is assistant professor of sociology at The Ohio State University.

REYNOLDS FARLEY is senior research scientist at the Population Studies Center of the University of Michigan.

JOE R. FEAGIN is the Ella C. McFadden Professor of Liberal Arts at Texas A&M University.

TYRONE A. FORMAN is associate professor of sociology and African American studies, faculty fellow at the Institute for Research on Race and Public Policy, and faculty affiliate at the Institute of Government and Public Affairs at the University of Illinois at Chicago.

EVELYN NAKANO GLENN is professor of women's studies and ethnic studies and founding director of the Center for Race and Gender at the University of California at Berkeley.

KAREN S. GLOVER is a doctoral student in sociology at Texas A&M University.

NAKISHA HARRIS is a graduate student in sociology at the University of Illinois at Chicago.

MANNING MARABLE is professor of public affairs, political science, and history at Columbia University, director of Columbia's Center for Contemporary Black History, and founding director of the Institute for Research in African-American Studies at Columbia University.

CHARLES W. MILLS is professor of philosophy at the University of Illinois at Chicago.

GEOFF WARD is assistant professor in the College of Criminal Justice at Northeastern University and faculty fellow at its Institute on Race and Justice.

Acknowledgments

THIS BOOK EMERGES from a set of conversations that began in the fall of 2000 with colleagues at the University of Illinois at Chicago (UIC). During these conversations, we discussed and debated what were the most pressing questions facing those trying to understand present day race relations and racial inequality. That group, initially convened by Bill Bridges and Phillip Bowman, and including ourselves, Maria Krysan and Amanda Lewis, along with Sharon Collins, Tyrone Forman, Cedric Herring, and Steve Warner, eventually transformed into a planning committee for a conference—"The Changing Terrain of Race and Ethnicity: Theory, Methods, and Public Policy." This conference ultimately brought together nearly three hundred fifty scholars from around the country for two days of lively and thought-provoking discussions. We need to begin by thanking all those involved in planning and carrying out that conference, which includes the aforementioned steering committee, the many participants, and those who provided financial and institutional support.

In addition to those on the steering committee, all of whom worked hard to plan and organize the event as well as participate as panelists or presiders, a number of other UIC colleagues contributed considerable time and scholarship to the conference. They include Richard Barrett, Bill Bridges, Constance Dallas, Leon Fink, Nilda Flores-Gonzalez, Rachel Gordon, Elena Gutierrez, Darnell Hawkins, Valerie Johnson, Jack Knott, Dwight McBride, Charles Mills, Suzanne Oboler, Tony Orum, Alice Palmer, David Perry, Pam Popielarz, Barbara Ransby, Beth Richie, Andrew Rojecki, Laurie Schaffner, and David Stovall. A number of other colleagues traveled to the conference to participate as panelists and plenary speakers, including Lawrence Bobo, Eduardo Bonilla-Silva, Bernardine Dohrn, Michael Emerson, Reynolds Farley, Joe Feagin, Philip Garcia, Evelyn Nakano Glenn, Greg Jao, Manning Marable, Omar

McRoberts, Aldon Morris, Robert L. Nelson, Mary Pattillo, Adolph Reed, Dorothy Roberts, Ellen Scott, Arlene Sanchez Walsh, and Geoffrey Ward. A number of staff and students provided critical administrative support, including Gary Miller, Jane Whitener, Natalie Henry, and Olga Padilla. We are very grateful to the contingent of UIC sociology graduate students who helped ensure that the conference proceeded smoothly. Finally, thanks to the efforts of Cedric Herring, the video of the proceedings of this conference can be viewed at http://www.uic.edu/depts/soci/.

We need to offer special thanks to two people without whom the conference would never have happened. First, Nakisha Harris, who, as a first year graduate student, worked tirelessly and contributed her extensive knowledge about the inner workings of UIC to make the conference happen and happen smoothly. She is a terrific young sociologist from whom we expect great things in the future. Second, Phillip Bowman, director of UIC's Institute for Research on Race and Public Policy (IRRPP) contributed his vision, energy, and the Institute's resources to bring the conference to reality. He also supported both of us at key moments with fellow positions to give us additional time to work on the conference and this volume. As he has for hundreds of other scholars in the academy, Phil has been an amazing mentor and supporter to us both.

The administration at UIC also generously supported the conference financially, and both Chancellor Sylvia Manning and Dean Stanley Fish offered opening remarks. In addition to IRRPP, the Departments of Sociology and African American Studies, the Institute for Government and Public Affairs, Great Cities Institute, and College of Liberal Arts and Sciences provided internal financial and administrative support. Early seed money was provided by the American Sociological Association's Fund for the Advancement of the Discipline, and a generous grant from the Russell Sage Foundation (RSF) provided the key resources for both the conference and the edited volume. We are especially grateful to Eric Wanner and his staff for their support and would like to offer a special thanks to Stephanie Platz who early on shared our vision of what the conference could be, and Suzanne Nichols who pushed us to make this book happen.

It took some time to convert a diverse and compelling collection of talks into a coherent volume, and we received a great deal of help along the way. Thanks to graduate students Nakisha Harris and Vickey Velazquez for their willingness to help us with both the intellectual and mundane tasks involved. Thanks also to the anonymous reviewers for their insightful feedback, and especially to those at the Russell Sage Foundation who have been working with us on the volume, including Suzanne Nichols, David Haproff, Cindy Buck, and Genna Patacsil.

Finally, we would like to offer a brief but very heartfelt thanks to our friends and family who continue to support us despite the strange hours that academic life sometimes requires and the mood swings it occasionally generates. Without them, our work would not be possible—nor would it be as rewarding or enjoyable. These include many friends (especially our game night comrades, Sharon and Ellen); our parents, Robert and Barbara Lewis and Jim and Carole Krysan; our siblings and nieces and nephews, Josh, Lisa, Becky, Chris, Charlie, Joey, Patrick, Bernadette, Damian, Sharon, Sarah and Mark; and our partners, Max and Tyrone. Collectively they keep us honest, grounded, and sane.

1

INTRODUCTION: ASSESSING CHANGES IN THE MEANING AND SIGNIFICANCE OF RACE AND ETHNICITY

ॐ

Amanda E. Lewis, Maria Krysan, and Nakisha Harris

THE MEANING AND significance of race and ethnicity in the United States have been of enduring interest inside and outside the halls of academia. Early social scientific work focused on such concerns as dismantling notions of biological determinism, identifying the deleterious consequences of legal segregation and blatant racial prejudice for individuals, communities, and nations, and understanding the demographic patterns associated with the migration of African Americans from the South to the North (McKee 1993).

As we begin the twenty-first century, it is difficult to survey the landscape of race and ethnicity—both the research and the reality—without recognizing that its meaning and significance have fundamentally shifted. These shifts include changes in the demographics of the nation, in the meaning and boundaries of racial categories, and in how race and racism operate in the social world. Although the vestiges of earlier patterns and systems undoubtedly persist, we are now confronted with more subtle and complex causes and consequences associated with racial stratification, discrimination, and prejudice. This becomes apparent in the diverse areas where researchers direct their attention: some examine the patterns and causes of racial inequality across a range of social institutions, while others focus on how people perceive and understand racial and ethnic groups, while still others seek to understand race and ethnicity as a feature of identity and group formation. And these discussions are being shaped by and are reflective of a necessary shift from the "black-white" model that characterizes most earlier work to what is better described as a "prism" (Zubrinsky and Bobo 1996) in light of the increasing immigration from Asia and from Central and South America.

Spanning virtually all domains of interest to scholars who focus on race and ethnicity are the common themes of transition and change. Those studying racial attitudes have observed a shift from the blatant "Jim Crow" racism of the past to more subtle forms (see, for example, Bobo, Kluegel, and Smith 1997; Bonilla-Silva and Forman 2000; Forman 2001; Kinder and Sanders 1996; Sears 1988). Scholars who focus on structural and behavioral patterns and their manifestations in social institutions point to new forms of racial segmentation in the workplace (Anderson 1999; Collins 1989, 1993, 1997a, 1997b), new kinds of statistical and indirect discrimination, unconscious stereotyping (Forman, Williams, and Jackson 1997; Neckerman and Kirschenman 1991; Reskin 2000), and more subtle employment and housing discrimination practices (Forman and Harris 1995; Myers 1993; Turner, Fix, and Struyk 1991; Yinger 1995).

The boundaries of race and ethnicity themselves and the very terrain upon which racial struggles take place are also changing. Witness the social scientific and political struggles associated with the U.S. government's attempts to assess racial identity in the 2000 decennial census, including the political and social struggles around the creation of multiracial categories and Arab American and Hawaiian attempts to be reclassified into different categories (Wright 1994). Not surprisingly, all of these changes have shifted the policy landscape, as controversies about racial profiling, zero-tolerance school policies, discrimination lawsuits, immigration policy, and anti–affirmative action referenda readily attest. It is essential for scholars not only to track these changes that have taken place in the real world but also to understand what is happening now and where we are headed (McKee 1993; Steinberg 1995).

In October 2001, a national conference convened at the University of Illinois at Chicago brought together prominent scholars to engage these issues directly. The conference, The Changing Terrain of Race and Ethnicity, assembled researchers who individually approach these issues from different angles but collectively push the boundaries of research on race and ethnicity. This volume grew out of that conference. As suggested by its title, the common thread across all of the chapters is an attempt to grapple with and push forward scholarship on race and ethnicity in this changing context. In part I (chapters 2 through 4), this takes the form of figuring out how to understand, measure, and interpret phenomena that have in many cases become more subtle and slippery. Chapters 2 and 3 focus on changes in racial attitudes, racial ideology, and racial politics, while chapter 4 reviews how race and ethnicity operate across a range of other social institutions. The two chapters in part II are the most explicit on the implications of the increasingly multiracial and multiethnic population of the United States. Both of these chapters call into question the very categories that are used to describe race and the boundaries that shape racial and ethnic identity. The four chapters in part III take a broader perspective and tackle the theoretical implications of contemporary racial and ethnic patterns and transformations. Taken together, they provide a road map for conceptualizing future research on race and ethnicity.

PART I: THE CHANGING MANIFESTATIONS OF
RACE IN ATTITUDES AND INSTITUTIONS

When racial attitudes were first measured in the 1940s, researchers focused on the important questions of the time: Do whites believe segregation should continue? Do whites believe blacks are innately inferior? At the time, explicitly—and often legally—sanctioned practices of exclusion restricted the opportunities of racial and ethnic minorities across a range of social institutions. These served to maintain strict patterns of segregation and ensured unfair and discriminatory treatment toward people of color. Researchers at the time were intent on measuring levels of support for or dissent from such policies and practices. By the beginning of the twenty-first century, many of the laws and statutes that created de jure segregation had been overturned and few Americans endorsed the blatant prejudices of the 1940s. Despite this seeming progress toward racial equality, racial attitude surveys and investigations of social institutions still highlight the continuing significance of race and the continuing presence of negative racial attitudes. For example, despite evidence of persistent discrimination across a number of different social arenas, the majority of whites believe that racial discrimination has ceased to be a problem and that racial inequality comes from a lack of motivation among nonwhites. In addition, though many whites support basic principles of racial equality, their support for race-targeted policies that would facilitate progress toward racial equality is much weaker (Herring and Amissah 1997; Schuman et al. 1997; Steeh and Krysan 1996; Williams et al. 1999).

Several new theoretical perspectives seek to explain these divergent patterns within racial attitudes, challenging our existing conceptions of racial attitudes and responding to changes in U.S. racial norms over the past half-century. Both Lawrence Bobo (chapter 2) and Tyrone Forman (chapter 3) argue, in essence, that the decrease in traditional prejudice does not mean that racial prejudice has disappeared. Rather, its form and expression have changed. Both of these chapters offer theories that challenge traditional notions of racial prejudice, offer a framework for understanding contemporary forms of prejudice, and draw attention to important methodological (Forman) and real-world implications (Bobo).

Bobo argues that we must attend to three key points if we are to understand race and attitudes in the contemporary United States. The first is a recognition of the crystallization of a new type of racism—laissez-faire racism. This form of racism operates in less formal structures than Jim Crow racism, but it reproduces, sustains, and rationalizes black-white inequality in much the same way that the Jim Crow laws of the twentieth century did. Second, race and racism remain powerful levers in American national politics, both in terms of their role in campaigns and in their impact on the likely success of a candidate depending on his or her racial background. In short, race and politics are deeply intertwined. Bobo then shines the spotlight on academia itself, arguing that scholars on both the left and the right have contributed to the problem of "race" by failing to come to grips—both theoretically and methodologically—with the conditions of embedded white privilege and the importance of black agency.

While Bobo takes on politics and the academy, Forman's perspective is social psychological. He begins with a discussion of color-blind racism. Intended to capture the pattern of many whites expressing their racial views in non-racial language, the term "color-blind racism" describes popular color-blind claims that are not accompanied by the alleviation of persisting racial inequality. Public officials, politicians, and average citizens often draw on the language of the civil rights movement when they declare that they no longer see color and simultaneously declare that discrimination is all but gone in the world at large. This claim allows them to regard themselves as not prejudiced, even as they endorse the currently unequal status quo. Forman uses color-blind racism as a theoretical lens but develops a new construct, racial apathy, which he argues is an especially good way to capture one manifestation of racial prejudice in the post–civil rights era. Racial apathy refers to indifference toward societal racial and ethnic inequality and a lack of engagement with race-related social issues.

Drawing on survey-based data, Forman shows the increase in whites' indifference about racial matters generally and argues that those interested in understanding contemporary racial attitudes must grapple with whites' passive support for the racially unequal status quo. Labeling whites' indifference "racial apathy," he argues that by ignoring the social reality of race in a racialized social system, whites and others sustain a system of inequality that restricts opportunities for many racial and ethnic minorities.

In chapter 4, Amanda Lewis, Maria Krysan, Sharon Collins, Korie Edwards, and Geoffrey Ward shift the focus away from attitudes and ideology specifically and examine how race is shaping social institutions. In particular, they emphasize the impact of race on opportunities and outcomes in these social institutions, changes in the mechanisms by which race operates in them, and what the future holds. They consider five key social institutions: housing, education, labor markets, criminal justice, and religion. Throughout the discussion of each of these institutions, we see the impact of the changing demographics of the United States and the increasingly subtle (and sometimes not so subtle) ways in which race and ethnicity are played out in contemporary American society.

PART II: CHANGES IN RACIAL CATEGORIES AND BOUNDARIES

Whereas chapter 4 highlights how the growing presence of racial and ethnic minorities is reshaping various institutions, both chapters in part II explore the shifts in the very definitions of existing racial categories and their boundaries—in both official racial designations and in the larger understanding of the racial system in the United States. Population dynamics over the past generation—including but not limited to immigration and intermarriage—have profoundly affected the racial topography of the United States. Whereas a generation ago racial boundaries in the United States were largely drawn along a dichotomized "black-white" axis—where "black" was understood fundamentally as "not white"—today the rapidly growing presence of Latino or Hispanic and Asian immigrants and the resurgence of Native American identification have greatly complicated cultural and official racial mapping. It is now possible for Americans to identify themselves—and indeed, to be classified by some official entities—as neither white nor black. Official boundaries and categorizations are being contested almost continuously now: some groups argue to be shifted from one category to another (for example, Native Hawaiians want to be included with "Native American" rather than "Asian or Pacific Islander"), and some argue for more options (for example, multiracial categories). Some Latinos or Hispanics—whom the U.S. census classifies in a separate "ethnicity" item but not as a "racial" group—have pushed for a racial classification that would uniquely identify them.

In chapter 5, Reynolds Farley uses the history of collecting racial data in the United States and the official racial designations as a vantage point from which to view the changes in racial identity and categorization. The complexity of racial and ethnic identity is highlighted by the social movement, which he describes in detail, that led to the most recent substantial change in how the census collects racial data: the multiracial movement of the 1990s. These efforts resulted in a new race question for the 2000 census that allowed people to indicate that they identified with more than one racial group. Farley connects this discussion of racial categorization in federal statistics to the larger context of race and ethnicity when he notes that the earliest racial data were collected to help *maintain* segregation and to *disadvantage* minorities, but that after the 1960s the data were used to help *overcome* traditional segregation practices. The move in the 1990s to permit Americans to identify themselves as multiracial represents a major shift in the collection of racial data that complicates the collection and analysis of data but also has the potential to shape how we as a society think about race. Farley then conducts a demographic analysis that answers the question: who marked all categories that applied? Based on these findings, Farley argues that while the multiracial movement has been successful in changing the way the government collects racial data, it is not clear that it has shifted how people think about race or how racial data are actually used. But this substantial change in how government agencies gather data on different racial groups may have significant consequences for the ability to understand, define, and characterize the experiences of different racial and ethnic groups in the United States.

Moving away from statistical agencies and self-reports of racial identity, Eduardo Bonilla-Silva and Karen Glover focus in chapter 6 on the larger racial stratification system. They ask critical questions about how Latino and Asian immigration challenge the centuries-old understanding of race in the United States and argue that the racial system in America is moving from a biracial to a more complex triracial system because of demographic changes, specifically the fact that most new immigrants are people of color. Bonilla-Silva and Glover argue that the triracial system will place "whites" (Euro-Americans, new whites, assimilated Latinos) at the top, "honorary whites" (white middle-class Latinos, Japanese Americans, Korean Americans, Asian Indians, Arab Americans) in the middle, and "collective blacks" (Filipinos, Vietnamese, dark-skinned poor Latinos, blacks, African immigrants, and reservation-bound Native Americans) at the bottom. America is headed in this direction, they suggest, because (1) an intermediate group is needed to buffer racial conflict; (2) with some newcomers labeled white, whites will retain their majority status; and (3) if most new immigrants are labeled "black," they will be unable to enjoy the full benefits of American citizenship.

PART III: THEORETICAL CONSIDERATIONS IN THE CHANGING TERRAIN OF RACE AND ETHNICITY

Spanning several academic disciplines, the authors of the four chapters in part III highlight three key issues—citizenship, structural racism, and white privilege—that are only briefly referenced in the earlier chapters in the volume. Each chapter offers a general theoretical perspective on race and ethnicity by identifying concepts and ideas that are important in the new landscape of race and ethnicity but are, as yet, underdeveloped or underacknowledged.

In chapter 7, Evelyn Nakano Glenn argues that we can understand how race relations have been constituted and contested in the United States by examining citizenship rights, defined broadly. In our exploration of these issues, she maintains, we cannot speak simply of race and ethnicity but must pay attention to the way race and ethnicity are gendered phenomenon that have quite different impacts on different race and gender groups. Glenn's central thesis is that citizenship has been used to draw boundaries between those included as members of the community (often defined along race and gender lines) and therefore entitled to respect, protection, and rights and those who are excluded and thus denied recognition and rights. Key to her argument is the idea that ultimately it is subtle everyday practices that reinforce exclusion more than the formal structures that have been put in place to delineate citizenship. She calls for a more sociological conception of citizenship as a product of both rhetorical and material practices, the latter including the everyday interactions that enforce and contest the boundaries of community.

The remaining three chapters in part III emphasize two key concepts that are in need of additional theoretical and empirical attention—the structural components of racism and white privilege. Joe R. Feagin and Manning Marable draw attention to the often-neglected material conditions that help to shape—and are shaped by—racism. Charles Mills argues that to fully understand racism in the United States, not only must we examine the manifestations and nuances of the oppression of people of color and the experiences of the subordinate groups, but we must turn this question on its head and give equal attention to the nuances and manifestations of white privilege.

In chapter 8, Feagin argues that past theorizing about racial and ethnic matters in the United States has placed too much emphasis on the ideological construction of racial meanings. He argues that racism is not just about the construction of images and identities but is centrally about the creation, development, and maintenance of white privilege and power. As such, theorizing about race must account for the material, social, educational, and political dimensions of racism. In developing his ideas, Feagin introduces several key concepts: systemic racism, exploitation, unjust enrichment and impoverishment, the social reproduction of enrichment and impoverishment, rationalizing oppression in racist ideology, and resistance to racism.

Focusing on a similar set of ideas but taking a slightly different approach, Manning Marable argues in chapter 9 that the central problem of the next century will be the problem of "structural racism," which he defines as the deeply entrenched patterns of inequality that are coded by race and justified by racist stereotypes in both public and private discourse. He uses the vast disparities in material resources and property between racial groups as evidence of structural racism. Marable attributes the existence of structural racism to the cumulative effects of four hundred years of white privilege. He develops this concept, reviews how African Americans have responded to the evolving domains of structural racism, and then suggests what can be done to challenge it. Among these suggestions are developing a richer theoretical and historically grounded understanding of diversity, establishing resistance organizations, and engaging issues related to the intersection of race, gender, sexuality, and class. Finally, Marable emphasizes the need to understand the global context of racism so that we can understand what is happening in the United States and gain perspective on how the U.S. system influences—and is influenced by—other systems around the world.

The themes of material conditions and white privilege emerge once again in chapter 10, where Charles Mills takes on what he labels "liberal" tendencies in both philosophy and other disciplines. Specifically, mainstream social and political theorizing about race has constructed racism as an anomaly. But this is an inappropriate characterization, Mills argues. Rather, we need a theory of race that properly captures the systemic and material components of racism—a subject on which mainstream American disciplines have heretofore remained silent. To do this successfully, a conceptual framework that is better formed and historically contextualized is necessary. Among other tasks, analysts must retrieve and build on the concept of white supremacy and develop an understanding of specifically *racial* forms of exploitation.

The ten chapters of this volume lay out a set of pressing challenges for those studying racial dynamics in the United States in the years to come. All of the authors are concerned with persisting racial inequalities and the social dynamics that are either exacerbating or mitigating these patterns. The research agenda that emerges reminds us to remain attentive to changes in social organization and social processes (to recognize, for instance, when innovation in methodological strategies is required) while also being cognizant of the social and historical contexts within which such changes are taking place. Without such contextual awareness, analyses can provide only attenuated understandings of social problems. All of these authors also remind us to recognize the interplay between racial ideologies, attitudes and understandings, and real life outcomes.

Although much of the volume is focused on racial dynamics in the United States, we recognize that there is much to be learned by expanding our comparisons to other nations. This is evidenced not only in Marable's reminder that globalization is as much a racial phenomenon as a class one but also in Bonilla-Silva and Glover's characterization of race in the United States as Latin Americanized. Still, racial dynamics vary considerably across different national racial landscapes (to the extent that they are still bound by national borders), and the United States presents us with abundant challenges to address and understand.

One of the key messages of this volume to all of us (policymakers, scholars, and citizens) is that racial dynamics continue to change but change does not always mean progress toward greater racial equality. In fact, some of the contributors—among whom are scholars who have been studying these issues for upward of three decades—express pessimism about what the immediate future holds. Whether our overall trajectory is good or bad—or perhaps more accurately, whether it reflects progress on some fronts and retrenchment on others—the point to stress is that if we are to assess the situation with accuracy, we must be attentive to shifting demographics and meanings.

The chapters that follow remind us that in everything from our research designs to our public policy recommendations we must be attentive to how racism is manifested structurally; to the intersections of race with other ascriptive categories (such as gender); to new and often subtle expressions of racial antipathy; to the role of whites as racial actors and the role of white privilege in shaping life outcomes; to the importance of indifference or apathy as an affective dimension of prejudice; and to the powerful effects of these issues on people's everyday lives. We hope that this volume inspires new research and reinvigorates existing efforts.

REFERENCES

Anderson, Elijah. 1999. "The Social Situation of the Black Executive." In *The Cultural Territories of Race,* edited by Michele Lamont. Chicago: University of Chicago Press.

Bobo, Lawrence, James Kluegel, and Ryan Smith. 1997. "Laissez-Faire Racism: The Crystallization of a Kinder, Gentler, Antiblack Ideology." In *Racial Attitudes in the 1990s: Continuity and Change,* edited by Steven A. Tuch and Jack Martin. Westport, Conn.: Praeger.

Bonilla-Silva, Eduardo, and Tyrone Forman. 2000. "'I'm Not a Racist, but . . .': Mapping White College Students' Racial Ideology in the USA." *Discourse and Society* 11(1): 50–85.

Collins, Sharon M. 1989. "The Marginalization of Black Executives." *Social Problems* 36(4): 317–31.

———. 1993. "Blacks on the Bubble: The Vulnerability of Black Executives in White Corporations." *Sociological Quarterly* 34(3): 429–47.

———. 1997a. "Black Mobility in White Corporations: Up the Corporate Ladder but Out on a Limb." *Social Problems* 44(l): 55–67.

———. 1997b. *Black Corporate Executives: The Making and Breaking of the Black Middle Class.* Philadelphia: Temple University Press.

Forman, Tyrone. 2001. "The Social Determinants of White Youths' Racial Attitudes." *Sociological Studies of Children and Youth* 8: 173–207.

Forman, Tyrone, and Kirk Harris. 1995. "Color-conscious or Color-blind? Employers' Hiring Decisions in Contemporary Urban Labor Markets." Paper presented to the annual meeting of the Society for the Study of Social Problems. Washington (August 18–20).

Forman, Tyrone, David R. Williams, and James S. Jackson. 1997. "Race, Place, and Discrimination." *Perspectives on Social Problems* 9: 231–61.

Herring, Cedric, and Charles Amissah. 1997. "Advance and Retreat: Racially Based Attitudes and Public Policy." In *Race and Public Policy,* edited by Steven Tuch. New York: Praeger.

Kinder, Donald, and Lynn Sanders. 1996. *Divided by Color: Racial Politics and Democratic Ideals.* Chicago: University of Chicago Press.

McKee, James B. 1993. *Sociology and the Race Problem: The Failure of a Perspective.* Urbana: University of Illinois Press.

Myers, Samuel L. 1993. "Measuring and Detecting Discrimination in the Post–Civil Rights Era." In *Race and Ethnicity in Research Methods,* edited by John H. Stanfield II and Rutledge M. Dennis. Newbury Park, Calif.: Sage.

Neckerman, Kathryn, and Joleen Kirschenman. 1991. "Hiring Strategies, Racial Bias, and Inner-City Workers." *Social Problems* 38(4): 801–15.

Reskin, Barbara. 2000. "Re-theorizing Employment Discrimination." Invited lecture, Department of Sociology, University of Illinois at Chicago (October 30).

Schuman, Howard, Charlotte Steeh, Lawrence Bobo, and Maria Krysan. 1997. *Racial Attitudes in America: Trends and Interpretations,* 2nd ed. Cambridge, Mass.: Harvard University Press.

Sears, David O. 1988. "Symbolic Racism." In *Eliminating Racism: Profiles in Controversy,* edited by Phyllis A. Katz and Dalmas A. Taylor. New York: Plenum Press.

Steeh, Charlotte, and Maria Krysan. 1996. "Trends: Affirmative Action and the Public, 1970–1995." *Public Opinion Quarterly* 60: 128–58.

Steinberg, Stephen. 1995. *Turning Back: The Retreat from Racial Justice in American Thought and Policy.* Boston: Beacon.

Turner, Margery Austin, Michael Fix, and Raymond J. Struyk. 1991. *Opportunities Denied, Opportunities Diminished: Racial Discrimination in Hiring.* Washington, D.C.: Urban Institute.

Williams, David R., James Jackson, Tony Brown, Myriam Torres, Tyrone Forman, and Kendrick Brown. 1999. "Traditional and Contemporary Prejudice and Urban Whites' Support for Affirmative Action and Government Help." *Social Problems* 46(4): 503–27.

Wright, Lawrence 1994. "One Drop of Blood." *The New Yorker,* July 25, 46–55.

Yinger, John. 1995. *Closed Doors, Opportunities Lost: The Continuing Costs of Housing Discrimination.* New York: Russell Sage Foundation.

Zubrinsky, Camille, and Lawrence Bobo. 1996. "Prismatic Metropolis: Race and Residential Segregation in the City of Angels." *Social Science Research* 25: 335–74.

PART I

THE CHANGING MANIFESTATIONS OF
RACE IN ATTITUDES AND INSTITUTIONS

2

INEQUALITIES THAT ENDURE?
RACIAL IDEOLOGY, AMERICAN POLITICS, AND THE
PECULIAR ROLE OF THE SOCIAL SCIENCES

∽

Lawrence D. Bobo

AS PART OF research on the intersection of poverty, crime, and race, I conducted two focus groups in a major eastern city in early September 2001, just prior to the tragic events of September 11. The dynamics of the two groups, one with nine white participants and another with nine black participants, drove home for me very powerfully just how deep but also just how sophisticated, elusive, and enduring a race problem the United States still confronts. An example from each group begins to make the point that the very nature of this problem and our vocabularies for discussing it have grown very slippery, very difficult to grasp, and therefore extremely difficult to name and to fight.

First let's consider the white focus group. In response to the moderator's early question, "What's the biggest problem facing your community?" a young working-class white male eagerly and immediately chimed in, "Section 8 housing." "It's a terrible system," he said. The racial implications hung heavy in the room until a middle-aged white bartender tried to leaven things a bit by saying:

> All right. If you have people of a very low economic group who have a low standard of living who cannot properly feed and clothe their children, whose speech patterns are not as good as ours [and] are [therefore] looked down upon as a low class. Where I live most of those people happen to be black. So it's generally perceived that blacks are inferior to whites for that reason.

The bartender went on to explain: "It's not that way at all. It's a class issue, which in many ways is economically driven. From my perspective, it's not a racial issue at all. I'm a bartender. I'll serve anybody if they're a class [act]." At this, the group erupted in laughter, but the young working-class male was not finished. He asserted, a bit more vigorously:

> Why should somebody get to live in my neighborhood that hasn't earned that right? I'd like to live [in a more affluent area], but I can't afford to live there so I don't. . . . So why should somebody get put in there by the government that didn't earn that right?

And then the underlying hostility and stereotyping came out more directly when he said: "And most of the people on that program are trashy, and they don't know how to behave in a working neighborhood. It's not fair. I call it unfair housing laws."

Toward the end of the session, when discussing why the jails are so disproportionately filled with blacks and Hispanics, this same young man said: "Blacks and Hispanics are more violent than white people. I think they are more likely to shoot somebody over a fender bender than a couple of white guys are. They have shorter fuses, and they are more emotional than white people."

In fairness, some members of the white group criticized antiblack prejudice. Some members of the group tried to point out misdeeds done by whites as well. But even the most liberal of the white participants never pushed the point, rarely moved beyond abstract observations or declarations against prejudice, and sometimes validated the racial stereotypes more overtly embraced by others. In an era when everyone supposedly knows what to say and what not to say and is artful about avoiding overt bigotry, this group discussion still quickly turned to racial topics and quickly elicited unabashed negative stereotyping and antiblack hostility.[1]

When asked the same question about the "biggest problem facing your community," the black group almost in unison said, "Crime and drugs," and a few voices chimed in, "Racism."[2] One middle-aged black woman reported: "I was thinking more so on the lines of myself because my house was burglarized three times. Twice while I was at work and one time when I returned from church, I caught the person in there."

The racial thread to her story became clearer when she later explained exactly what happened in terms of general police behavior in her community:

> The first two robberies that I had, the elderly couple that lived next door to me, they called the police. I was at work when the first two robberies occurred. They called the police two or three times. The police never even showed up. When I came in from work, I had to go . . . file a police report. My neighbors went with me, and they had called the police several times and they never came. Now, on that Sunday when I returned from church and caught him in my house, and

the guy that I caught in my house lives around the corner, he has a case history, he has been in trouble since doomsday. When I told [the police] I had knocked him unconscious, oh yeah, they were there in a hurry. Guns drawn. And I didn't have a weapon except for the baseball bat, [and] I wound up face down on my living room floor, and they placed handcuffs on me.

The moderator, incredulous, asked: "Well, excuse me, but they locked you and him up?" "They locked me up and took him to the hospital."

Indeed, the situation was so dire, the woman explained, that had a black police officer who lived in the neighborhood not shown up to help after the patrol car arrived with sirens blaring, she felt certain the two white police officers who arrived, guns drawn, would probably have shot her. As it was, she was arrested for assault, spent two days in jail, and now has a lawsuit pending against the city. Somehow I doubt that a single, middle-aged, churchgoing white woman in an all-white neighborhood who had called the police to report that she apprehended a burglar in her home would end up handcuffed, arrested, and in jail alongside the burglar. At least, I am not uncomfortable assuming that the police would not have entered a home in a white community with the same degree of apprehension, fear, preparedness for violence, and ultimate disregard for a law-abiding citizen as they did in this case. But it can happen in black communities in America today.[3]

To say that the problem of race endures, however, is not to say that it remains fundamentally the same and essentially unchanged. I share the view articulated by historians such as Barbara Fields (1982) and Thomas Holt (2000) that race is both socially constructed and historically contingent.[4] As such, it is not enough to declare that race matters or that racism endures. *The much more demanding challenge is to account for how and why such a social construction comes to be reconstituted, refreshed, and enacted anew in very different times and places.* How is it that in 2001 we can find a working-class white man who is convinced that many blacks are "trashy people" controlled by emotions and clearly more susceptible to violence? How is it that a black woman defending herself and her home against a burglar ends up apprehended as if she were one of the "usual suspects"? Or cast more broadly, how do we have a milestone like the *Brown* decision and pass a Civil Rights Act, a Voting Rights Act, a Fair Housing Act, and numerous acts of enforcement and amendments to all of these, including the pursuit of affirmative action policies, and yet still continue to face a significant racial divide in America?

The answer I sketch here is but a partial one, focusing on three key observations. First, as I have argued elsewhere and elaborate in important ways here, I believe that we are witnessing the crystallization of a new racial ideology here in the United States. This ideology I refer to as laissez-faire racism. We once confronted a slave labor economy with its inchoate ideology of racism and then watched it evolve in response to war and other social, economic, and cultural trends into an explicit Jim Crow racism of the de jure segregation era. We have more recently seen the biological and openly segregationist thrust of twentieth-century Jim Crow racism change into the more cultural, free-market, and ostensibly color-blind thrust of laissez-faire racism in the new millennium. But make no mistake—the current social structure and attendant ideology reproduce, sustain, and rationalize enormous black-white inequality (Bobo and Kluegel 1997).

Second, race and racism remain powerful levers in American national politics. These levers can animate the electorate, constrain and shape political discourse and campaigns, and help direct the fate of major social policies. From the persistently contested efforts at affirmative action through a historic expansion of the penal system and the recent dismantling of "welfare as we know it," the racial divide has often decisively prefigured and channeled core features of our domestic politics (Bobo 2000).

Third, social science has played a peculiar role in the problem of race. And here I wish to identify an intellectual and scholarly failure to come to grips with the interrelated phenomena of white privilege and black agency. This failure may present itself differently depending on the ideological leanings of scholars. I critique one line of analysis on the left and one on the right. On the left, the problem typically presents as a failure of sociological imagination. It manifests itself in arguments that seek to reduce racialized social dynamics to some ontologically more fundamental nonracialized factor. On the right, the problem is typically the failure of explicit victim-blaming. It manifests itself in a rejection of social structural roots or causation of racialized social conditions. I want to suggest that both tactics—the left's search for some structural force more basic than race (such as class or skill levels or child-rearing practices) and the right's search for completely volitional factors (cultural or individual dispositions) as final causes of "race" differences—reflect a deep misunderstanding of the dynamics of race and racism. Race is not just a set of categories, and racism is not just a collection of individual-level anti–minority group attitudes. Race and racism are more fundamentally about sets of intertwined power relations, group interests and identities, and the ideas that justify and make sense out of (or challenge and delegitimate) the organized racial ordering of society (Dawson 2000). The latter analytic posture and theory of race in society is embodied in the theory of laissez-faire racism.[5]

ON LAISSEZ-FAIRE RACISM

There are those who doubt that we should be talking about racism at all. The journalist Jim Sleeper (1997) denounces continued talk of racism and racial bias as mainly so much polarizing "liberal racism." The political scientists Paul Sniderman and Edward Carmines (1997) write of the small and diminishing effects of racism in white public opinion and call for us to "reach beyond race." And the linguist John McWhorter (2000) writes of a terrible "culture of victimology" that afflicts the nation and ultimately works as a form of self-sabotage among black Americans. Even less overtly ideological writers talk of the growing victory of our Myrdalian "American Creed" over the legacy of racism. Some prominent black intellectuals, such as the legal scholar Randall Kennedy (1997), while not as insensitive to the evidence of real and persistent inequality and discrimination, raise profound questions about race-based claims on the polity.

These analysts, I believe, are wrong. They advance a mistaken and counterproductive analysis of where we are today, how we got here, and the paths that we as a nation might best follow in the future. In many respects, these analysts are so patently wrong that it is easy to dismiss them.

Let's be clear first on what I mean by "racism." Attempts at definition abound in the scholarly literature. William Julius Wilson (1973, 32) offers a particularly cogent specification when he argues that racism is an "an ideology of racial domination or exploitation that (1) incorporates belief in a particular race's cultural and/or inherent biological inferiority and (2) uses such beliefs to justify and prescribe inferior or unequal treatment for that group." I show here that there remains a profound tendency in the United States to blame racial inequality on the group culture and active choices of African Americans. This is abundantly clear in public opinion data (Kluegel and Smith 1986), and it is exemplified by more than a few intellectual tracts, including McWhorter's *Losing the Race* (2000). Closely attendant to this pattern is the profound tendency to downplay, ignore, or minimize the contemporary potency of racial discrimination (Kluegel 1990). Again, this tendency is clear in public opinion and finds expression in the scholarly realm in the Thernstroms' book *America in Black and White* (1997). These building blocks become part of the foundation for rejecting social policy that is race-targeted and aims to reduce or eliminate racial inequality. In effect, these attitudes facilitate and rationalize continued African American disadvantage and subordinated status. Our current circumstances, then, both as social structure and ideology, warrant description and analysis as a racist regime. Yet it is a different, less rigid, more delimited, and more permeable regime as well.

Laissez-faire racism involves persistent negative stereotyping of African Americans, a tendency to blame blacks themselves for the black-white gap in socioeconomic status, and resistance to meaningful policy efforts to ameliorate U.S. racist social conditions and institutions. It represents a critical new stage in American racism. As structures of racial oppression became less formal, as the power resources available to black communities grew and were effectively deployed, as other cultural trends paved the way for an assault on notions of biologically ranked "races," the stage was set for displacing Jim Crow racism and erecting something different in its place.

I have taken up a more complete development of the historical argument and the contemporary structural argument elsewhere (Bobo, Kluegel, and Smith 1997; Bobo and Smith 1998).[6] What is worth emphasizing here is, first, the explicit social groundedness and historical foundation of our theoretical logic—something that sets this theory of racial attitudes apart from notions like symbolic racism. Although not directly inspired by his work, our theoretical logic is a direct reflection of ideas articulated by the historian Thomas Holt (2000, 21–22). As he explains: "Racial phenomena and their meaning do change with time, with history, and with the conceptual and institutional spaces that history unfolds. More specifically they are responsive to major shifts in a political economy and to the cultural systems allied with that political economy."

The second point to emphasize here is that this is an argument about general patterns of group relations and ideology—not merely about variation in views among individuals from a single racial or ethnic category. As such, our primary concern is with the central tendency of attitudes and beliefs within and between racial groups and the social system as such, not within and between individuals. It is the collective dimensions of social experience that I most intend to convey with the notion of laissez-faire racism—not a singular attitude held to a greater or lesser degree by particular individuals. The intellectual case for such a perspective has been most forcefully articulated by the sociologist Mary R. Jackman (1994, 119). We should focus an analysis of attitudes and ideology on group-level comparisons, she writes, because doing so

> draws attention to the structural conditions that encase an intergroup relationship and it underscores the point that individual actors are not free agents but caught in an aggregate relationship. Unless we assume that the individual is socially atomized, her personal experiences constitute only one source of information that is evaluated against the backdrop of her manifold observations of the aggregated experiences (both historical and contemporaneous) of the group as a whole.

The focus is thus more on the larger and enduring patterns and tendencies that distinguish groups than on the individual sources of variation.

With this in mind, I want to focus on three pieces of data, the first of which concerns the persistence of negative stereotypes of African Americans. Figure 2.1 reports data from a national Web-based survey I recently conducted using eight of Paul Sniderman's stereotype questions (four dealing with positive social traits and four dealing with negative social traits) (Sniderman and Piazza 1993).[7] Several patterns stand out. It is easier for both blacks and whites to endorse the positive traits when expressing views about the characteristics of blacks than the negative traits. However, African Americans are always more

FIGURE 2.1 STEREOTYPE ITEMS, BY RACE

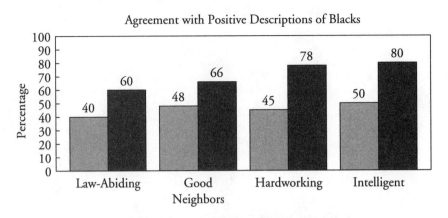

Agreement with Positive Descriptions of Blacks

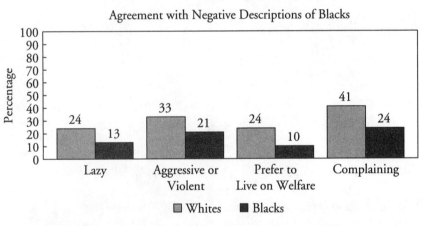

Agreement with Negative Descriptions of Blacks

□ Whites ■ Blacks

Source: Race, Crime, and Public Opinion Study (2001).

favorable and less negative in their views than whites. Some of the differences are quite large. For instance, there is a thirty-percentage-point difference between white and black perceptions on the trait of intelligence and a thirty-three-percentage-point difference on the "hardworking" trait.

A fuller sense of what these patterns mean for group differences can be seen in figure 2.2. It provides a cumulative assessment of the positive and negative ratings. Here we see that whites are more than twice as likely as blacks to have attributed none of the positive traits to blacks and that blacks are essentially twice as likely as whites to attribute all four positive traits to members of the group. On the flip side, nearly two-thirds of blacks reject all of the negative

FIGURE 2.2   SUMMARY STEREOTYPE MEASURES, BY RACE

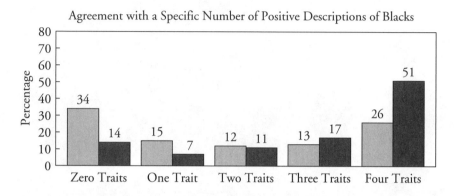

Agreement with a Specific Number of Positive Descriptions of Blacks

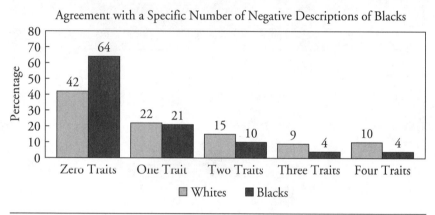

Agreement with a Specific Number of Negative Descriptions of Blacks

Source: Race, Crime, and Public Opinion Study (2001).

stereotypes of the group, in contrast to the 58 percent of whites who accept at least one negative trait perception and the nearly one-third who accept three or more.

Negative stereotypes of African Americans are common, though not uniform, and to a distressing degree they exist among both blacks and whites and presumably influence perceptions and behaviors for both groups.[8] However, there is a sharp difference in central tendency within each group, in predictable directions. One cannot escape the conclusion that most whites have different and decidedly lesser views of the basic behavioral characteristics of blacks than do blacks themselves. And that generally these patterns indicate that African Americans remain a culturally dishonored and debased group in the American psyche.

Stereotypes as measured here are arguably more cognitive in nature and tell us a bit less about racism as an active force than do more overt expressions of social distance. We asked three questions about interracial relationships in a 1997 national telephone survey.[9] The questions dealt with general approval of black-white dating and marriage, and black-white marriages of family members. To provide a strong assessment of the extent of non- or antiracist thinking, we present the data in three broad categories: we distinguished those who gave the highest "strongly approve" response across all three items from those who gave the consistent overtly racist response of "strongly disapprove" and treated everyone else as in the middle. As figure 2.3 shows, large fractions of whites and blacks end up in the middle category under this scheme. Perhaps not too surprising is the higher percentage of African Americans in the consistently "strongly approve" category (48 percent versus 31 percent).

It is the committed racist category to which I most want to draw attention. Barely 2 percent of African Americans fall into this category, compared to

FIGURE 2.3   WHITE AND BLACK LEVELS OF APPROVAL OF INTERRACIAL ITEMS

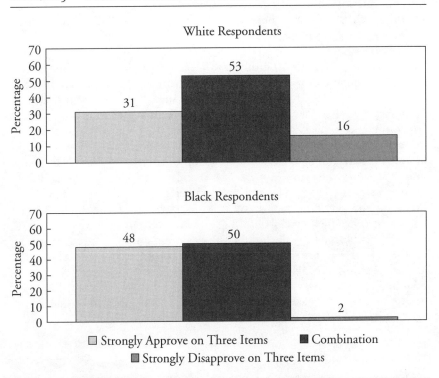

Source: National Omnibus Survey (1997).

16 percent of whites (or slightly less than one in six). Given that these are nationally representative data, given that they yield a ratio of committed racists, comparing black to white, of eight to one, and assuming that these figures probably underestimate (particularly among whites) racist leanings, these numbers point to a serious ongoing problem of racism.

Alternatively, these data could be interpreted as showing the essential ambivalence of racial attitudes today, especially among most whites. This is the view adopted by Robert Entman and Andrew Rojecki (2000) in their very important book, *The Black Image in the White Mind: Media and Race in America*. I want to suggest that, sociologically speaking, the view that most whites are ambivalent on race, while politically strategic, is also probably a good deal too generous. There are two reasons for this conclusion that are tightly interrelated. First, I think genuine ambivalence requires a fairly high level of what Howard Schuman once called "sympathetic identification" with the underdog (Schuman and Harding 1963). Most of the cultural and social structural pressures in the United States still arguably tilt in an antiblack direction. So, second, without strong underlying sympathetic identification, the extant patterns of economic inequality, segregation by race, and political polarization and the long-standing failures of American political culture (discussed later) heavily weight the scale toward ambivalence that usually (if not invariably) resolves itself on the side of acting against, recoiling from, or disparaging blacks rather than actively, sympathetically embracing blacks.

More specifically, we can produce some empirical evidence on this point. In the same national survey we included the distinguished social psychologist Tom Pettigrew's (1997) intergroup affect measures. These questions ask how often the respondent has felt sympathy for blacks and how often he or she has felt admiration for blacks. Again, to pose a strong test, we focus our attention on those respondents who said "very often" in response to both questions. As figure 2.4 shows, a vanishingly small fraction of whites fall into this category, only 5 percent, while fully 37 percent of African Americans do, for a ratio of more than seven to one. Moreover, fully 35 percent of whites consistently said that they "not very often" or "never" felt sympathy or admiration for blacks. Viewed as central tendencies within major social groups—not individuals— these results bespeak the likelihood of a profound and widespread tendency on the part of whites to regard blacks as "the other." Many individuals may indeed be ambivalent. Nonetheless, the larger social context and climate remain seriously doubtful of the full humanity of African Americans. At a minimum, the immediate sense of commonality assumed in much of the current "color-blind" discourse is simply not in evidence here.

ON AMERICAN POLITICS

As a historic fact and experience as well as a contemporary political condition, racial prejudice has profoundly affected American politics. A wide body of

FIGURE 2.4   WHITE AND BLACK AFFECTS TOWARD AFRICAN AMERICANS

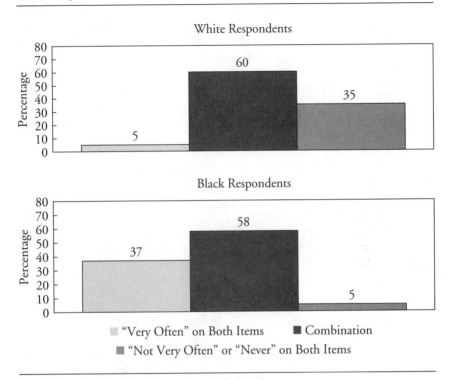

Source: Race, Crime, and Public Opinion Study (2001).

evidence is accumulating to show that racial prejudice still affects politics. Black candidates for office typically encounter severe degree of difficulties securing white votes, partly owing to racial prejudice (Citrin, Green, and Sears 1990; Kaufman 1998; Callaghan and Terkildsen 2002). There is some evidence, to be sure, that the potency of racial prejudice varies with the racial composition of electoral districts and the salience of race issues in the immediate political context (Reeves 1997; Kaufman 2003).

Moreover, political candidates can use covert racial appeals to mobilize a segment of the white voting public under some circumstances. For example, the deployment of the infamous Willie Horton political ad during the 1988 presidential campaign heightened the voting public's concern over race issues. It also accentuated the impact of racial prejudice on electoral choices and did so in a way that did not increase concern with crime per se (Kinder and Sanders 1996; Mendelberg 1997). That is, what appears to give a figure like Willie Horton such efficacy as a political symbol is not his violent criminal behavior per se, but rather his being a violent black man whose actions upset a racial order that should privilege and protect whites.

Major social policy decisions may also be driven by substantially racial considerations. The political psychologists David Sears and Jack Citrin (1985) make a strong case that antiblack prejudice proved to be a powerful source of voting in favor of California's historic property tax reduction initiative (Proposition 13), a change in law that fundamentally altered the resources available to government agencies.

On an even larger stage, the very design and early implementation of core features of the American welfare state were heavily shaped by racial considerations. Robert Lieberman (1998) has shown that the programs that became Social Security, Aid to Families with Dependent Children (AFDC), and unemployment insurance were initially designed to either exclude the great bulk of the black population or leave the judgment of qualification and delivery of benefits to local officials. The latter design feature of AFDC (originally ADC) had the effect in most southern states of drastically curtailing the share of social provision that went to African Americans. As Lieberman (1998, 216–17) explains:

> Any possibility for broader racial inclusion in social policy evaporated before the ink from the president's pen was dry on 14 August 1935; the moment Franklin Roosevelt affixed his signature to the Social Security Act, a particular racial compromise became law—a compromise not of generalities but of specifics. A new set of rules was in place that would define for a generation and more who was in and who was out of American social provision. African-Americans were decidedly out, but the terms on which they were excluded, the institutions designed to keep them out, differed in their racial porousness. . . . Although different policies affect race relations in different ways—by challenging or buttressing particular legal, political, economic, or social relations—American social policies share a legacy of race-laden institutional structures. The ability to exclude African-Americans from benefits has been a central factor in the adoption of national policies, and the parochialism of other policies has often effectively restricted African-American participation.

Lieberman shows that it was white southern legislators who insisted upon many of these racialized features of the early American welfare state and that they often spoke directly about the impact of the policies on blacks and labor relations in the South. It was mainly early black civil rights organizations, he also shows, that argued against these policies and political compromises with racism.

There are good reasons to believe that the push to "end welfare as we know it"—which began as a liberal reform effort but was hijacked by the political right and became, literally, the end of welfare as we had known it—was just as surely impelled by heavily racial considerations. The political sociologist Martin Gilens (1999) has carefully analyzed white opinion on the welfare state in the United States. Some features of the welfare state, he finds, lack an overtone of black dependency (such as Social Security) and enjoy high consensus support. Other programs (AFDC, food stamps, general relief) are heavily racialized, with much of the white voting public regarding these programs as helping lazy and undeserving blacks.

Indeed, the fundamental alignment of the U.S. national political parties has been centrally driven by a racial dynamic (Frymer 1999; Glaser 1996). Over the past thirty-five years we have witnessed a fundamental transformation in the Democratic and Republican party system, a transformation that political scientists call realignment. The more the Democratic Party was seen as advancing a civil rights agenda and black interests—in a manner that clearly set them apart from the Republican Party—the more race issues and race itself became central to party affiliations, political thinking, and voting in the mass white public (Carmines and Stimson 1989). What was once a solid white Democrat-controlled South has thus shifted to a substantially white Republican-controlled South.

The end result of all of these patterns, simply put, is that African Americans do not enjoy a full range of voice, representation, and participation in politics. Black candidates, particularly if they are identified with the black community, are unlikely to be viable in majority white electoral districts. Even white candidates who come to be strongly associated with black interests run the risk of losing many white voters. As a consequence, party leaders on both sides have worked to organize the agenda and claims of African Americans out of national politics. In particular, the national Democratic Party, which should arguably reward its most loyal constituents in the black community, instead has often led the way in pushing black issues off the stage (Frymer 1999; Edsall and Edsall 1991). As the political scientist Paul Frymer (1999) has explained, party leaders do so because they are at risk of losing coveted white "swing voters" in national elections if they come to be perceived as catering to black interests. Thus is the elite discourse around many domestic social policies, and their ultimate fate, bound up in racial considerations.

Against this backdrop it becomes difficult, if not counterproductive, to accept the widely shared view that American democracy is on an inexorable path toward ever-greater inclusivity and fuller realization of its democratic potential. In the context of such enduring and powerful racialization of American politics, such an assumption is naive at best.

There is an even more incisive point to be made. The presumption of ever-expanding American liberalism is mistaken. For example, the Pulitzer Prize winning–historian Joseph Ellis (2001) writes of the terrible "silence" on the subject of slavery and race that the "founding fathers" *deliberately* adopted. They waged a Revolutionary War for freedom, declared themselves the founders of a new nation, and in very nearly the same moment *knowingly* wedded democracy to slave-based racism. The philosopher Charles Mills (1997) extends the reach of this observation by showing the deep bias of Enlightenment thinkers toward a view of those on the European continent—whites—as the only real signatories to the "social contract." Others, particularly blacks, were never genuinely envisioned or embraced as fully human and thus were never intended to be covered by the reach of the social contract.

Considerations of this kind led the political theorist Rogers Smith (1993) to suggest that the United States has not one but rather multiple political traditions. One tradition is indeed more democratic, universalistic, egalitarian, and expansive. But this tradition competes with and sometimes decisively loses out to a sharply hierarchical, patriarchal, and racist civic tradition (see also Gerstle 2001; Glenn 2002). The ultimate collapse of Reconstruction following the Civil War and the subsequent gradual development of de jure segregation and the Jim Crow racist regime provide one powerful case in point.

On the Peculiar Role of Social Science

Mainstream scholars on the left tend to treat race as a categorical designation that affects the outcomes that matter to us for reasons that have nothing to do with race as a sociological phenomenon. If African Americans have lower employment chances or earnings than whites, this is not a function of race but rather of purely "statistical discrimination" or other factors, such as different levels of education and skill, that somehow "explain" the extraneous influence of race. Since we do not believe in race as an inherent biological or primordial cultural factor that produces social outcomes, there must be other nonracial social conditions that account for any effect of race on outcomes that matter. The analog to this line of reasoning in examinations of political attitudes and public opinion is the treatment of African Americans as an out-group attitude object, an object toward which individual whites have been socialized to hold more or less negative attitudes.

To the credit of liberal social analysts, both approaches reject biological and inflexible cultural understandings of race and racial differences. Yet both approaches fail to come to grips with the condition of embedded white privilege and the import of constrained but quite real black agency. That is, there are sociologically meaningful "imagined communities," communities of identity as well as of typical residence, interaction, family connection, and larger interest defined as black and white that exist in relation to one another in the United States. And indeed, race has been used at various points and in various ways as one of the fundamental principles in organizing an array of conditions that define the relationship between those sociological units or imagined communities. Hence, its effects are not reducible to other, putatively more fundamental causes.

Let me be more specific by taking an example from the realm of racial attitudes and public opinion. The theory of symbolic racism contends that a new form of antiblack prejudice has arisen among whites reflecting a blend of early learned traditional values (for example, individualism and the Protestant work ethic) and early learned negative feelings and beliefs about blacks.[10] This new attitude is an amalgamation. It consists of a resentment of demands made by blacks, a resentment of special favors received, especially from government, by blacks, and a denial of the contemporary relevance of discrimination. These views constitute a coherent attitude, an attitude not bearing any functional relation to white advantage or privilege or to real-world black challenge and resistance to white privilege. Rather, the attitude is a learned ideation of centrally unreasoned, emotion-laden content. When political issues arise that make race and African Americans salient, this underlying psychological disposition becomes the basis of whites' political response. Hence, prejudice *intrudes* into politics.

What I want to suggest is that prejudice is *in and of* politics—not an ideational intrusion of the individual's emotionally expressive and irrational impulses upon the political sphere (Bobo and Tuan, forthcoming). As I have argued elsewhere, intergroup attitudes are not principally individual-level judgments of like and dislike (Bobo, Kluegel, and Smith 1997; Bobo and Smith 1998). Instead, following the inspiration of Herbert Blumer (1958), I argue that these attitudes centrally involve beliefs and feelings about the proper relation between groups. Racial attitudes capture aspects of the preferred group positions and those patterns of belief and affect that undergird, mobilize as needed, and make understandable the prevailing racial order.

These remarks have specific meaning with regard to the conceptualization and measurement of a notion like symbolic racism. Beliefs and feelings about whether blacks receive special treatment, favors, or an unfair advantage or have leaders and a political agenda that demand too much are not merely ventilations of atomistic feelings of resentment or hostility. These are highly political judgments about the status, rights, and resources that members of different *groups* are rightly entitled to enjoy or make claims on.

This difference in conceptualization is an important one and is directly linked to my concern with white privilege and black agency. From the vantage point of symbolic racism theory, there is no instrumental or rational objective whatsoever behind the intrusion of prejudice into politics. Whites are neither seeking the maintenance of privilege nor responding in any grounded fashion to real social, political, and economic demands arising from the black community and its leaders. Instead, the theory holds, a mixture of emotions, fears, anxieties, and resentments combines with important social values to occasion a hostile response when African Americans and their concerns are made politically salient (Kinder and Sanders 1996; Sears, van Laar, and Kosterman 1997).

Although not intended as such, this view trivializes African Americans' political activism and struggle that put issues like desegregation, antidiscrimination,

affirmative action, and increasingly the matter of reparations on the national political agenda. Real political actors pursued deliberate strategies and waged hard-
fought legal, electoral, and protest-oriented battles to advance the interests
of black communities. These actions had powerful effects on the larger dynamics of politics and public opinion (Lee 2002). And however imperfect and
imbued with exaggerated apprehensions they may have been, white Americans
nonetheless perceived and responded to these very substantively political struggles (Bobo 1988). Hence, to classify white attitudes and beliefs about black
demands, black leadership, and black responses to disadvantage as some sort
of "pre-political," completely emotional ideation is to trivialize black America,
to infantalize white America, and to skirt serious engagement with the many
powerful "wages" that still accrue to whiteness.

Empirically and in terms of measurement, this argument raises serious
doubts about how to understand the meaning of responses to the questions
used to tap symbolic racism. For example, my own research suggests that when
many whites say that blacks (or any other minority group) are "taking unfair
advantage of privileges given to them by the government," these are not vague
resentments (Bobo 1999). These sentiments are almost certainly not precisely
calculated assessments of real risks and actual losses, but they are still expressly
political judgments about the quality of life and about important resources, at
once material and symbolic, that groups may get from the state.

In particular, whites who answer in the affirmative to this sort of survey question frequently speak of their tax dollars and their work effort going to support
others, in the concrete language of a zero-sum resource transfer. A good illustration of the point comes from the cultural sociologist Michele Lamont's important new book, *The Dignity of Working Men: Morality and the Boundaries of
Race, Class, and Immigration* (2000, 60–61). She writes of one of her subjects:

> . . . Vincent is a workhorse. He considers himself "top gun" at his job and makes
> a very decent living. His comments on blacks suggest that he associates them
> with laziness and welfare and with claims to receiving special treatment at work
> through programs such as affirmative action. He says: "Blacks have a tendency
> to . . . try to get off doing less, the least possible . . . to keep the job where whites
> will put in that extra oomph. I know this is a generality and it does not go for
> all, it goes for a portion. It's this whole unemployment and welfare gig. A lot of
> the blacks on welfare have no desire to get off it. Why should they? It's free
> money. I can't stand to see my hard-earned money [*said with emphasis*] going
> to pay for someone who wants to sit on his ass all day long and get free money."

As Lamont (2000, 62) concludes about a number of the white working-class men
she interviewed: "They underscore a concrete link between the perceived dependency of blacks, their laziness, and the taxes taken from their own paychecks."

This is not an isolated finding of Lamont's in-depth interviews. For example, the sociologist Mary Waters (1999, 177) observed a very similar pattern among the white managers and employers she studied. She writes:

> Most white respondents were much more able to tap into their negative impressions of black people, especially "underclass" blacks whom they were highly critical of. These opinions were not just based on disinterested observation. There was a direct sense among many of the whites that they personally were being taken advantage of and threatened by the black population.

The language used is one of traits (laziness) and violations of values (hard work and self-reliance) coupled with moral condemnation, but the group comparison, sense of threat, and identity-engaging element is equally clear. Indeed, as the experimental social psychologist Eliot Smith (1993, 308–9) has persuasively argued, it is exactly this blend of important group identity and resource threat to the group that *should* be emotionally arousing: "These items and the definition all involve appraisals of an outgroup as violating ingroup norms or obtaining illegitimate advantages, leading to the emotion of anger." Conceptualizing such responses as the ventilation of resentment distorts the critical point that "the focus in the model advanced here is not the intrinsically negative qualities attributed to blacks themselves (which are the theoretical key in concepts of prejudice as a negative attitude) but *appraisals of the threats posed by blacks to the perceiver's own group*" (309, emphasis in original).

The substance of the theory and the interpretation of the measures of symbolic racism thus suffer from a failure of sociological imagination. The theory pushes out of analytical view the real and substantial linkage between the facts of white privilege and the facts of active black challenge to it. In their place, the theory gives us but the phantasms of racial resentments in the minds of individual whites. These phantasms somehow—but apparently unintentionally—enter politics, take note of black agitation and disruption, and then release in a spasm of reaction against race-targeted social policies. I would like to suggest that there is something decidedly wrong with the theory and conceptualization, even though the many sentiments identified in the concepts of symbolic racism and racial resentment are indeed at the heart of the contemporary political struggle over race (Krysan 2000).

On the right side of the political spectrum, the example I wish to draw attention to is the mounting speculation, most prominently offered by Stephan and Abigail Thernstrom (1997), that the pervasive patterns of racial segregation we observe in the United States are a function of "black self-segregation." In this case, African Americans are credited with agency, but that agency is said to be exercised in a manner that continues to disadvantage blacks. Only this time it is blacks themselves who, by choosing a self-handicapping preference, are responsible. The argument is a troubling one for anyone who believes that neighborhoods vary in school quality, safety, social services and amenities, and all that goes into the phrase "quality of life." It says that blacks are, perforce and of their own free will, placing racial solidarity above social mobility and a better quality of life.

The failure here is twofold. First, the Thernstroms' argument is contingent on the rejection of compelling empirical evidence of racial bias and discrimination in the housing market (for an authoritative review, see Charles 2003). It is clear that a powerful racial hierarchy continues to permeate thinking about communities, neighborhoods, and where to live. Using experimental data, Camille Z. Charles and I show that white Americans are systematically more open to residential contact with Asians and Latinos than with blacks—holding every other consideration constant (Zubrinsky and Bobo 1996). Several studies have now made it clear that antiblack racial stereotypes are direct predictors of willingness to live in more integrated communities (Farley et al. 1994; Bobo and Zubrinsky 1996; Charles 2000).

These results are consistent with other demographic and behavioral data (Yinger 1998). Researchers at the State University of New York at Albany document the very small changes in high rates of black-white residential segregation between 1990 and 2000. Indeed, HUD auditing studies in 1989 found overall rates of discrimination in access to housing for African Americans that were only trivially different from those observed a decade earlier (for the most up-to-date review of the literature, see Charles 2003).

Second, the theory of black self-segregation treats black choice and action as if it exists in a vacuum. That is, it ignores altogether what are almost surely important feedback mechanisms that prompt many blacks to self-select into black neighborhoods out of the reasonable expectation that they would encounter hostility from some white neighbors. As formulated by the Thernstroms and others, the self-segregation hypothesis fails to address the immediately relevant question of whether African Americans would self-select into predominantly black communities in the absence of historic experience, current collective memory, and ongoing encounters with contemporary racism. The best available empirical evidence suggests that blacks as a group are the people who are the most likely to prefer integration and to comfortably accept living in minority group status in a neighborhood (Charles 2000).

Part of the message here concerning theoretical interpretation on the right and the left is that variables and data never speak for themselves. It is the questions we pose (and those we fail to ask) as well as our theories, concepts, and ideas that bring a narrative and meaning to marginal distributions, correlations, regression coefficients, and statistics of all kinds. If we suffer from failures of sociological imagination, if we conceive of race and racism in ways that disassociate them from white privilege, black agency, and the interrelations between the two phenomena, then we are bound to get things wrong however much we may have followed formal statistical criteria and other normative canons of science. Or, as the sociologist Tukufu Zuberi (2001, 144) puts it in his new book, *Thicker Than Blood: How Racial Statistics Lie:* "Most racial statistics lack a critical evaluation of racist structures that encourage pathological interpretations. These pathological interpretations have had a profound impact on our causal theories and statistical methods. Our theories of society, not our empirical evidence, guide how we interpret racial data."

Indeed, it is that perspective on racist structures, or what the political scientists Michael Dawson (2001) and Claire Jean Kim (2000) call the American racial order, that informs a very different reading of the import of white privilege and black agency.

CAVEATS

A series of interpretative caveats should be borne in mind here. First, although I have spoken extensively about black-white relations, I am mindful of the extent to which this is an increasingly partial view of American race relations. The rapid and continuing expansion of the Asian and Latino populations in the United States and the unique experiences and issues faced by members of these internally diverse communities will inevitably reshape the American social landscape. However, it is not at all clear that the continued diversification of the United States in any way fundamentally destabilizes the historic black-white divide. The urban sociologist Herbert Gans (1999) has written a provocative and I think more than suggestive essay arguing that we are evolving as a nation toward a new major racial dichotomy: the black versus the nonblack. Accordingly, we would still have racial hierarchy and some degree of heterogeneity, especially within the nonblack category (which include whites and those effectively earning the title of honorary whites, such as successful middle-class Asians). And much of the arsenal of analytical tools and perspectives that long helped to make sense of the black-white divide would have applicability in such a new context. Similarly, my colleague Mary Waters's (1999) powerful recent book, *Black Identities: West Indian Immigrant Dreams and American Realities,* makes clear just how salient the black-white divide remains even for an immigrant population that arrived committed to transcending race.

Second, wartime and the social upheaval occasioned by war can present a powerful opportunity for reshaping the landscape of race relations. Indeed, the political scientists Philip Klinkner and Rogers Smith (1999) craft a persuasive claim that war is a necessary but not sufficient precondition for improvements in the status of blacks. They argue that far-reaching qualitative changes in the status of African Americans have typically involved the convergence of three factors: a major wartime mobilization that ultimately required a large number of black troops; an enemy viewed as profoundly antidemocratic, thereby heightening the claims for fuller realization of democratic ideals at home;

and significant internal political mobilization and contestation from below demanding reform.

Viewed in this light, the terrorist attacks on the United States of September 11, 2001, and the subsequent military actions in Afghanistan against the al Qaeda network and the ruling Taliban regime and the later war in Iraq raise again the possibility of this convergence of circumstances. That the early televised images of the devastation at the World Trade Center in New York were so thoroughly multiracial and multiethnic only heightens this potential. And that African Americans in the persons of Colin Powell and Condoleezza Rice occupy such high leadership posts adds to the salutary import of the moment. Certainly we are already witnessing journalistic accounts of a nation pulling together and uniting in ways that may heal otherwise deep racial divisions.[11]

Yet at this moment there are no strong indications that these events will seriously shift the landscape of black-white relations. Not all wartime moments do, as Klinkner and Smith note with regard to the Spanish-American War, the Korean War, and the Vietnam War.

Third, I have scarcely touched upon the matter of class divisions within the African American community and the growth of the black middle class. Nor, for that matter, have I wrestled with the ways in which gender and sexuality also condition life along the color line. It must be stressed that class, gender, and sexuality all become dividing lines within the African American community (and outside it) in ways that shape agendas, the capacity for mobilization, and even ideas about who is a full member of the community (Cohen 1999; Dawson 1994, 2001). My objective has been to focus on those aspects of contemporary race relations that largely cut across these cleavages and thus are centrally experienced as "race," rather than examine the intersection of race with other statuses and identities. I do not mean to dismiss or disregard these other factors, but rather to stress that there remain social conditions we must understand and engage as a distinctive racial divide.

CONCLUSION

I opened with the words of a young, angry white male who saw "trashy" Section 8 blacks coming into his neighborhood with government subsidies and diminishing what he perceived as a standard of life that he had earned and that set him above and apart from them. And with the words of a middle-aged, churchgoing black woman who returned to her home one Sunday morning not only to do battle with a burglar but later with the racially biased police and criminal justice system. As these two cases attest, race remains a deep divide in America.

Of course, black and white Americans could scarcely be further apart in their own judgments about the severity of the racial divide. As part of an election study in 2000, Michael Dawson and I asked a large national sample of blacks and whites about the likelihood of achieving racial equality in America.[12] Figure 2.5 shows the results. A full one-third of whites said that we had already achieved it, in contrast to a mere 6 percent of African Americans. One in five blacks said that we never would achieve it, and another two out of five said that it would never happen in their lifetimes. Blacks see a deep and lingering social ill, and whites see a problem that is just about resolved. Without claiming to "know" the answer, I interpret responses of "have already achieved racial equality" and perhaps even of "will soon achieve racial equality" to constitute a deliberate evasion of responsibility more than a thoughtful assessment or response to social realities (Kluegel and Smith 1986; Kluegel and Bobo 2001). Too many friction points, inequalities, and signs of discrimination remain to take such views at face value.

FIGURE 2.5   RESPONDENTS' RACE AND BELIEFS ABOUT RACIAL EQUALITY

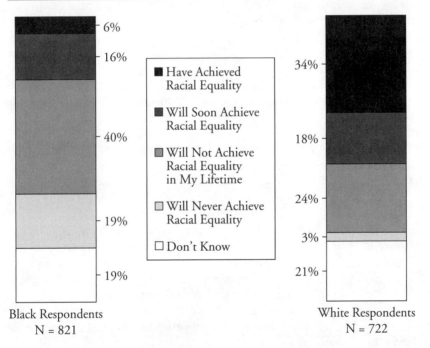

Do you think that blacks have achieved racial equality, will soon achieve racial equality, will not achieve racial equality in your lifetime, or will never achieve racial equality?

Source: National African American Election Study (2000).

Indeed, it is fair to still speak of white supremacy in America and of racism in America (Bonilla-Silva 2001; Feagin 2001). The persistence of white supremacy and the enduring potency of racism, I believe, trace to the adaptive capacity of racial ideologies. As Thomas Holt (2000, 27–28) has explained: "Race is ideological, but, being embedded in political economies that are quite historically specific, it cannot long survive changes in the material base from which it draws sustenance." The defeat of Jim Crow racism and the victories of the civil rights era did not eradicate black-white economic inequality, labor market discrimination, or gargantuan disparities in accumulated wealth; they did not end residential segregation by race and randomly disperse people in physical space; they did not reallocate political power; and they did not completely repudiate the racist stereotypes and other elements of American political culture and whites' sense of entitlement that feed and sustain racism.

These victories did, however, fundamentally restructure the terrain on which racism is now enacted, understood, and reproduced. This new regime of laissez-faire racism is more fluid and permeable than the Jim Crow regime. It works in ways that permit, on the one hand, the carefully delimited and controlled success of a Colin Powell, a Condoleezza Rice, or even an Oprah Winfrey, but that, on the other hand, do not eliminate the ghetto, black joblessness, and poverty and do not even wince at a despicable effort at black voter disenfranchisement. Indeed, it works in ways that allow a young working-class white man to seethe with anger at a social policy effort to extend a step up for poor blacks and in ways that allow a churchgoing black woman to endure the tragic burden of fighting a black burglar and the white police. These are all manifestations of our continued entrapment in the snare of racism.

I have no battle plan for defeating laissez-faire racism. What we can do as scholars is, first, to struggle to conceptualize, name, and understand as accurately as possible what is happening and to make those ideas widely available. Let's tell the story of enduring inequality in its fullness and according to the highest standards that we can attain.

Second, we can push for changes and social policies that speak to what our analyses tell us are the central structural and cultural problems. In that regard, the push for a serious dialogue about race—for truth and reconciliation, for an apology, and most of all for reparations—is a major element of the next stage of the struggle (Dawson and Popoff 2004). Liberal and progressive voices must turn away from the demand that the black political agenda be entirely suppressed in favor of a race-neutral, purely universalistic or centrist political agenda (see Thompson 1998).

And third, I do not believe it is possible to accomplish a recognition of one's full humanity without demanding it as such. Careful political thinking and organizing is necessary, to be sure. Strategic coalitions reaching across lines of class, color, and ethnicity will be essential. Working through conventional legal and political channels will be necessary too. But I remain doubtful that hidden agendas and half-measures will do what it takes to finally crush the legacy of white supremacy in America, to dislodge laissez-faire racism, and to lead us to that mountaintop that Martin Luther King spoke of the night before he was assassinated.

NOTES

1. The white focus group, led by a white, professional focus group moderator, had nine participants, six men and three women. Everyone in the group had at least a high school education, with an average of 15.1 years of schooling. The average age was 48.3, and participants had an average income of $66,700. The group lasted for two hours and after some opening general topics moved to issues of crime and criminal justice.

2. The black focus group, led by a black, professional focus group moderator, had nine participants, five men and four women. Everyone in the group had at least a high school education, with an average of 14.2 years of schooling. The average age of participants was 40.6, and participants had an average income of $51,900. The group lasted for two hours and after some opening general topics moved to issues of crime and criminal justice.

3. Two recent series of events underscore just how arbitrarily and unjustly the criminal justice system can act in black communities, especially low-income ones. Based on an erroneous tip from a police informant, New York City police officers used a concussion grenade to enter, without knocking or providing any warning, the home of a fifty-seven-year-old Harlem woman. She was a career civil servant with no criminal history or involvement in drug-dealing, and she was dressing to go to work at the time of the 6:00 A.M. raid. Officers broke down her door and tossed in the grenade, and she was initially handcuffed by police officers. Within two hours she had died of a heart attack (Rashbaum 2003). Of somewhat broader notoriety are the Tulia, Texas, drug arrests carried out by a white undercover agent who provided the only evidence and testimony against a number of defendants, the overwhelming majority of whom were African American. In August 2003, the governor of Texas pardoned thirty-five people (thirty-one of whom were black), many of whom had already served lengthy years in jail, when that evidence turned out to be fabricated (Liptak 2003).

4. As I develop later, race is neither a biological nor a primordial cultural imperative or affiliation, but a historically contingent social construction. It also varies in configuration and salience over time (Collins 2001). The experience of race may be importantly conditioned by and intersect

with class, gender, and sexuality, among other variables (Cohen 1999). It nonetheless has powerful social effects (for other definitional issues, see Bobo [2001] and Bobo and Tuan [forthcoming]), but these effects are best understood as part of a social process (Zuberi 2001) that is greatly influenced by significant social actors, as expressed in such forms as government policy (Nobles 2000), rather than as static demographic categories.

5.   This critique of the left and the right with regard to race is very similar to the historian Alice O'Connor's (2001) definitive analysis of the shortcomings of social science examinations of poverty in the post–World War II era. She finds that larger economic structures and racial dynamics were often obscured by a narrow focus on the specific circumstances or behaviors of those who were poor. The consequence, she suggests, has been a set of analyses and policy prescriptions too heavily tilted toward altering individual behavior and insufficiently focused on the larger and more fundamental social and political forces that constrain opportunity.

6.   The laissez-faire racism argument rests on an analysis of the critical historical changes in the configuration of demographic, economic, political, and cultural forces that, on the one hand, opened the door to a sustained and effective attack on Jim Crow institutional arrangements and ideas. These factors include the waning economic and political power of the old southern planter elite, the urban and northern migration of African Americans and attendant growth in human capital and social capital in black hands, and the growing intellectual and cultural assault on notions of "biological racism." On the other hand, the laissez-faire racism theory also points to the persistence of residential segregation, enormous economic inequality (especially in terms of accumulated assets or wealth), limited political representation, and deep reservoirs of antiblack attitudes and beliefs that have powerfully constrained and channeled progressive racial reform. This historical argument provides the basis for contemporary empirical analyses showing how whites' attitudes shifted toward more qualified stereotyping of blacks, away from biological attributions for black-white differences to cultural attributions, and toward resistance to strong integrationist and equal opportunity policies.

7.   The data come from my 2001 Race, Crime, and Public Opinion Study. These data were collected by Knowledge Networks using a nationally representative, Web-based social survey design, with 978 white and 1,010 black respondents. The within-panel response rate for blacks was 72 percent and it was 61 percent for whites. Fuller information on the sample and respondent characteristics are reported in Bobo and Johnson (2004).

8. That stereotypes are likely to influence blacks as well as whites is strongly suggested by the pioneering work of the social psychologist Claude Steele (1998) on the notion of stereotype threat. Insightful work by Kimberly Torres and Camille Charles (2004), based on in-depth interviews with black students on an elite college campus, shows how these students are aware of whites' negative stereotypes about blacks and strive to differentiate themselves from stigmatizing group images, which they too take seriously.

9. The data come from the 1997–1998 National Omnibus Survey conducted by the University of Maryland Survey Research Center. It involved a random digit dial telephone survey of 838 white, 115 black, and 51 other race respondents. The survey had an overall cooperation rate of 68 percent and a conservatively estimated response rate of 55 percent.

10. Several scholars, most notably David O. Sears (1988), Donald R. Kinder (Kinder and Sanders 1996), and John B. McConahay (1986), have advocated for the theory. Over time some differences in usage, labeling, and measurement have emerged among these (and other) scholars. For example, both McConahay and Kinder have moved away from the label "symbolic racism," the former preferring "modern racism" and the latter "racial resentment." Sears retains the original concept label.

11. Immediately following the events of September 11, the *New York Times* reported on newfound interracial harmony, particularly between police and the African American community (Sengupta 2001).

12. The 2000 National African American Election Study was a nationally representative, Web-based survey conducted by Knowledge Networks. It included a preelection panel of 831 African Americans and post-election panel of 605 African Americans and a fresh sample of 724 whites. Fuller details on the sample characteristics and respondents may be found in Dawson and Popoff (2004) and Bobo and Johnson (2004).

REFERENCES

Blumer, Herbert. 1958. "Racial Prejudice as a Sense of Group Position." *Pacific Sociological Review* 1: 3–7.

Bobo, Lawrence D. 1988. "Attitudes Toward the Black Political Movements: Trends, Meaning, and Effects on Racial Policy Attitudes." *Social Psychology Quarterly* 51(4): 287–302.

———. 1999. "Prejudice as Group Position: Microfoundations of a Sociological Approach to Racism and Race Relations." *Journal of Social Issues* 55(3): 445–72.

————. 2000. "Reclaiming a DuBoisian Perspective on Racial Attitudes." *Annals of the American Academy of Political and Social Science* 568: 186–202.

————. 2001. "Racial Attitudes and Relations at the Close of the Twentieth Century." In *America Becoming: Racial Trends and Their Consequences,* vol. 1, edited by Neil J. Smelser, William J. Wilson, and Faith N. Mitchell. Washington, D.C.: National Academy Press.

Bobo, Lawrence D., and Devon Johnson. 2004. "A Taste for Punishment: Black and White Americans' Views on the Death Penalty and the War on Drugs." *Du Bois Review* 1: 151–80.

Bobo, Lawrence, and James R. Kluegel. 1997. "Status, Ideology, and Dimensions of Whites' Racial Beliefs and Attitudes: Progress and Stagnation." In *Racial Attitudes in the 1990s: Continuity and Change,* edited by Steven A. Tuch and Jack K. Martin. New York: Praeger.

Bobo, Lawrence, James R. Kluegel, and Ryan A. Smith. 1997. "Laissez-Faire Racism: The Crystallization of a Kinder, Gentler Antiblack Ideology." In *Racial Attitudes in the 1990s: Continuities and Change,* edited by Steven Tuch and Jack K. Martin. New York: Praeger.

Bobo, Lawrence D., and Ryan A. Smith. 1998. "From Jim Crow Racism to Laissez-Faire Racism: The Transformation of Racial Attitudes." In *Beyond Pluralism: The Conception of Groups and Group Identities in America,* edited by Wendy F. Katkin, Ned Landsman, and Andrea Tyree. Urbana, Ill.: University of Illinois Press.

Bobo, Lawrence D., and Mia Tuan. Forthcoming. *Prejudice in Politics: Group Position, Public Opinion, and the Wisconsin Treaty Rights Controversy.* Cambridge, Mass.: Harvard University Press.

Bobo, Lawrence, and Camille L. Zubrinsky. 1996. "Attitudes on Residential Integration: Perceived Status Differences, Mere In-group Preference or Racial Prejudice?" *Social Forces* 74(3): 883–909.

Bonilla-Silva, Eduardo. 2001. *White Supremacy and Racism in the Post–Civil Rights Era.* Boulder, Colo.: Lynne Rienner.

Callaghan, Karen, and Nayda Terkildsen. 2002. "Understanding the Role of Race in Candidate Evaluation." *Political Decision Making, Deliberation, and Participation* 6: 51–95.

Carmines, Edward G., and James A. Stimson. 1989. *Issue Evolution: Race and the Transformation of American Politics.* Princeton, N.J.: Princeton University Press.

Charles, Camille Z. 2000. "Neighborhood Racial-Composition Preferences: Evidence from a Multiethnic Metropolis." *Social Problems* 47(3): 379–407.

————. 2003. "The Dynamics of Racial Residential Segregation." *Annual Review of Sociology* 29: 67–107.

Citrin, Jack, Donald Green, and David O. Sears. 1990. "White Reactions to Black Candidates: When Does Race Matter?" *Public Opinion Quarterly* 54: 74–96.

Cohen, Cathy J. 1999. *The Boundaries of Blackness: AIDS and the Breakdown of Black Politics.* Chicago: University of Chicago Press.

Collins, Randall. 2001. "Ethnic Change in Macrohistorical Perspective." In *Problem of the Century: Racial Stratification in the United States,* edited by Elijah Anderson and Douglas S. Massey. New York: Russell Sage Foundation.

Dawson, Michael C. 1994. *Behind the Mule: Race and Class in African American Politics.* Princeton, N.J.: Princeton University Press.

———. 2000. "Slowly Coming to Grips with the Effects of the American Racial Order on American Policy Preferences." In *Racialized Politics: The Debate on Racism in America,* edited by David O. Sears, James Sidanius, and Lawrence D. Bobo. Chicago: University of Chicago Press.

———. 2001. *Black Visions.* Chicago: University of Chicago Press.

Dawson, Michael C., and Ravana Popoff. 2004. "Reparations: Justice and Greed in Black and White." *Du Bois Review* 1: 47–92.

Edsall, Thomas B., and Mary D. Edsall. 1991. *Chain Reaction: The Impact of Race, Rights, and Taxes on American Politics.* New York: Hill & Wang.

Ellis, Joseph J. 2001. *Founding Brothers: The Revolutionary Generation.* New York: Knopf.

Entman, Robert M., and Andrew Rojecki. 2000. *The Black Image in the White Mind: Media and Race in America.* Chicago: University of Chicago Press.

Farley, Reynolds, Charlotte Steeh, Maria Krysan, Tara Jackson, and Keith Reeves. 1994. "Stereotypes and Segregation: Neighborhoods in the Detroit Area." *American Journal of Sociology* 100(3): 750–80.

Feagin, Joe R. 2001. *Racist America: Roots, Current Realities, and Future Reparations.* New York: Routledge.

Fields, Barbara J. 1982. "Ideology and Race in American History." In *Region, Race, and Reconstruction: Essays in Honor of C. Vann Woodward,* edited by J. Morgan Kousser and James M. McPherson. New York: Oxford University Press.

Frymer, Paul. 1999. *Uneasy Alliances: Race and Party Competition in America.* Princeton, N.J.: Princeton University Press.

Gans, Herbert J. 1999. "The Possibility of a New Racial Hierarchy in the Twenty-first-Century United States." In *The Cultural Territories of Race: Black and White Boundaries,* edited by Michele Lamont. New York: Russell Sage Foundation.

Gerstle, Gary. 2001. *American Crucible: Race and Nation in the Twentieth Century.* Princeton, N.J.: Princeton University Press.

Gilens, Martin I. 1999. *Why Americans Hate Welfare: Race, Media, and the Politics of Antipoverty Policy.* Chicago: University of Chicago Press.

Glaser, James M. 1996. *Race, Campaign Politics, and the Realignment in the South.* New Haven, Conn.: Yale University Press.

Glenn, Evelyn Nakano. 2002. *Unequal Freedom: Gender, Race, and Labor in American Citizenship.* Cambridge, Mass.: Harvard University Press.

Holt, Thomas. 2000. *The Problem of Race in the Twenty-first Century.* Cambridge, Mass.: Harvard University Press.

Jackman, Mary R. 1994. *The Velvet Glove: Paternalism and Conflict in Gender, Class, and Race Relations.* Berkeley: University of California Press.

Kaufman, Karen M. 1998. "Racial Conflict and Political Choice: A Study of Mayoral Voting Behavior in Los Angeles and New York." *Urban Affairs Review* 33: 655–85.

———. 2003. *The Urban Voter: Group Conflict and Mayoral Voting Behavior in American Cities.* Ann Arbor: University of Michigan Press.

Kennedy, Randall. 1997. "My Race Problem—And Ours." *Atlantic Monthly* 279: 55–66.

Kim, Claire Jean. 2000. *Bitter Fruit: The Politics of Black-Korean Conflict in New York City.* New Haven, Conn.: Yale University Press.

Kinder, Donald R., and Lynn M. Sanders. 1996. *Divided by Color: Racial Politics and Democratic Ideals.* Chicago: University of Chicago Press.

Klinkner, Philip, and Rogers Smith. 1999. *The Unsteady March: The Rise and Decline of Racial Equality in America.* Chicago: University of Chicago Press.

Kluegel, James R. 1990. "Trends in Whites' Explanations of the Gap in Black-White Socioeconomic Status, 1977–1989." *American Sociological Review* 55(4): 512–25.

Kluegel, James R., and Lawrence D. Bobo. 2001. "Perceived Group Discrimination and Policy Attitudes: The Sources and Consequences of the Race and Gender Gaps." In *Urban Inequality: Evidence from Four Cities,* edited by Alice O'Connor, Chris Tilly, and Lawrence D. Bobo. New York: Russell Sage Foundation.

Kluegel, James R., and Eliot R. Smith. 1986. *Beliefs About Inequality: Americans' Views About What Is and What Ought to Be.* New York: Aldine de Gruyter.

Krysan, Maria. 2000. "Prejudice, Politics, and Public Opinion: Understanding the Sources of Racial Policy Attitudes." *Annual Review of Sociology* 26: 135–68.

Lamont, Michele. 2000. *The Dignity of Working Men: Morality and the Boundaries of Race, Class, and Immigration.* Cambridge, Mass.: Harvard University Press.

Lee, Taeku. 2002. *Mobilizing Public Opinion: Black Insurgency and Racial Attitudes in the Civil Rights Era.* Chicago: University of Chicago Press.

Lieberman, Robert C. 1998. *Shifting the Color Line: Race and the American Welfare State.* Cambridge, Mass.: Harvard University Press.

Liptak, Adam. 2003. "Texas Governor Pardons 35 Arrested in Tainted Sting." *New York Times,* August 23.

McConahay, John B. 1986. "Modern Racism, Ambivalence, and the Modern Racism Scale." In *Prejudice, Discrimination, and Racism,* edited by John F. Dovidio and Samuel Gaertner. Orlando, Fla.: Academic Press.

McWhorter, John. 2000. *Losing the Race: Self-sabotage in Black America.* New York: HarperCollins.

Mendelberg, Tali. 1997. "Executing Hortons: Racial Crime in the 1988 Presidential Campaign." *Public Opinion Quarterly* 61(1): 54–71.

Mills, Charles W. 1997. *The Racial Contract.* Ithaca, N.Y.: Cornell University Press.

Nobles, Melissa. 2000. *Shades of Citizenship: Race and the Census in Modern Politics.* Stanford, Calif.: Stanford University Press.

O'Connor, Alice. 2001. *Poverty Knowledge: Social Science, Social Policy, and the Poor in Twentieth-Century U.S. History.* Princeton, N.J.: Princeton University Press.

Pettigrew, Thomas F. 1997. "The Affective Component of Prejudice: Empirical Support for the New View." In *Racial Attitudes in the 1990s: Continuity and Change,* edited by Steven A. Tuch and Jack K. Martin. New York: Praeger.

Rashbaum, William K. 2003. "Woman Dies After Officers Mistakenly Raid Her Home." *New York Times,* May 17.

Reeves, Keith. 1997. *Voting Hopes or Fears? White Voters, Black Candidates, and Racial Politics in America.* New York: Oxford University Press.

Schuman, Howard, and John Harding. 1963. "Sympathetic Identification with the Underdog." *Public Opinion Quarterly* 27: 230–41.

Sears, David O. 1988. "Symbolic Racism." In *Eliminating Racism: Profiles in Controversy,* edited by Phyllis A. Katz and Dalmas A. Taylor. New York: Plenum.

Sears, David O., and Jack Citrin. 1985. *Tax Revolt: Proposition 13 and Something for Nothing in California.* Cambridge, Mass.: Harvard University Press.

Sears, David O., Collette van Laar, and Rick Kosterman. 1997. "Is It Really Racism? The Origins of White Americans' Opposition to Race-Targeted Policies." *Public Opinion Quarterly* 61: 16–53.

Sengupta, Somini. 2001. "September 11 Attack Narrows the Racial Divide." *New York Times,* October 10.

Sleeper, Jim. 1997. *Liberal Racism.* New York: Viking.

Smith, Eliot R. 1993. "Social Identity and Social Emotions: Toward New Conceptualizations of Prejudice." In *Affect, Cognition, and Stereotyping: Interactive Processes in Group Perception,* edited by Diane M. Mackie and David L. Hamilton. New York: Academic Press.

Smith, Rogers M. 1993. "Beyond Tocqueville, Myrdal, and Hartz: The Multiple Traditions in America." *American Political Science Review* 87: 549–66.

Sniderman, Paul M., and Edward G. Carmines. 1997. *Reaching Beyond Race.* Cambridge, Mass.: Harvard University Press.

Sniderman, Paul M., and Thomas Piazza. 1993. *The Scar of Race.* Cambridge: Harvard University Press.

Steele, Claude. 1998. "A Threat in the Air: How Stereotypes Shape Intellectual Identity and Performance." In *Confronting Racism: The Problem and the Response,* edited by J. L. Eberhardt and Susan T. Fiske. Thousand Oaks, Calif.: Sage Publications.

Thernstrom, Stephan, and Abigail Thernstrom. 1997. *America in Black and White: One Nation, Indivisible.* New York: Simon & Schuster.

Thompson, J. Phillip. 1998. "Universalism and Deconcentration: Why Race Still Matters in Poverty and Economic Development." *Politics and Society* 26: 181–219.

Torres, Kimberly C., and Camille Z. Charles. 2004. "Metastereotypes and the Black-White Divide: A Qualitative View of Race on an Elite College Campus." *Du Bois Review* 1: 115–50.

Waters, Mary C. 1999. *Black Identities: West Indian Immigrant Dreams and American Realities.* Cambridge, Mass.: Harvard University Press.

Wilson, William J. 1973. *Power, Racism, and Privilege: Race Relations in Theoretical and Sociohistorical Perspectives.* New York: Free Press.

Yinger, John. 1998. "Housing Discrimination Is Still Worth Worrying About." *Housing Policy Debate* 9: 893–927.

Zuberi, Tukufu. 2001. *Thicker Than Blood: How Racial Statistics Lie.* Minneapolis: University of Minnesota Press.

Zubrinsky, Camille L., and Lawrence Bobo. 1996. "Prismatic Metropolis: Race and Residential Segregation in the City of Angels." *Social Science Research* 24: 335–74.

3

COLOR-BLIND RACISM AND RACIAL INDIFFERENCE: THE ROLE OF RACIAL APATHY IN FACILITATING ENDURING INEQUALITIES

୨୦

Tyrone A. Forman

THE CIVIL RIGHTS movement prompted several important changes in American society. One significant change has been the decline in overt expressions of racial prejudice over the past four decades (Schuman et al. 1997). This decline has led some observers to argue that white racial antipathy has virtually disappeared in the United States (D'Souza 1995; Steele 1990; Thernstrom and Thernstrom 1997). Others have argued, however, that rather than an actual *disappearance* in white racial antipathy, there has instead been a change in its *expression* (Bobo, Kluegel, and Smith 1997; Bonilla-Silva and Forman 2000; Dovidio 2001; Forman 2001; Gould 1999; Myers and Williamson 2001; Pettigrew and Meertens 1995; Sears and Henry 2003). These authors have drawn attention to the fact that despite the rather dramatic increase in the acceptance of the principle of racial equality and integration among large numbers of whites over the past four decades, there remain indications of persisting racial antipathy and enduring racial inequalities (Crosby, Bromley, and Saxe 1980; Darity and Myers 1998; Forman 2001; Pettigrew 1985).

There is abundant evidence that racial prejudice persists as an important problem. For example, while large-scale surveys show overwhelming liberalization in racial thinking in response to traditional survey items, on survey items designed to capture the present-day racial climate there is evidence for the actual worsening of racial prejudice (see Forman 2004). As recent experimental results illustrate, the change in racial prejudice is one of kind rather than of degree. Using laboratory experiments, John Dovidio and his colleagues have shown that white college students are more likely to express distaste for or to discriminate against blacks when conditions enable them to do so without having to directly acknowledge or confront their racist attitudes or behavior—for example, when their views can be masked by some other motive (see Dovidio 2001; Dovidio and Gaertner 2000; Hodson, Dovidio, and Gaertner 2002). Thomas Pettigrew and Roel Meertens (1995, 73) note that many individuals "express their negative views only in ostensibly nonprejudiced ways that 'slip under the norm.' " Increasingly it seems apparent that those measures of racial attitudes traditionally deployed in surveys and other studies have limited utility for capturing racial dynamics in the post–civil rights period, a time when overt expressions of racial prejudice are discouraged (Bonilla-Silva and Forman 2000; Myers and Williamson 2001).

As many analysts have argued, tapping into these newer, subtler forms of racial prejudice requires the use of new measures (Bobo, Kluegel, and Smith 1997; Dovidio 2001; Forman 2001, 2004; Henry and Sears 2002; Pettigrew and Meertens 1995; Sears and Henry 2003). But measuring contemporary racial prejudice is not straightforward.[1] New measures must be able to capture the more passive and less explicit ways in which white racial antipathy is increasingly expressed. Building on Pettigrew and Meertens's (1995) formulation of the absence of sympathy for an out-group (that is, the denial of emotions) as a new form of prejudice, in this chapter I develop a construct, *racial apathy,* that I argue is an especially good way to capture at least one manifestation of newer and subtler racial prejudice in the post–civil rights era. Broadly, racial apathy refers to lack of feeling or indifference toward societal racial and ethnic inequality and lack of engagement with race-related social issues. It is expressed in at least two ways: a lack of concern about racial and ethnic disparities and an unwillingness to address proximal and distal forms of racially disparate treatment. As Paul Wachtel (1999, 35–36) points out, this dimension has too often been overlooked:

> Perhaps most important of all for whites to acknowledge and understand is [racial] indifference. . . . Perhaps no other feature of white attitudes and of the underlying attitudinal structure of white society as a whole is as cumulatively responsible for the pain and deprivation experienced by [racial minorities] at this point in our history as is [racial] indifference. At the same time, perhaps no feature is as misunderstood or overlooked.

Whereas historically most scholars have characterized racial prejudice as an overt manifestation of negative feelings about an out-group, in this chapter I focus instead on the expression of racial apathy toward, lack of care for, or disinterest in the social circumstances of racial and ethnic minorities as a new form of racial prejudice. I argue that contemporary racism plays an essential part in the construction of this newer and more subtle form of prejudice. Before examining the parameters and extent of this new prejudice, I explore an important antecedent to its expression, namely, contemporary racism.

THE NATURE OF CONTEMPORARY RACISM

Researchers have labeled these more subtle and covert forms of racism as laissez-faire racism (Bobo, Kluegel, and Smith 1997), color-blind racism (Bonilla-Silva and Forman 2000), cultural racism (Jones 1999), aversive racism (Dovidio 2001), symbolic racism (Henry and Sears 2002; Sears and Henry 2003), racial resentment (Kinder and Sanders 1996), modern racism (McConahay 1986), and subtle racism (Pettigrew and Meertens 1995). Despite the fact that these authors differ in how they conceptualize the nature and content of contemporary racism, they share two common features. First, these authors theorize that new forms of racism emerged in the aftermath of the civil rights movement. Second, they argue that racism is not motivated by irrationality but rather by the desire to maintain a dominant social position in the racialized social system. I use the term "racism" here to represent a widely held ideology that enables either the full or—in more recent times—partial denial of opportunity and resources to particular racial and ethnic groups (for a similar perspective, see Mills 1997, 2000).[2]

I argue that the post–civil rights racial ideology should be called *color-blind racism*.[3] As I use it here, color-blind racism encapsulates the general set of ideas that race does not matter in post–civil rights America and the claim by many Americans that they are personally color-blind and do not see race (see Gallagher 2003; Lewis 2001; Lewis, Chesler, and Forman 2000).[4] The main beliefs of this racial ideology are: (1) U.S. society functions as a racial meritocracy; (2) for the most part these days people do not care about or even notice race; (3) any racialized patterns of social inequality that do persist are outcomes of individual and/or group-level cultural deficiency; and (4) because of the first three beliefs, nothing systematic (such as affirmative action) needs to be or should be done to redress racialized outcomes.

Color-blind ideology largely explains contemporary racial and ethnic inequality as the result of nonracial dynamics. It fosters a view that existing racial inequality must be the result of personal choices, not blocked opportunity. As Lewis Killian (1990, 4) observes, many whites

> have accepted the victories of the Civil Rights Movement. They don't object to sharing public accommodations with blacks and they will let their children go to school with them as long as there aren't too many. They believe that blacks should have equal job opportunities and if a lot of them remain poor it must be because they don't take advantage of the changes open to them.

It is important to note that, because color-blindness provides a seemingly neutral or nonracial basis for not redressing racial and ethnic inequalities, it serves as a barrier to doing so. Color-blindness explains away inequities, blaming the victims of racial discrimination for their situation and, as Charles Gallagher (2003, 6) puts it, rendering the true origins of such inequality invisible: "Color-blindness hides white privilege behind a mask of assumed meritocracy while rendering invisible the institutional arrangements that perpetuate racial inequality." In this way color-blindness is a central mechanism used today in the United States to defend the racial status quo.

It is essential to point out, however, that the importance of color-blind racism in the post–civil rights era is not necessarily in the direct harm it inflicts on individual racial minorities, as was the case with Jim Crow racism. The importance of color-blindness lies instead in its indirect impact on racial and ethnic minorities' life chances through its creation of a societal climate that prevents many whites and some minorities from recognizing or taking actions to redress persistent and pervasive racial inequality. That is, a crucial limitation to the color-blind discourse is that it "blinds [us] to the effects of race and color in the world around us" (Lewis 2003, 192). The ethical protection of color-blindness ("I'm color-blind and therefore not responsible"), which leaves many whites free to participate in a system of inequality without feeling any accountability, is one of the main pillars of contemporary racial and ethnic inequality. In this way, whites are taken off the moral hook and individual and group cultural deficiencies are made the culprit for any persistent racial inequity.

As color-blind racism gains normative dominance in U.S. society, targeted efforts perceived as addressing contemporary racial and ethnic inequality in our society (affirmative action, for example) are increasingly deemed illegitimate and therefore stigmatized. Another important consequence of this emergent post–civil rights racial ideology is that individuals are not likely to express their prejudices toward racial minorities explicitly but rather are more likely to express their negative feelings in ways that are subtle or covert and enable plausible deniability, both to themselves and to others (Bonilla-Silva and Forman 2000; Myers and Williamson 2001). Racial apathy represents one new manifestation of negative feelings toward racial minorities. Unfortunately, our traditional conceptualization of prejudice does not allow us to fully capture this new development.

RECONCEPTUALIZING PREJUDICE

A review of the race and ethnic relations literature reveals broad diversity in conceptualizations and definitions of prejudice. In fact, this diversity prompted Patricia Devine and her colleagues to note that more than any other phenomenon, "how social psychologists have conceptualized prejudice has changed over time" (Devine, Plant, and Blair 2001, 198). The following lists present a number of the definitions of prejudice that are provided in the research literature. The thread connecting these diverse definitions is the idea that prejudice is negative and contains both affective and cognitive components. However, it is also at this point that the varying definitions of prejudice part ways conceptually. To highlight these different conceptualizations of prejudice I have separated the definitions into two categories: traditional and alternative views of prejudice.

TRADITIONAL DEFINITIONS OF PREJUDICE

"Prejudice is an antipathy based upon a *faulty* and inflexible generalization" (Allport 1954, 10, emphasis added).

"Prejudice is a pattern of hostility in interpersonal relations which is directed against an entire group or against its individuals members; it fulfills a specific *irrational* function for its bearer" (Ackerman and Jahoda 1950, 3–4, emphasis added).

"Prejudiced attitudes . . . are *irrational,* unjust, intolerant dispositions towards other groups" (Milner 1975, 9, emphasis added).

"Prejudice is an *irrational* attitude of hostility directed against an individual, a group, a race, or their supposed characteristics, an unreasonable prejudgment" (Better 2002, 19, emphasis added).

"Prejudice is an *unreasonable* negative attitude towards others because of their membership in a particular group" (Fishbein 1996, 5, emphasis added).

"Prejudice is shared feelings of acceptance-rejection, trust-distrust, and liking-disliking that characterizes attitudes toward specific groups" (Brewer and Kramer 1985, 230).

ALTERNATIVE DEFINITIONS OF PREJUDICE

"Prejudice is a failure of rationality or a *failure of justice* or a *failure of human-heartedness* in an individual's attitude toward members of another ethnic group" (Harding et al. 1969, 6, emphasis added).

"Prejudice against racial and ethnic groups is an antipathy [that] simultaneously violates two basic norms—the norm of rationality and the *norm of human-heartedness*" (Pettigrew 1980, 2–14, emphasis added).

"Prejudice refers to attitudes or propensities to *act in ways which disadvantage* individuals because of their group affiliation" (Leggon 1979, 9, emphasis added).

"Prejudice refers to an *organized predisposition* to respond in an unfavorable manner toward people from an ethnic group because of their ethnic affiliation" (Aboud 1988, 4, emphasis added).

"Prejudice is a set of attitudes which *causes, supports, or justifies* discrimination" (Rose 1951, 5, emphasis added).

The traditional conceptualization of prejudice has a number of advantages; most important is its focus on the negative and hostile nature of prejudice. Further, it typically focuses on the irrationality, faultiness, or unreasonableness of prejudice. An unfortunate consequence of this focus has been a tendency to narrowly conceptualize prejudice as a personality disorder. According to the sociologist Robin Williams (1988, 345), this view makes two important assumptions: "(1) The individual is a unit separable from 'society'; and (2) prejudices involve distortions of an external reality or departures from rationality." Thus, a common criticism of the traditional view of prejudice is that it ignores the larger social structure and power dynamics (see Blumer 1958; Bobo and Fox 2003; Jackman 1994; Williams 1988). By focusing on the irrationality of prejudice and ignoring social structural dynamics, the traditional conceptualization of prejudice is unable to account for some of the newer, subtler, and more covert manifestations of contemporary prejudice.

In contrast, the five alternative definitions of prejudice highlight the notion that prejudice is linked to a larger social system. This linkage results in a conceptualization of prejudice that acknowledges the role of irrationality but also considers the *failure of justice* (Harding et al. 1969) and the *violation of the norms of human-heartedness and justice* (Pettigrew 1980). Interestingly, two of the traditional definitions of prejudice highlight the role of unjust attitudes (see Milner 1975; Stephan 1999). For example, according to J. H. Harding and his colleagues, "prejudice violates the norm of rationality by being overgeneralized, rigid, and based on inadequate evidence; it violates the norm of justice because it fails to accord equal treatment to all members of society; and it violates the norm of human-heartedness in denying the basic humanity of [the] other" (cited in Duckitt 1992, 15). The incorporation of unjust attitudes and/or failure of human-heartedness into our definition of prejudice also provides conceptual leverage for understanding the changing expression of racial prejudice in U.S. society.

Moreover, the traditional view's focus on the irrationality or unreasonableness of prejudice implies that people have no rational reason (that is, nothing to gain) for expressing racial prejudice. In contrast, others have pointed out that "far from being deviant or abnormal, prejudice often becomes the normal and expected state of affairs in a society" (Levin and Levin 1982, 76). In line with this perspective, Richard Schermerhorn (1970, 6) argues that if social scientists have learned anything from their long-term study of the concept of prejudice, it is that prejudice "is *not* a little demon that emerges in people because they are depraved." Therefore, I argue that the expression of racial prejudice is not simply irrational but in fact serves an important social function in a racialized social system. Typically this function is to disadvantage an individual or socially defined group viewed as subordinate (see also Pettigrew 1980). As such, *racial prejudice* must be understood in a wider sense to include a possible irrational component and/or to include a failure of justice component. Further, this alternative conceptualization provides an important basis for considering racial apathy a contemporary form of racial prejudice.

Although racial prejudice has long been recognized to have both affective and cognitive dimensions, most of the previous research on contemporary racial prejudice has focused on the cognitive dimension (Pettigrew 1997, 2000; Shelton 2000). As Eric Vanman and Norman Miller (1993, 215) note, "A consideration of prejudice as a phenomenon in the mind rather than in the guts has its limits." Furthermore, the predominant focus on cognition in the study of prejudice is quite limited, since "affect is an inexonerable force in intergroup relations. Encounters with members of different groups might activate beliefs and thoughts, but they are also likely to activate feelings and emotions" (Stroessner and Mackie 1993, 63). In fact, recent research has begun an important corrective by emphasizing the affective dimension of prejudice. For instance, Eliot Smith and his colleagues (Smith 1993; Smith and Ho 2002) have developed a new conceptualization of prejudice that highlights the affective dimension. Smith (1993, 304) defines prejudice as "a social emotion experienced with respect to one's social identity as a group member, with an outgroup as a target." Consistent with this definition, Marilyn Brewer and Roderick Kramer (1985, 231) note that although "the term 'prejudice' could be applied to the cognitive content of intergroup perceptions as well, typically it is used with reference to the affective or emotional component." In essence, by defining prejudice in this manner, it highlights the notion that feelings and emotions are central to intergroup dynamics.

This theoretical insight has spawned a number of empirical investigations concerning the role of intergroup emotions in shaping a range of outcomes. For instance, Thomas Pettigrew and his colleagues (Meertens and Pettigrew 1997; Pettigrew and Meertens 1995; Pettigrew et al. 1998; Pettigrew 2000) have investigated an important dimension of affective prejudice in Europe and the United States, namely, subtle prejudice. They argue that individuals express prejudice toward out-groups in ways that shift over time in response to changes in societal norms about socially appropriate ways to express dislike. Thus, subtle prejudice consists of three ways to express distaste in modern-day Europe and the United States that are thought to be socially acceptable: defense of traditional values, exaggeration of cultural differences, and denial of positive emotion. Drawing on large, nationally representative survey data from four European nations, Pettigrew and his colleagues show that subtle prejudice is distinct from blatant prejudice and is independently linked to a variety of social policies concerning out-group members, even when other important factors are simultaneously controlled (see Meertens and Pettigrew 1997; Pettigrew and Meertens 1995; Pettigrew et al. 1998; Pettigrew 2000). Especially noteworthy in this work is the focus of Pettigrew and his colleagues on the withholding of positive emotions, such as sympathy or admiration, toward out-group members as an important dimension of subtle prejudice. In the next section, I build on this formulation of subtle prejudice as the denial of emotions by focusing on the absence of human-heartedness or denial of care as another form of subtle prejudice (that is, racial apathy). I speculate that the expression of racial apathy reflects not a true lack of care but a subtler distaste for out-group members.

RACIAL APATHY: THE NEW FACE OF RACIAL PREJUDICE

Several decades ago Jack Levin claimed that "if we fail to take action to halt discrimination or redress the grievances of minorities, we are acting against them" (Levin and Levin 1982, 58). Here he highlights the importance of recognizing a lack of action (for example, a failure to intervene in the face of injustice) as equivalent in some important ways to direct action against a group. In a similar vein I argue that the expression of racial apathy serves functions similar to those of explicit forms of prejudice of the past. In the post–civil rights era the expression of racial apathy represents passive support for the racial status quo in society. It facilitates the racial status quo by paralyzing individuals from acting to redress injustice. As color-blind racism becomes hegemonic in U.S. society more individuals are becoming indifferent to racial inequality. Racial apathy is often expressed because individuals believe that any existing racial inequities are the result of individual or group cultural deficiencies, not racial discrimination. Thus, the racially apathetic see little reason to be bothered by or to care about lingering inequities. Racial apathy is a subtle expression of a particular kind of dislike.

Theorizing the negative consequences of racial apathy is not entirely new. For instance, Daniel Katz (1960, 182) noted almost fifty years ago that

> most research on attitudes has been directed at beliefs concerning the undesirable character of minority groups or of deviants, with accompanying feelings of distrust, contempt, and hatred. Many attitudes, however, are not the projection of repressed aggression but are expressions of apathy or withdrawal. The individual protects himself from a difficult or demanding world and salvages his self-respect by retreating within his own shell.

Here Katz argues that apathy is not truly a lack of opinion about a group, but an expression of a particular kind of dislike. Pettigrew (1980, 2–14) has also discussed indifference as a form of prejudice. He argues that "violating the norm of 'human-heartedness' can result from fear and threat, or jealousy and envy; it can range from intense hatred to simple *indifference* and an *absence of human sympathy.*" In fact, in recent work Pettigrew and his colleagues have argued that the absence of sympathy for out-group members in a number of European countries represents a new form of subtle prejudice (Pettigrew and Meertens 1995; Pettigrew et al. 1998; Pettigrew 2000). These patterns have also been observed in the United States. For instance, a recent study found that 43 percent of whites reported that they seldom (not too often, hardly ever, never) feel sympathy for blacks, and 48 percent indicated that they seldom feel admiration for blacks (Williams et al. 1999). As another analyst has recently pointed out, often when individuals say they do not feel anything or they are apathetic, "it can mask and underlie great cruelty . . . [and] can shape how [individuals] behave in powerful ways" (Johnson 1997, 66). This is quite consistent with the view that the "mind rarely, probably never, perceives any object with absolute indifference, that is, without feeling" (Sherrington 1890, as cited in Blumenthal 1977). Moreover, recent qualitative research confirms that expressions of racial apathy as conceptualized here easily coexist with persistent negative views about racial minorities. For example, studying everyday life in a white suburban enclave, recent ethnographic research describes the way in which young, middle-class whites discussed race-related matters: "When the topic of racial difference was posed to SWR [abbreviation for town name] students directly and in a more public context, they made it clear that they thought race was someone else's issue, one [with] which they did not need to bother" (Kenny 2000, 171). In more private settings, however, these same students were quite willing to express negative feelings toward racial minorities (Kenny 2000). As a construct, racial apathy captures the ways in which whites may publicly express indifference or lack of care about racial inequality while at the same time continuing to hold antiminority views.

There are at least two possible reasons why individuals express racial apathy. First, individuals may express indifference to racial inequality because they view those racial minorities who experience difficulty as having individual or group cultural deficiencies that justify their disadvantaged status. As a result, these individuals feel they have little reason to care about the social circumstances of these minorities. In essence, they deny the humanity of the disadvantaged. Daniel Bar-Tal (1990) has labeled this phenomenon *delegitimization,* by which he means the categorization of certain groups into negative social categories so as to exclude them from social acceptability. This view is also captured in Michael Katz's (1989) concept of the "undeserving poor." Although this term ostensibly refers to the work effort of the poor, in the post–civil rights era these moral judgments have been extended to racial minorities. The perception is that the deserving poor are white and work hard, whereas the undeserving poor are black or Latino as well as unemployed and receiving government assistance.

Thus, the disadvantaged status of many racial minorities is attributed to their lack of motivation and non-normative values.

Another possible reason for the expression of racial apathy is ignorance about the persistent nature of racial and ethnic inequality. One advantage of a focus on racial apathy is its ability to capture not only white indifference to racial inequality—their lack of an opinion or interest in the subject—but also the expression of whites' privileged status in the racialized social system in their ability to be structurally ignorant about racial discrimination or to not even think much about racial matters. Rather than being a thoughtful response to social realities, such a lack of thought about racial matters in some ways represents a strategic evasion of responsibility, or what Lorraine Kenny (2000) has called "sanctioned ignorance." James Baldwin (1955, 166) discussed the power of this sanctioned ignorance in his classic essay "Stranger in the Village," in which he argues that

> there is a great deal of will power involved in the white man's naïveté . . . [he prefers] to keep the black man at a certain human remove because it is easier for him thus to preserve his simplicity and avoid being called to account for crimes committed by his forefathers, or his neighbors. He is inescapably aware, nevertheless, that he is in a better position in the world than black men are.

What Baldwin highlights here is the fact that despite being profoundly ignorant about the social circumstance of racial minorities, in many ways whites occupy a privileged position because of that very ignorance. For if they were to dispense with this ignorance, they would ultimately have to change their views and behavior toward racial minorities. This "naïveté" or "sanctioned ignorance" is an evasion that is closely linked to the pervasive racial residential segregation in our society.

Whites continue to be the most racially isolated group in the country (Lewis 2001; Massey and Fischer 1999; Orfield and Lee 2004). Many whites live in almost-all-white suburban communities; a large body of recent work has clearly demonstrated that these communities are not accidentally this way (Lipsitz 1998; Massey and Denton 1993; Sugrue 1996). That is, living in such largely homogenous communities is representative not of a lack of racial dynamics but of participation (whether deliberate or accidental) in the very racialized phenomenon of segregation. On the other hand, although there is a racial component to the composition of these spaces, the racial motives, history, and practices that have led to their current demographics are largely unacknowledged, if not explicitly denied (see Lewis 2001). For example, Lorraine Kenny (2000, 6), in her ethnography of everyday life in white suburbia, describes the segregated spaces as the " 'anti-OtherAmerica'—a place intentionally built on imposing distance between white America and its Others" and based on both "the exclusion of the Other and the denial of this practice." Thus, whites are often today deliberately situated so that they do not have to think about race regularly and can remain ignorant about contemporary discrimination, largely because they have insulated themselves from the racial "other." The construct of racial apathy represents a way to capture these kinds of deliberate evasions, destructive indifference, and powerful inaction.

NATIONAL FINDINGS

What is the extent of racial apathy and indifference in the United States? To answer this question I draw on survey data from several nationwide surveys. As a first step in examining changes in racial indifference among whites, figure 3.1 reports results for a measure of racial apathy and generalized apathy drawn from a large-scale survey of young people called the Monitoring the Future Survey, an annual survey since 1976 of young people about their social attitudes toward a broad range of questions. *Racial apathy* was measured by asking respondents whether they agreed or disagreed (on a scale from 1 = "disagree" to 5 = "agree") with the statement: "Maybe some minority groups do get unfair treatment, but that's no business of mine." The statement with which

FIGURE 3.1   CHANGES IN YOUNG WHITES' EXPRESSION OF RACIAL APATHY AND
             GENERALIZED APATHY, 1976 TO 2000

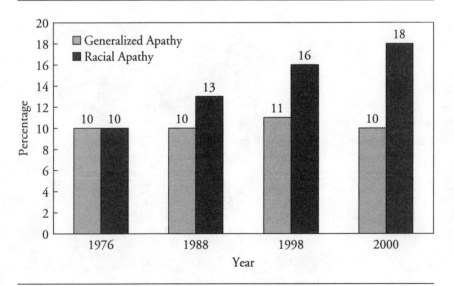

Source: Author's compilation.
Note: p ≤ .05.

generalized apathy was measured was: "It's not really my problem if others are in trouble and need help." Here I am interested in comparing white youths' responses in 2000 with those given in 1998, 1988, and 1976. Two patterns are worth highlighting from these data. First, racial apathy shows movement toward increasing racial intolerance. That is, more young whites today agree (18 percent) with the statement that minority groups may receive unfair treatment but that is not their concern than did so in 1976 (10 percent). Second, there appears to be virtual stability in young whites' expression of generalized apathy. For example, approximately one in ten young whites today agree that it is not their problem if others need help; a similar number shared this view in 1976. This pattern of results indicates, at least with respect to young whites, that racial indifference is a perspective held by an increasing number of white youth. Further, this expressed racial apathy is distinct from the generalized apathy that is often attributed to young people. Rather, it is specific to a racialized notion of apathy.

Figure 3.2 reports the proportion of young whites responding "never" over time to the question: "How often do you worry about race relations?" (scale

FIGURE 3.2   CHANGE IN THE PERCENTAGE OF YOUNG WHITES REPORTING THEY NEVER WORRY ABOUT RACE RELATIONS, 1976 TO 2000

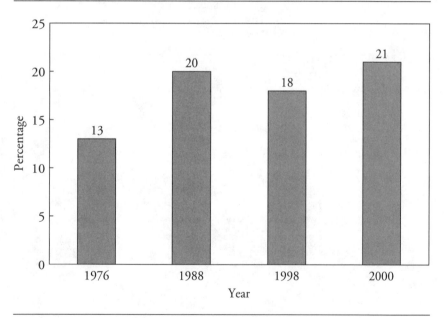

Source: Author's compilation.
Note: $p \leq .05$.

from 1 = "never" to 4 = "often"). An increasing number of young whites report never being concerned about race relations. For instance, whereas 13 percent of young whites reported never being concerned with race in 1976, by 2000, 21 percent of white youth expressed this view. Again, this pattern of change suggests that racial apathy in particular is on the rise, not generalized apathy.

Is racial indifference specific to the young? Unfortunately, comparable survey questions have not been asked of the general adult population. However, other questions have been asked of white adults continuously, in many cases for at least four decades (1964 to 2000). These questions provide some insight, albeit indirectly, about the prevalence of and shifts in racial indifference among white adults. The first set of questions comes from the Institute for Social Research (ISR) at the University of Michigan. Surveys from ISR have included three questions about government intervention in matters of school integration, neighborhood integration, and workplace integration (see appendix to this chapter). Figure 3.3 graphically depicts changes over the past four decades in the proportion of white adults saying they have no interest in these questions on integration. These data indicate that increasing numbers of white adults are responding that they have no interest in the role that the government should play in ensuring integration in several life domains. For instance, the proportion of white adults saying they had no interest in the issue of school integration rose from approximately 11 percent in 1964 to 34 percent in 2000.

Does the rise in "no interest" and "don't know" responses reflect racial apathy and more general racial intolerance? I argue that it does. My interpretation of these survey responses is quite consistent with other recent research that has shown that some whites who harbor negative racial attitudes hide behind "don't know" responses (see Berinsky 1999). Furthermore, analysis of longitudinal data spanning the 1960s through the 1990s indicates that the pattern among whites of responding "don't know" or "no interest" is more likely today than it was in the past to reflect a strategic move to mask socially undesirable responses (Berinsky 2002). Similarly, Moshe Semyonov and his colleagues (2001), in a study of antiforeigner sentiment in Germany, found that 29 percent of their German respondents refused to answer a question on the perceived size of the foreign population. When they examined these respondents' views on other questions in the survey, it was clear that they were more likely to have a deep hatred for foreigners than those who had responded.

Figure 3.4 provides data that enable us to get a better assessment of the extent of racial apathy among white adults. It shows white and black responses to the "better break" question: "On the whole, do you think most white people want to see blacks get a better break, or do they want to keep blacks down, or don't you think they care either way?" Figure 3.4 reports the proportion of whites and blacks who say that whites "don't care either way." Two patterns

Federal Job Intervention, 1964 to 2000

Federal School Intervention, 1964 to 2000

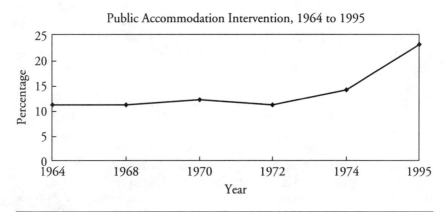

Public Accommodation Intervention, 1964 to 1995

Source: Author's compilation.
Note: p ≤ .05.

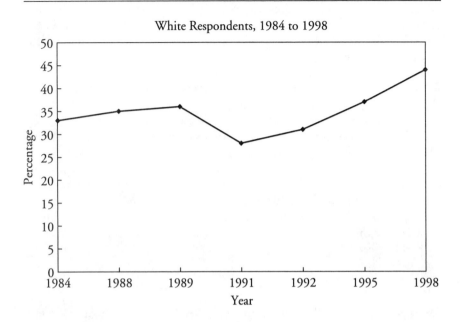

White Respondents, 1984 to 1998

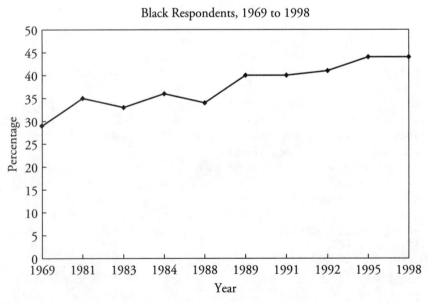

Black Respondents, 1969 to 1998

Source: Author's compilation.
Note: p ≤ .05.

revealed in this figure are worth emphasizing. First, in 1984, 33 percent of whites responded that "whites don't care"; by 1998, 44 percent of whites responded in this fashion. Second, there is substantial agreement among blacks and whites on this question, a rare occurrence in survey research on racial attitudes (see Kinder and Sanders 1996)! Whereas 29 percent of blacks reported in 1969 (at the height of the urban riots) that "whites don't care," by 1998, 44 percent of blacks held this view. In short, there was an upward shift in the proportion of whites and blacks who believed that "whites don't care" about the plight of African Americans.

I believe that taken together these patterns of change in social attitudes reveal a growing level of racial apathy among young and old whites alike in the United States. These results are especially important because they provide additional empirical evidence for the changes that have occurred over the past three decades in whites' racial attitudes. They highlight the need to refine our measurement of racial attitudes to incorporate the increasingly subtle forms of their expression (Bobo, Kluegel, and Smith 1997; Bonilla-Silva and Forman 2000; Dovidio 2001; Forman 2001).

CONCLUSION

As Lawrence Bobo highlights in this volume, "it is not enough to declare that race matters or that racism endures. The more demanding challenge is to account for how and why such a social construction comes to be reconstituted, refreshed, and enacted anew in very different times and places." Clearly, our efforts to eradicate racial and ethnic inequality will not be successful until we better understand the precise mechanisms reproducing it. In this chapter, I have argued that the expression of racial apathy is one mechanism by which racial and ethnic inequality endures. By being indifferent or ignoring the social reality of race in a racialized social system, whites and others sustain a system of inequality that restricts opportunities for many racial and ethnic minorities. As Bryan Fair (1997, xxiii) recently noted: "The problem of the twenty-first century will be the problem of color-blindness—the refusal of legislators, jurists, and most of American society to acknowledge the causes and current effects of racial caste and to adopt remedial policies to eliminate them." Those who are color-blind and racially apathetic to pervasive racial and ethnic inequality represent a "silent majority" in our society (Wiley 1973).

Almost four decades ago the Reverend Martin Luther King Jr. (1996, 745) remarked in his famous "Letter from a Birmingham Jail" that "we will have to repent in this generation not merely for the vitriolic words and actions of the bad people, but for the appalling silence of the good people." In other words, "what counts isn't just what [people] do, but even more what they don't do" (Johnson 2001, 114). The continued focus on traditional, overt Jim Crow prejudice as the main cause of the dire circumstances that many racial and ethnic minorities experience, ironically, enables many whites to overlook their role in facilitating enduring racial and ethnic inequalities.

If in the face of entrenched, systemic, and institutionalized racism most whites say that they have no negative feelings toward racial minorities but that they feel no responsibility to do anything about enduring racial and ethnic inequalities and in fact object to any programmatic solutions to addressing those inequalities—is that progress or merely a new form of prejudice in its passive support for an unequal racial status quo? It is my view that it is the latter rather than the former. The expression of racial apathy in the post–civil rights era represents an action that is racist at least in its effect, if not in its intent. Hence, we must pay closer attention to its manifestation as an important and destructive force. Although this chapter represents just a first step in detailing the nature and extent of racial apathy in the United States today, it does highlight some possible new expressions of prejudice that demand methodological as well as conceptual innovation.

APPENDIX: QUESTION WORDING

MONITORING THE FUTURE SURVEY

Racial Apathy Respondents were asked to rate on a five-point Likert-type scale the following statement: "Maybe some minority groups do get unfair treatment, but that's no business of mine." Possible responses ranged from "disagree" (1) to "agree" (5). High scores represent greater racial apathy.

Generalized Apathy Respondents were asked to rate on a five-point Likert-type scale the following statement: "It's not really my problem if others are in trouble and need help." Possible responses ranged from "disagree" (1) to "agree" (5). High scores represent greater apathy.

Concern About Race Relations Respondents were asked to answer the following question on a four-point Likert-type scale: "Of all the problems facing the nation today, how often do you worry about race relations?" Possible responses ranged from "never" (1) to "often" (4).

INSTITUTE FOR SOCIAL RESEARCH SURVEY

Federal School Intervention "Some people say that the government in Washington should see to it that white and black children go to the same schools. Others claim that this is not the government's business. Have you been interested enough in this question to favor one side over the other? [If yes] Do you think the government in Washington should see to it that white and black children go to the same schools, or stay out of this area, as it is not its business?" Possible responses were "government should see to it" (1), "government should stay out" (2), or "no interest" (3).

Federal Job Intervention   "Some people feel that if black people are not getting fair treatment in jobs, the government in Washington ought to see to it that they do. Others feel that this is not the federal government's business. Have you had enough interest in this question to favor one side over the other? [If yes] How do you feel? Should the government in Washington see to it that black people get fair treatment in jobs or is this not the federal government's business?" Possible responses were "government should see to it" (1), "government should stay out" (2), or "no interest" (3).

Public Accommodations Intervention   "As you may know, Congress passed a bill that says that black people should have the right to go to any hotel or restaurant they can afford, just like anybody else. Some people feel that this is something the government in Washington should support. Others feel that the government should stay out of this matter. Have you been interested enough in this to favor one side over the other? [If yes] Should the government support the right of black people to go to any hotel or restaurant they can afford, or should it stay out of this matter?" Possible responses were "government should see to it" (1), "government should stay out" (2), or "no interest" (3).

GALLUP SURVEY

Better Break   "On the whole, do you think most white people want to see blacks get a better break, or do they want to keep blacks down, or do you think they care either way?" Possible responses were "better break" (1), "keep blacks down" (2), or "don't care either way" (3).

This chapter was completed while I was a visiting fellow at the Research Institute of Comparative Studies in Race and Ethnicity (RICSRE) at Stanford University. I am grateful to colleagues Thomas Guglielmo, Maria Krysan, Thomas Pettigrew, Kerry Ann Rockquemore, Ulrich Wagner, and participants in Stanford's RICSRE Fellows Forum—Tom Biolsi, James Campbell, George Fredrickson, Hazel Markus, Thomas Pettigrew, Ann Pettigrew, Robert Smith, and Dorothy Steele—for their insightful comments and suggestions. I am especially indebted to Amanda Lewis for her thoughtful comments on earlier versions of this chapter. Support for this project was provided by the Institute for Research on Race and Public Policy at the University of Illinois at Chicago and the Russell Sage Foundation.

NOTES

1. Given the continuing existence of racial prejudice in society, albeit covertly expressed, some social psychologists have focused in recent years on more unobtrusive measures of prejudice. One form that this line of inquiry has taken has been to study implicit prejudice—biases of which individuals themselves may not even be aware (see Fazio et al. 1995; Blair 2001). One of the most common methods of measuring implicit prejudice is to use response-time latency procedures—in essence, the length of time it takes respondents to make particular associations that are either stereotypic or counterstereotypic (Cunningham, Preacher, and Banaji 2001). Several recent studies indicate that these implicit measures are an important predictor of socially sensitive behaviors, above and beyond traditional self-report measures of racial prejudice (Dovidio 2001; McConnell and Leibold 2001). Although these new developments in the study of racial prejudice are clearly important, a full discussion and integration of these works are beyond the scope of this chapter. Furthermore, I contend that more refined survey items can capture the new forms of prejudice.

2. By ideology I mean, following Jeffrey Prager (1982, 101), "an organized set of assumptions and presuppositions concerning social organization that orient thought and action in society and, if need be, are capable of articulation and rational defense."

3. There are clear conceptual similarities between laissez-faire racism and color-blind racism. They both highlight the importance of whites' beliefs in the cultural inferiority of racial minorities and their resistance to efforts that promote racial equality. The two conceptualizations differ in important respects as well. For instance, laissez-faire racism focuses on the persistence of negative racial stereotypes, whereas color-blind racism focuses on individuals' belief that U.S. society functions as a racial meritocracy and that people do not care about or even notice race. Nevertheless, it may well be the case that these differences mainly concern a difference in emphasis rather than substantive content.

4. I use the term "color-blind" here to highlight the idea that these beliefs are rooted in the notion of not seeing race. Though the irony of color-blindness is that, as Amanda Lewis (2003, 34) points out, "it attempts to mask the power of race as it simultaneously demonstrates precisely the difference race does make (that is, when one asserts that one does not pay attention to race, the implication is that to notice it would have deleterious outcomes)." That is, color-blindness contains within it implicit cynicism about our capacity to recognize and appreciate difference without also engaging in discrimination. As Michelle Alexander (2003, 10) puts

it, "The colorblindness ideal is premised on the notion that we, as a society, can never be trusted to see race and treat each other fairly, or with genuine compassion."

REFERENCES

Aboud, Frances. 1988. *Children and Prejudice*. New York: Basil Blackwell.

Ackerman, Nathan, and Marie Jahoda. 1950. *Anti-Semitism and Emotional Disorder: A Psychoanalytic Interpretation*. New York: Harper.

Alexander, Michelle. 2003. *Against Color-blindness*. Paper presented to the conference "Color-blind Racism? The Politics of Controlling Racial and Ethnic Data." Stanford University, Stanford, Calif. (October 2–3).

Allport, Gordon. 1954. *The Nature of Prejudice*. Reading, Mass.: Addison-Wesley.

Baldwin, James. 1955. *Notes of a Native Son*. Boston: Beacon Press.

Bar-Tal, Daniel. 1990. "Causes and Consequences of Delegitimization: Models of Conflict and Ethnocentrism." *Journal of Social Issues* 46(1): 65–81.

Berinsky, Adam. 1999. "The Two Faces of Public Opinion." *American Journal of Political Science* 43(4): 1209–30.

———. 2002. "Political Context and the Survey Response: The Dynamics of Racial Policy Opinion." *Journal of Politics* 64(2): 567–84.

Better, Shirley. 2002. *Institutional Racism: A Primer on Theory and Strategies for Social Change*. Chicago: Burnham.

Blair, Irene. 2001. "Implicit Stereotypes and Prejudice." In *Cognitive Social Psychology*, edited by Gordon Moskowitz. Mahwah, N.J.: Lawrence Erlbaum.

Blumenthal, Arthur. 1977. *The Process of Cognition*. Englewood Cliffs, N.J.: Prentice-Hall.

Blumer, Herbert. 1958. "Race Prejudice as a Sense of Group Position." *Pacific Sociological Review* 1: 3–7.

Bobo, Lawrence, and Cybelle Fox. 2003. "Race, Racism, and Discrimination: Bridging Problems, Methods, and Theory in Social Psychological Research." *Social Psychology Quarterly* 66(4): 319–32.

Bobo, Lawrence, James Kluegel, and Ryan Smith. 1997. "Laissez-faire Racism: The Crystallization of a Kinder, Gentler, Antiblack Ideology." In *Racial Attitudes in the 1990s: Continuity and Change*, edited by Steven A. Tuch and Jack Martin. Westport, Conn.: Praeger.

Bonilla-Silva, Eduardo, and Tyrone Forman. 2000. " 'I'm Not a Racist, but . . .': Mapping White College Students' Racial Ideology in the USA." *Discourse and Society* 11(1): 50–85.

Brewer, Marilyn, and Roderick Kramer. 1985. "The Psychology of Intergroup Attitudes and Behavior." *Annual Review of Psychology* 36: 219–43.

Crosby, Faye, Stephanie Bromley, and Leonard Saxe. 1980. "Recent Unobtrusive Studies of Black and White Discrimination and Prejudice: A Literature Review." *Psychological Bulletin* 87(3): 546–63.

Cunningham, William, Kristopher Preacher, and Mahzari Banaji. 2001. "Implicit Attitude Measures: Consistency, Stability, and Convergent Validity." *Psychological Science* 121(2): 163–70.

Darity, William, Jr., and Samuel Myers. 1998. *Persistent Disparity: Race and Economic Inequality in the United States Since 1945.* Cheltenham, Eng.: Edward Elgar.

Devine, Patricia, E. Ashby Plant, and Irene Blair. 2001. "Classic and Contemporary Analyses of Racial Prejudice." In *The Blackwell Handbook in Social Psychology*, vol. 4, *Intergroup Processes*, edited by Rupert Brown and Samuel Gaertner. Oxford: Blackwell.

Dovidio, John. 2001. "On the Nature of Contemporary Prejudice." *Journal of Social Issues* 57(4): 829–49.

Dovidio, John, and Samuel Gaertner. 2000. "Aversive Racism and Selection Decisions: 1989 and 1999." *Psychological Science* 11(4): 319–23.

D'Souza, Dinesh. 1995. *The End of Racism: Principles for a Multiracial Society.* New York: Free Press.

Duckitt, John. 1992. *Social Psychology of Prejudice.* New York: Praeger.

Fair, Bryan. 1997. *Notes of a Racial Caste Baby.* New York: New York University Press.

Fazio, Russell, Joni Jackson, Bridget Dunton, and Carol Williams. 1995. "Variability in Automatic Activation as an Unobtrusive Measure of Racial Attitudes: A Bona Fide Pipeline?" *Journal of Personality and Social Psychology* 69(6): 1013–27.

Fishbein, Harold. 1996. *Peer Prejudice and Discrimination.* Boulder, Colo.: Westview Press.

Forman, Tyrone. 2001. "The Social Determinants of White Youths' Racial Attitudes." *Sociological Studies of Children and Youth* 8: 173–207.

———. 2004. "Beyond Prejudice? Young Whites' Racial Attitudes in Post–Civil Rights America, 1976–1998." Unpublished paper. University of Illinois, Chicago.

Gallagher, Charles. 2003. "Color-blind Privilege: The Social and Political Functions of Erasing the Color Line in Post-Race America." *Race, Gender, and Class* 10(4): 1–17.

Gould, Mark. 1999. "Race and Theory: Culture, Poverty, and Adaptation to Discrimination in Wilson and Ogbu." *Sociological Theory* 17(2): 171–200.

Harding, John, Harold Prochansky, Bernard Kutner, and Isidor Chein. 1969. "Prejudice and Ethnic Relations." In *Handbook of Social Psychology*, vol. 5, 2nd ed., edited by Gardner Lindzey and Elliot Aronson. Reading, Mass.: Addison-Wesley.

Henry, P. J., and David Sears. 2002. "The Symbolic Racism 2000 Scale." *Political Psychology* 23(2): 253–83.

Hodson, Gordon, John Dovidio, and Samuel Gaertner. 2002. "Processes in Racial Discrimination: Differential Weighting of Conflicting Information." *Personality and Social Psychology Bulletin* 28(4): 460–71.

Jackman, Mary. 1994. *The Velvet Glove: Paternalism and Conflict in Gender, Class, and Race Relations.* Berkeley: University of California Press.

Johnson, Allan G. 1997. *The Forest and the Trees: Sociology as Life, Practice, and Promise.* Philadelphia: Temple University Press.

———. 2001. *Power, Privilege, and Difference.* Mountain View, Calif.: Mayfield.

Jones, James. 1999. "Cultural Racism: The Intersection of Race and Culture in Intergroup Conflict." In *Cultural Divides: Understanding and Overcoming Group Conflict,* edited by Deborah Prentice and Dale Miller. New York: Russell Sage Foundation.

Katz, Daniel. 1960. "The Functional Approach to the Study of Attitudes." *Public Opinion Quarterly* 24(2): 163–204.

Katz, Michael. 1989. *The Undeserving Poor.* New York: Pantheon.

Kenny, Lorraine Delia. 2000. *Daughters of Suburbia: Growing Up White, Middle-class, and Female.* New Brunswick, N.J.: Rutgers University Press.

Killian, Lewis. 1990. "Race Relations and the Nineties." *Social Forces* 69(1): 1–13.

Kinder, Donald, and Lynn Sanders. 1996. *Divided by Color: Racial Politics and Democratic Ideals.* Chicago: University of Chicago Press.

King, Martin Luther, Jr. 1996. "Letter from a Birmingham Jail." In *African Intellectual Heritage,* edited by Molefi Asante and Abu Abarry. Philadelphia: Temple University Press.

Leggon, Cheryl. 1979. "Theoretical Perspectives on Race and Ethnic Relations: A Sociohistorical Approach." *Research in Race and Ethnic Relations* 1: 1–15.

Levin, Jack, and William Levin. 1982. *The Functions of Discrimination and Prejudice.* New York: Harper & Row.

Lewis, Amanda. 2001. "There Is No 'Race' in the Schoolyard: Color-blind Ideology in an (Almost) All-White School." *American Educational Research Journal* 38(4): 781–812.

———. 2003. *Race in the Schoolyard: Negotiating the Color Line in Classrooms and Communities.* New Brunswick, N.J.: Rutgers University Press.

Lewis, Amanda, Mark Chesler, and Tyrone Forman. 2000. "The Impact of 'Color-blind' Ideologies on Students of Color: Intergroup Relations at a Predominantly White University." *Journal of Negro Education* 69(1–2): 74–91.

Lipsitz, George. 1998. *The Possessive Investment in Whiteness: How White People Profit from Identity Politics.* Philadelphia: Temple University Press.

Massey, Douglas, and Nancy Denton. 1993. *American Apartheid: Segregation and the Making of the Underclass.* Cambridge, Mass.: Harvard University Press.

Massey, Douglas, and Mary Fischer. 1999. "Does Rising Income Bring Integration? New Results for Blacks, Hispanics, and Asians in 1990." *Social Science Research* 28(3): 316–26.

McConahay, John. 1986. "Modern Racism, Ambivalence, and the Modern Racism Scale." In *Prejudice, Discrimination, and Racism,* edited by John F. Dovidio and Samuel L. Gaertner. Orlando, Fla.: Academic Press.

McConnell, Allen, and Jill Leibold. 2001. "Relations Among the Implicit Association Test, Discriminatory Behavior, and Explicit Measures of Racial Attitudes." *Journal of Experimental Social Psychology* 37(5): 435–42.

Meertens, Roel, and Thomas Pettigrew. 1997. "Is Subtle Prejudice Really Prejudice?" *Public Opinion Quarterly* 61(1): 54–71.

Mills, Charles. 1997. *The Racial Contract.* Ithaca, N.Y.: Cornell University Press.

———. 2000. "Race and the Social Contract Tradition." *Social Identities* 6(4): 441–62.

Milner, David. 1975. *Children and Race.* Harmondsworth, Eng.: Penguin.

Myers, Kristen, and Passion Williamson. 2001. "Race Talk: The Perpetuation of Racism Through Private Discourse." *Race and Society* 4(1): 3–26.

Orfield, Gary, and Chungmei Lee. 2004. *Brown at Fifty: King's Dream or Plessy's Nightmare?* Report. Cambridge, Mass.: Harvard University, Civil Rights Project.

Pettigrew, Thomas. 1980. "Prejudice." In *Dimensions of Ethnicity: Prejudice,* edited by Stephen Thernstrom, Ann Orlov, and Oscar Handlin. Cambridge, Mass.: Harvard University Press.

———. 1985. "New Black-White Patterns: How Best to Conceptualize Them?" *Annual Review of Sociology* 11: 329–46.

———. 1997. "The Affective Component of Prejudice: Empirical Support for the New View." In *Racial Attitudes in the 1990s,* edited by Steven Tuch and Jack Martin. Westport, Conn.: Praeger.

———. 2000. "Systematizing the Predictors of Prejudice." In *Racialized Politics: The Debate About Racism in America,* edited by David Sears, Jim Sidanius, and Lawrence Bobo. Chicago: University of Chicago Press.

Pettigrew, Thomas, and Roel Meertens. 1995. "Subtle and Blatant Prejudice in Western Europe." *European Journal of Social Psychology* 25(1): 57–75.

Pettigrew, Thomas, James Jackson, Jeanne Ben Brika, Gerard Lermain, Roel Meertens, Ulrich Wagner, and Andreas Zick. 1998. "Out-group Prejudice in Western Europe." *European Review of Social Psychology* 8: 241–73.

Prager, Jeffrey. 1982. "American Racial Ideology as Collective Representation." *Ethnic and Racial Studies* 5(1): 99–119.

Rose, Arnold M. 1951. *The Roots of Prejudice.* Paris: UNESCO.

Schermerhorn, Richard. 1970. *Comparative Ethnic Relations: A Framework for Theory and Research.* New York: Random House.

Schuman, Howard, Charlotte Steeh, Lawrence Bobo, and Maria Krysan. 1997. *Racial Attitudes in America.* Cambridge, Mass.: Harvard University Press.

Sears, David, and P. J. Henry. 2003. "The Origins of Symbolic Racism." *Journal of Personality and Social Psychology* 85(2): 259–75.

Semyonov, Moshe, Rebecca Raijman, Anat Yom Tov, and Peter Schmidt. 2001. "Does Size Matter? Actual Size, Perceived Size, and Antiforeigner Sentiments." Unpublished paper. Chicago: University of Illinois.

Shelton, J. Nicole. 2000. "A Reconceptualization of How We Study Issues of Racial Prejudice." *Personality and Social Psychology Review* 4(4): 374–90.

Smith, Eliot. 1993. "Social Identity and Social Emotions: Toward New Conceptualizations of Prejudice." In *Affect, Cognition, and Stereotyping: Interactive Processes in Group Perception,* edited by Diane Mackie and David Hamilton. San Diego: Academic Press.

Smith, Eliot, and Colin Ho. 2002. "Prejudice as Intergroup Emotion." In *Relative Deprivation: Specification, Development, and Integration,* edited by Iain Walker and Heather Smith. New York: Cambridge University Press.

Steele, Shelby. 1990. *The Content of Our Character: A New Vision of Race in America.* New York: St. Martin's Press.

Stephan, Walter. 1999. *Reducing Prejudice and Stereotyping in Schools.* New York: Teachers College Press.

Stroessner, Steven, and Diane Mackie. 1993. "Affect and Perceived Group Variability: Implications for Stereotyping and Prejudice." In *Affect, Cognition, and Stereotyping: Interactive Processes in Group Perception,* edited by Diane Mackie and David Hamilton. San Diego: Academic Press.

Sugrue, Tom. 1996. *The Origins of the Urban Crisis.* Princeton, N.J.: Princeton University Press.

Thernstrom, Stephan, and Abigail Thernstrom. 1997. *America in Black and White.* New York: Simon & Schuster.

Vanman, Eric, and Norman Miller. 1993. "Applications of Emotion Theory and Research to Stereotyping and Intergroup Relations." In *Affect, Cognition, and Stereotyping: Interactive Processes in Group Perception,* edited by Diane Mackie and David Hamilton. San Diego: Academic Press.

Wachtel, Paul. 1999. *Race in the Mind of America.* New York: Routledge.

Wiley, Nobert. 1973. "The Silent Majority." In *Through Different Eyes: Black and White Perspectives on American Race Relations,* edited by Peter Rose, Stanley Rothman, and William J. Wilson. New York: Oxford University Press.

Williams, David, James Jackson, Tony Brown, Myriam Torres, Tyrone Forman, and Kendrick Brown. 1999. "Traditional and Contemporary Prejudice and Urban Whites' Support for Affirmative Action and Government Help." *Social Problems* 46(4): 503–27.

Williams, Robin. 1988. "Racial Attitudes and Behavior." In *Surveying Social Life: Papers in Honor of Herbert H. Hyman,* edited by Hubert O'Gorman. Middletown, Conn.: Wesleyan University Press.

4

Institutional Patterns and
Transformations: Race and Ethnicity in
Housing, Education, Labor Markets,
Religion, and Criminal Justice

*Amanda E. Lewis, Maria Krysan,
Sharon M. Collins, Korie Edwards, and Geoff Ward*

WHERE PEOPLE LIVE, go to school, work, and pray—as well as the system purported to protect them as they go about these and other pursuits—continues to be fundamentally shaped by race and ethnicity. An individual's race and ethnicity shapes how he or she is treated by the institutions of housing, education, labor markets, religion, and the criminal justice system, and issues of race and ethnicity are embedded in how these institutions operate. This is not a new story. But what is new are the particulars of how race and ethnicity operate and the larger context within which they operate. Specifically, the manifestations and expressions of racial stratification, prejudice, and discrimination have become more subtle, and the causes and consequences correspondingly more complex. Increases in immigration from Asia and Latin America, which have resulted in a dramatic demographic change in the racial-ethnic composition of the United States, have also made the dynamics of race and ethnicity more complex.

In this chapter, we examine five social institutions, providing a brief historical context for each institution before reviewing recent trends in racial and ethnic inequality within it. We highlight the current key debates on the impact of race and ethnicity on each of these institutions and then pose key questions for the future. Within our discussion of each institution, our aim is to clarify how race and ethnicity play out at the beginning of the twenty-first century. Taken together, these detailed examinations of five institutions provide important insights into how race and ethnicity continue to affect individuals in their everyday life.

HOUSING

Throughout our nation's history, there have been few moments when whites and blacks shared residential space. During some times and in some places the separation was not as severe, and in recent decades the levels of integration have risen modestly in some areas, but it is still difficult to survey America's landscape without concluding that whites and blacks live in different neighborhoods and communities. Although the overall terrain has changed only somewhat, the context in which these patterns are created and perpetuated has shifted substantially, and the causes of these patterns continue to be the subject of much research and debate.

Prior to 1968, explicit and in many cases legally and politically mandated laws and public policies kept African Americans out of white neighborhoods. These policies shaped where people moved, encouraged neighborhood turnover, and turned a blind eye to the deterioration of the communities in which African Americans predominated. For example, local governments instituted restrictive zoning ordinances to keep blacks out of certain neighborhoods, and the federal government's policies on public housing and other housing programs were complicit in these efforts as they encouraged white movement to the suburbs and discouraged investment in urban housing stock, where most African Americans lived (Oliver and Shapiro 1995).

These patterns were exacerbated by actions taken in the private realm. Neighborhood improvement associations and the real estate industry used restrictive covenants to prohibit white owners from selling to African Americans. Brokers and lenders were often bound by their codes of practice and ethics to refuse their services to those who were making pro-integrative moves, and others in the industry took direct action to prompt racial turnover through various "block-busting" strategies (Massey and Denton 1993; Meyer 2000). In fact, as Stephen Meyer (2000) has recently argued, government policies were constructed in part as a response to the civil disruption created by whites—individually as well as collectively through homeowners' associations, neighborhood groups, and mobs—upon the arrival of African Americans on their block. Whites responded with intimidation, scare tactics, buyouts, and protests (see also Sugrue 1996).

After years of resistance through the work of individual black homeowners making integrative moves and through collective action by civil rights groups waging legal and political battles, the passage of the 1968 Fair Housing Act signaled the end of "legal" housing segregation. Although explicit barriers and policies limiting blacks' housing choices were made illegal by the act, continued research and persisting patterns of segregation reveal that free and open access to housing is still not a reality for racial and ethnic minorities in the twenty-first-century United States. The most recent census data document modest declines in black-white residential segregation, mainly in newer areas and the West (Farley and Frey 1994), but many of our nation's largest metropolitan areas continue to be residentially divided along racial lines. In addition, evidence suggests that Latinos and Asians, though not as residentially segregated as African Americans, were actually becoming more segregated during the past decade (Charles 2003). However, the Fair Housing Act has led to changes in the patterns and sources of residential segregation. Current debates about the origins of segregation highlight some of these new dynamics, though many are simply new variations on three old themes: preferences, discrimination, and economics.

THE CAUSES OF PERSISTENT RACIAL
RESIDENTIAL SEGREGATION

Racial Preferences   One subject of considerable debate during the last decade or so is the degree to which residential segregation is the outcome of blacks and whites preferring to live in neighborhoods composed of people of their own race. At issue has been both the meaning of these preferences and the question of whose preferences fuel the process: is it that whites prefer to live with whites, that blacks prefer to live with blacks, or both? During the 1950s and 1960s the research focused on patterns of white departure from the neighborhoods into which African Americans were moving. But during the 1990s the focus turned to: (1) the role of whites' decisions, not about which neighborhoods to *leave,* but about which neighborhoods to *enter;* (2) the role of African American preferences; and (3) the motivations underlying these various preferences.

Although there is considerable debate about whether "white flight" appropriately describes contemporary population distribution patterns, there is substantial agreement that the corollary decision—about which areas whites are willing to move into—is critical. The evidence is quite clear: residential segregation is perpetuated in part because whites are significantly less likely to move into a neighborhood where African American residents are already living (South and Crowder 1998; Crowder 2000).

The second theory—that African American segregation is a result of African American preferences to live in black neighborhoods—argues that even if white aversion to living with blacks was eliminated, segregation would persist because of the "neutral" preferences of African Americans to live "among their own kind" (Clark 1986, 1992; Patterson 1997; Thernstrom and Thernstrom 1997). A number of scholars have refuted this "black preference" theory of residential segregation. For example, Camille Charles (2001) and Maria Krysan and Reynolds Farley (2002) find that many African Americans are willing to consider moving into neighborhoods with few African Americans and that African Americans, compared to Asians, Latinos, and whites, have the lowest level of "in-group preference." In short, African American preferences are complex and flexible and thus do not support the argument that African Americans live in largely black communities because of a preference to do so.

A growing body of research has sought to answer the question that is implicit in this debate about the role of African American preferences: what are the motivations underlying expressed preferences? Those who attribute segregation to the preferences of African Americans argue that such preferences are motivated by neutral ethnocentrism—a desire to live among one's "own kind" where shared culture and values predominate. But others suggest that black preferences are driven by concerns about the possibility of racial hostility and discrimination in predominantly white neighborhoods (Feagin and Sikes 1994; Bobo and Zubrinsky 1996). This possibility suggests that even to the degree that African American "preferences" contribute to segregation, they are motivated by concerns that are far from benign and neutral.

There are also a number of competing interpretations of the origins of white preferences. Some analysts have suggested that whites do not object to living with African Americans per se but to the conditions they associate with living with African Americans—or what David Harris (2001) calls "racial proxy" considerations. Here the argument is that whites want to avoid living in African American neighborhoods because these neighborhoods are run-down, have low property values, and suffer from high crime rates—not because they want to avoid African Americans. Ingrid Ellen (2000) offers a variant on this argument—the neighborhood stereotyping hypothesis. Others have refuted this interpretation, arguing that objections to integrated neighborhoods that are based on supposedly "race-neutral" characteristics of the neighborhood—declining property values, run-down housing, and high crime rates—may not be so racially benign (Charles 2000; Krysan 2002).

Discrimination   Although many of the public and private practices and policies of explicit discrimination in the housing market have been outlawed, various forms of discriminatory treatment by a range of social institutions and actors persist. Audit studies in which housing is sought by paired individuals who are comparable on a number of characteristics but differ in their race or ethnicity have documented discriminatory treatment toward African Americans searching for housing, purchasing a mortgage, and securing insurance (Yinger 1995). Though outright refusals to sell or to show a home are rare, these studies have consistently found more subtle forms of differential treatment: giving minority home-seekers fewer options, showing them fewer units, or steering them to neighborhoods with higher numbers of other racial-ethnic minorities (Turner and Wienk 1993).

Discrimination also can occur beyond the point of simply finding a home to purchase or an apartment to rent. When attention turned to "the color of credit" during the 1990s (Ross and Yinger 2002), several studies documented that, controlling for numerous other relevant characteristics, blacks and Hispanics are denied loans at a much higher rate than whites (Munnell et al. 1996; Oliver and Shapiro 1995). Disparate treatment can be subtle: for example, when white applicants arrive with flaws in their credit histories, they may be more likely to be given information and assistance to help them fix the flaws; minority customers, by contrast, are more likely to simply be denied the loan. Or when customers get behind in payments, mortgage companies can decide either to foreclose or to help the customers through their problems. The latter approach appears to be taken more often with white customers than with minority customers. Finally, loan officers can make the process more difficult by encouraging buyers to shop around, emphasizing the complicated application procedures, sending them to other branch offices (where interest rates are higher), or encouraging them to apply for FHA loans (which have less favorable terms) (Wyly and Holloway 1999). In short, at all the points in the mortgage process where discretion can be exercised, minorities are at a disadvantage. The result may be that the search for housing involves more psychological, emotional, and economic costs for minorities than for whites. Not only do these various forms of disparate treatment contribute to residential segregation, but they may create more general barriers to homeownership among African Americans and Latinos.

Redlining—a discriminatory practice used by the banking industry for much of the twentieth century—continues today, although, again, in more subtle forms. Currently such practices include differential placement of branch offices, advertising approaches, and pre-application procedures. Each such practice can result in fewer banks competing for minority loans, higher interest rates, and less favorable terms for minority borrowers (Oliver and Shapiro 1995; Smith and DeLair 1999). This complex chain of events can set in motion a self-fulfilling prophecy, as Melvin Oliver and Thomas Shapiro (1995, 144) suggest:

> Minority customers are perceived as being higher risk borrowers and are rejected more frequently for conventional loans. So they take their business to finance companies and pay higher rates than they would have paid on a conventional mortgage. In the process they actually become the higher-risk borrowers that banks originally perceived them to be. Ironically, minority customers would be lower-risk borrowers if their monthly payments were not inflated by high rates of finance-company interest.

Economic Causes   The general public most commonly offers an economic explanation for residential segregation: whites and blacks live in different areas because blacks, on average, cannot afford to live in the same kinds of neighborhoods as whites (Krysan and Faison 2002). The validity of this explanation has been largely refuted by studies of the 1960 to 1980 censuses showing that high-income African Americans were just as segregated from high-income whites as poor blacks were segregated from poor whites (Denton and Massey 1988; Farley 1977b). More recent analyses are less clear on this question: some show that social class may play some role, but others continue to find negligible effects (Alba, Logan, and Stults 2000; Clark and Ware 1997; Darden and Kamel 2000; Krivo and Kaufman 1999; Massey and Fischer 1999; St. John and Clymer 1999).

One of the recent contributions to the debate about the relationship between economics and residential segregation turns the question around and asks: to what extent is economic inequality due to residential segregation? As Oliver and Shapiro (1995) demonstrate, while there has been some progress toward reducing black-white *income* inequality, a tremendous racial gulf in *wealth* remains: for every $1 in wealth held by a black household, white households have $12. Oliver and Shapiro (1995) and more recently Dalton Conley (1999) argue persuasively that homeownership is a key to wealth accumulation; thus, one of the outcomes and implications of housing segregation is that African Americans have been shut out of a critical avenue to wealth accumulation and economic stability. Differential homeownership rates are not the only culprit: segregated housing markets also suppress for black homeowners the increases in property values that whites enjoy, largely because of the discriminatory "tastes" of whites. Government policies and practices have been complicit in this development, and its effects go beyond simple homeownership: "Black Americans who failed to secure this economic base [through homeownership] were much less likely to be able to provide educational access for their children, secure the necessary financial resources for self-employment, or participate effectively in the political process" (Oliver and Shapiro 1995, 23).

In addition to residential segregation's effects on wealth differentials, the 1990s saw a number of studies that provide substantial evidence of other deleterious consequences of segregation for African Americans across a wide range of economic and health outcomes, including single-motherhood, infant mortality, homicide rates, and adult mortality rates (Collins and Williams 1999; Cutler and Glaeser 1997; Hart et al. 1998; LaViest 1989, 1993; Peterson and Krivo 1991, 1999; Polednak 1990).

THE FUTURE OF RACE, ETHNICITY, AND HOUSING

What Are the Implications of an Increasingly Multiethnic Population?   The nation's changing racial-ethnic composition raises critical questions about the future of housing patterns. Asians and Latinos continue to be less segregated from whites than blacks are segregated from whites, but analyses of the 2000 census reveal that these groups are becoming more segregated over time. The dynamics of immigration contribute to this pattern of isolation (Charles 2003). At the same time, analyses of Hispanics and Asians reveal that levels of segregation differ considerably depending on subgroup: for example, Puerto Ricans are more segregated than Mexicans and Cubans. Several questions arise: Will these new immigrant groups from Latin America and Asia substantially alter patterns of segregation, both in cities where they join large populations of African Americans and in areas where they are the only or the largest racial-ethnic minority group? Will Latino and Asian immigrants eventually become less segregated, as earlier European ethnic groups have done over time? Or will there be persistent segregation across all of these groups? What are the attitudes of immigrants toward living with whites and blacks? And conversely, what are the attitudes of whites and blacks toward living with Asians and Latinos? Charles (2000) has provided some of the only answers to these questions; much remains to be done.

What About Revitalization?   During the 1990s several of our nation's largest metropolitan areas showed substantial signs of revitalization of their inner-city neighborhoods. What influence will such efforts have on overall patterns of segregation? Will segregation be reduced as a result of this flow back into the city? Or will this movement simply re-create patterns of segregation within the city? What will happen to those who are being displaced, and how will their displacement affect overall patterns of segregation?

What Will Black Suburbanization Do to the Future of Residential Segregation?   Black suburbanization has increased over the last few decades; for example, the census of 2000 reports fewer all-white neighborhoods than in the past (Glaeser and Vigdor 2001). What are the implications of this movement? Who will move into these suburbs, and who will stay? Will others follow? What impact do gated communities in these suburbs have on residential processes? Will increased suburbanization result in resegregation in the suburbs? Or will different patterns emerge?

Will Changes in Technology Use in the Housing Industry Influence Patterns of Segregation?   Technology has transformed aspects of the mortgage industry, particularly through the increased use of automated underwriting techniques. In the aggregate, this may make the mortgage industry more willing to assume more credit risk, but would this have a positive or negative effect on minorities (Gates, Perry, and Zorn 2002; LaCour-Little 2000; Straka 2000)? Does such a process eliminate the discretion of the manual methods that resulted in discriminatory treatment? Or will the models upon which the automated processes are based have a disparate impact on minorities (Ross and Yinger 2002)? Will the lack of information about an applicant's racial identity—when, for example, mortgage loans are secured over the Internet—help to equalize these markets? Or will other tactics emerge that are more subtle yet equally discriminatory in their impact? Outside the realm of the mortgage industry, there are other areas where technology is transforming how people do real estate business. Will the "digital divide" make disparities between whites and blacks who are searching for housing even greater in access to information and resources that make it possible to succeed in this search (Gates, Perry, and Zorn 2002)?

EDUCATION

Residential segregation has been called the "structural lynchpin" that maintains racial inequality in the United States (Bobo 1989; Pettigrew 1979). One of the consequences of segregated housing, for example, is that it feeds directly into segregated schools and racial inequality in education. Throughout the history of the United States, educational institutions have at times reproduced or maintained racial inequality, and at other times have challenged it. From the systematic denial of education to black slaves, Japanese field workers, and Mexican laborers to the provision of distinctly separate but equal schools in the South, to the development of freedom schools (Anderson 1988; Franklin 2000; Montejano 1987; Takaki 1989), education has been a key arena in which racial hierarchies have been negotiated and contested (Walters 2001).

Much as occurred with housing, the 1950s and 1960s featured legal and political battles, first simply to gain access to schools and educational opportunities, and then to gain access to white schools. One of the key legal decisions in the arena of schools was a dismantling of Jim Crow laws in the South by the 1954 Supreme Court decision *Brown v. Board of Education,* which outlawed segregation in public schooling. Some of the early and influential social scientific research on race and education provided key evidence in this ruling— specifically, studies showing the negative effects of segregated schooling on African American children (McKee 1993). As with housing, then, the battle to dismantle de jure segregation in education was eventually won.

By the 1990s, however, these civil rights successes had been turned on their head. The legal battles now being waged focus on *dismantling* the very policies that were put in place to integrate educational institutions, such as challenges to affirmative action and the ending of many court-ordered desegregation plans. As such, schools—more so than many other institutions—are at the center of the most contested policy issues pertaining to race and ethnicity in the contemporary United States. In addition to the lawsuits against affirmative action and school desegregation plans, there are political battles being waged to equalize school funding, to institute a voucher system, and to change bilingual education. The core issues within the arena of race, ethnicity, and education are changing school demographics, current patterns of school desegregation, and debates about the causes of racial inequality in school achievement.

School Demographics   The demographic changes in the United States are magnified in the context of schools, given the age distribution of the newly arriving immigrants and birthrates among different racial-ethnic groups. There are now 7.9 million more black and Latino students in U.S. public school systems and 6.1 million fewer whites than there were in the 1960s (Orfield and Lee 2004). Latinos are by far the fastest-growing group of public school students, with a 305 percent increase since 1968. The number of black students has also increased (29 percent), while the number of white students has declined by 18 percent. By 2001 only 60.3 percent of all U.S. public school students were white. The biggest changes in public school demographics have taken place in the West and Southwest, where there are high numbers of immigrants from Asia and Latin America; in many of these states public school systems already have nonwhite majorities (Orfield and Lee 2004; Orfield and Gordon 2001).

As is most evident in California and Texas—the states where the demographic changes have been the greatest—these shifting demographics have resulted in a number of public policy debates about whom public schools should serve (as reflected, for example, in laws that bar children of illegal immigrants from receiving public services), the best means to educate diverse populations (as evidenced by both vigorous public opposition to and support for bilingual education), and what criteria are most important for admissions to public higher educational systems (as argued, for example, in affirmative action lawsuits). Similar to the rethinking of education that followed large population influxes from southern and eastern Europe in the early 1900s, current demographic changes may well lead to reexaminations of the proper means and ends of public education in the United States.

The Dismantling of Desegregation   The school desegregation success story was relatively short-lived. While the emphasis in housing has been on modest—though inadequate—improvements in integration, in education the story is one of regression. Indeed, given the large transformations in school demographics and the increasing numbers of students of color in the schools, we might assume that schools generally are becoming more diverse. But the actual picture of school racial composition is much more complicated. In the decades following *Brown v. Board of Education,* the segregation of black students declined dramatically and steadily (Frankenberg, Lee, and Orfield 2003; Orfield and Gordon 2001; Orfield and Yun 1999). The South was in many ways the biggest success story: those states that had state-mandated segregation were the states where desegregation orders were most carefully and forcefully enforced, and thus where schools were most successfully integrated. The result has been that whites in the South attend schools with more minority students than do whites in any other region in the United States (Orfield and Yun 1999). But many of the gains in the South and elsewhere were lost during the 1990s. Partly as a result of the termination of a number of desegregation orders by state and appellate courts and the Supreme Court, racial segregation in U.S. public schools intensified throughout the 1990s—in contrast to the patterns in housing, which either improved somewhat or remained stagnant (Frankenberg, Lee, and Orfield 2003). Erica Frankenberg and Chungmei Lee (2002, 4, emphasis in original), using national data, find that "*virtually all* school districts analyzed are showing lower levels of inter-racial exposure since 1986, suggesting a trend towards resegregation," with sharp declines in some districts. These patterns are true not only for public schools but for private schools: indeed, a recent study of national trends for private schools found that they are more segregated than public schools (Reardon and Yun 2002).

One emerging issue in the discussion of school segregation is the experiences of Latinos, who are now one of the largest minority groups in the country and will soon be the largest within public schools. Educationally, they are also the most segregated minority group by both race-ethnicity and poverty and have been for over a decade. Partly as a result, Latinos have the highest dropout and lowest graduation rates. Many also face the additional challenges of subpar bilingual education. Of the 9 percent of students nationally who are limited English proficient (LEP), 75 percent are native Spanish speakers. Many of these students attend schools where the quality of the teaching and the facilities is poor and where resources are inadequate (Ma 2002).

Despite the overall fluctuations in school segregation patterns, it remains true today that most white students in the United States attend schools with few minority peers. Whites are, in fact, the most segregated group in terms of their schooling. Moreover, most black and Latino students remain in predominantly minority schools. This is not an issue merely because of concerns about diversity and interracial exposure. Partly because of segregation patterns, minority students are also much more likely to attend schools with concentrated poverty—that is, schools where over 50 percent of the student body lives in poverty.

The recent retreat from desegregation has taken place despite the many demonstrated benefits of desegregation (for example, improved test scores, higher rates of college attendance and success, and greater confidence in interracial situations). As recent work by the Civil Rights Project makes clear, the period from the 1960s through the 1980s, a time when major gains were made in integration, was also a time of major gains for black students in closing academic achievement gaps (Orfield and Lee 2004; Orfield and Gordon 2001). By contrast, the last few decades, a period of resegregation, are showing increasing gaps and loss of progress. This is especially alarming given that many of the alternative strategies for equalizing separate schools (such as compensatory education and raising standards) have not been successful. For example, the 1990s movement to stimulate improvement by raising standards was not very successful. Racial differences in achievement and graduation actually grew during the 1990s after several decades of shrinking (Orfield and Gordon 2001). These patterns of retrenchment mirror resegregation patterns almost exactly.

Racial Inequality in School Outcomes   Another major issue in race and education has been racial differences in both the quantity and quality of schooling. On the one hand, high school graduation rates for all groups have increased steadily since the 1960s. In the year 2000, according to the 2000 census, Asians and whites had the highest graduation rates (around 85 percent), and blacks had achieved substantial progress, with graduation rates close to 79 percent. While widely varying among different nationality groups, Latinos remain substantially behind (U.S. Census 2001). By contrast, gaps in the acquisition of a college degree remain high. Relative to whites, blacks are only 65 percent as likely to have attained a bachelor's degree and only 58 percent as likely to have achieved an advanced degree. Rates for Latinos are even lower (42 percent and 38 percent, respectively). Asians have the highest educational attainment rates, though again, there remains substantial variation within the category among different national-origin groups. For example, while many East and South Asian groups (Chinese, Japanese, Asian-Indians) have college graduation rates around 40 percent, Southeast Asian (Vietnamese, Cambodian, Laotian) rates are one-half to one-eighth as high. This bimodal distribution of educational attainment among Asians is quite important, because it stands in stark contrast to the model minority myth that all Asians groups have high academic achievement.

Despite some progress with regard to the *amount* of education different groups receive, there is still substantial evidence that large gaps remain in the *quality* of their educational experiences. As noted earlier, blacks and Latinos in particular are more likely to attend high-poverty schools; these schools also tend to have fewer resources. For example, as we learned from the 2000 census, schools with high minority enrollments are less likely to have Internet access in the classroom, and they have more students per computer available; black and Latino students are also less likely to have access to computers in the early grades. Schools with black majorities are much more likely to have under-qualified instructors or to use long-term substitutes to fill teacher vacancies (Darling-Hammond 2003; Nettles and Perna 1997). Recent studies have also shown that black and Latino students are less likely to have access to instructional materials, safe facilities, college preparatory curricula, and advanced placement courses and less likely to take either the SAT or ACT (Allen, Bonous-Hammarth, and Ternishi 2002; Harris 2004; IDEA 2004). These examples of gaps in the quality of education are most often not a result of explicit segregation and direct action to limit minority access to quality education, as they were in the past. Instead, they are more typically both the direct and indirect outcome of a number of school and nonschool processes, such as the segregation of communities, the concentration of poverty, the dependence on local property taxes to fund schools, and whites' aversion to sending their children to minority schools. Some of these processes involve seemingly "race-neutral" public policies (such as local funding for schools), and some involve private practices (such as families' school choices). Their cumulative impact, however, is unquestionable. For example, while only 15 percent of segregated white schools had concentrated poverty, 88 percent of segregated minority schools were predominantly poor (Orfield and Lee 2004).

These differences in educational quality are receiving growing attention because of the persistence in racial gaps in school achievement. Though the gaps narrowed in the 1970s and 1980s, they leveled off or increased in the 1990s (Lee 2002). There are competing explanations for these gaps. Individual-level explanations include those emphasizing innate or genetic factors (for example, Herrnstein and Murray 1994) and those pointing to community or family factors (for example, Coleman et al. 1966). Currently, there is a considerable debate about whether students of color, particularly blacks and Latinos, have a culture of opposition that might explain their underperformance. While John Ogbu and Signithia Fordham (Ogbu 1978; Fordham and Ogbu 1986) have received much attention for making these arguments, substantial recent research suggests that school practices, personnel, and institutional cultures— rather than student cultures—may be the more important factors (Ainsworth-Darnell and Downey 1998; Carter 2003; Horvat and O'Connor, forthcoming; Mickelson 1990; O'Connor 2001; O'Connor, Lewis, and Mueller, forthcoming). Like other school-level or structural explanations, this work has focused on how schools support some students and families more than others; how resource differences across schools or communities shape different outcomes (Kozol 1991; Hanushek 1994; Card and Krueger 1996; Conley 1999); and how racial dynamics play out in teacher expectations, home-school relations, rewards for cultural resources, and school discipline (Ainsworth-Darnell and Downey 1998; Lareau and Horvat 1999; Delpit 1990; R. Ferguson 1998a, 1998b; A. Ferguson 2000). For example, a number of studies recently have documented dramatic differentials in school disciplinary rates and the school processes that produce such differentials (Ayers, Dohrn, and Ayers 2001; A. Ferguson 2000; Johnson, Boyden, and Pittz 2001). Linked at least figuratively to the criminalization of minority communities in general (see the last section of this chapter for more on this issue), the rates at which students of color are targeted for punishment and excluded from school have been increasing.

THE FUTURE OF RACE, ETHNICITY, AND EDUCATION

Will the Trend Toward "Regression" Continue?   One thing that stands out about the changing terrain of education is how it differs from other areas, such as housing. For example, one key finding from housing research is stagnation— that is, segregation in many of our nation's largest metropolises is stuck at very high levels. But the patterns in segregated schools tell a story of regression: we are undoing what has been accomplished. In other arenas the story is more complex. Gaps in school completion rates have narrowed—clearly a sign of progress—but there are still major inequities in the schools that different students attend. The question remains: will the trend toward undoing integrated schools continue, and if so, what consequences will this have for persisting inequalities in educational outcomes?

How Will Changing Demographics Affect Schools and Education?   The changing demographics of the United States—which are magnified in the public schools—raise a number of important scholarly and policy questions. How will such changes affect the educational outcomes of various groups? What will race relations look like in schools with substantial numbers of three, four, or five racial-ethnic groups present? How will public school districts faced with shrinking budgets address the growing needs of new populations? Why are Latino school achievement levels still so low? What will be the effects of patterns of growing Latino school segregation? How much progress on educational outcomes will be lost if school segregation overall continues to be dismantled? Relatedly, more research is needed on diversity within populations: we need to understand not only how the experiences of different subgroups diverge (for example, Mexican American versus Puerto Rican students) but also how race intersects with immigration status, class, and gender (for example, why college graduation rates are higher for black women).

How Do Schools "Teach" Race to Students?   Historically, educational research has examined race by comparing the education and achievement levels of racial groups and focusing on the causes for these differences. That is, research has emphasized the expression or exacerbation of racial inequality in education and schools. But given the important socialization role of schools, it is equally important to understand how race, as a social phenomenon, is constructed "in the schoolyard" (Lewis 2003)—that is, understanding how schools as social institutions are a venue in which racial identities and meanings are negotiated (Davidson 1996; Dolby 2001; Lewis 2003; Perry 2002). Schools are clearly places where children learn not only about belonging to a "racial group"—"being," for instance, white, black, or Asian—but also about the rules of classification and how race works (Van Ausdale and Feagin 2001; Lewis 2003). This area of research, though still in its early stages, has demonstrated the powerful way in which this occurs. Future research needs to build on these ideas and create more theoretically sophisticated treatments of the interaction between race and education. For example, what lessons do schools "teach" students about race? How are students' racial identities and understandings shaped by explicit and hidden curricula, interracial interactions, and experiences in and across different school buildings? Given the shifting ways in which racism is manifested in the larger society, how do we then study these phenomena of color-blind or laissez-faire racism in everyday school practices?

What Are the Policy Implications of This Changing Terrain in Education?   The policy implications of all of these changing patterns are substantial, and several arenas have been identified here. One additional arena would be linking research on housing segregation to research on education. We need to understand the ways in which educational opportunities and segregation in housing are connected. In particular, how are data on schools used by individuals to make housing decisions? Is race used as a proxy for measuring school quality? How do school funding mechanisms (for example, funding schools primarily through local property taxes) continue to link the "public" good of education with "private" choices in housing?

LABOR MARKETS

As with education and housing, policies and practices of exclusion have shaped the experiences of racial and ethnic minorities in labor markets for decades. Also as with the institutions of housing and education, there has been in some cases substantial progress in labor markets toward equality. But the patterns are complex, and inequalities persist despite the passage of laws, much like those in housing and education, that outlaw discrimination based on race or ethnicity. A review of the historical and contemporary patterns of racial inequality in occupation and labor market status highlights what has changed and what remains the same. After summarizing these trends, we turn to the question of the underlying causes of racial inequality—a debate that mirrors similar debates in the arenas of housing and education that we just discussed.

Before the 1960s, in both the South and the North, blacks were cast in servant roles and almost unilaterally barred from lucrative industries and establishments—in short, from any jobs that white workers found attractive. Between 1960 and 1980 there was a dramatic change in blacks' ability to compete in the broader labor force. Blacks entered white-collar jobs at a rate much faster than that of whites: the proportion of blacks in white-collar jobs increased 80 percent between 1960 and 1970, and 44 percent more between 1970 and 1979. By 1980 the proportion of blacks in white-collar jobs had increased 120 percent, compared to only 25 percent for whites.

This period was also marked by substantial improvement in black-white male earnings ratios (Smith and Welch 1977, 1978), and the occupational distribution for employed black men began to approximate that of employed white men (Farley 1977a; Featherman and Hauser 1976; Hauser and Featherman 1974). The most dramatic occupational advancements occurred as black men moved into professional jobs, including management and the business-oriented professions, such as accounting and law. For the first time in U.S. history, highly educated black men broke into these traditionally closed, higher-paying, white-collar jobs. Thus, the relative occupational gap between skilled black and white men began to shrink (Freeman 1976; Featherman and Hauser 1976;

Smith and Welch 1977). As is the case with housing and education, despite the progress, closer examination of the labor market across a range of economic indices reveals persistent disparities.

PERSISTENT DISPARITIES AT THE BOTTOM AND
TOP RUNGS OF LABOR MARKETS

African Americans continue to face challenges at both the bottom and the top rungs of the labor market. At the very bottom, underemployment and unemployment persist. For example, the size of the black-white unemployment gap was as wide in the early 1990s as it was in 1970 (Harris and Farley 2000), remaining roughly twice the rate of whites for decades. African Americans are also greatly overrepresented in unskilled work and thus concentrated in economic sectors that pay unlivable wages. At the other end of the occupational spectrum, despite substantial gains, African Americans remain far underrepresented among skilled blue-collar workers, higher-paid managers, and professionals and overrepresented in low-wage service-sector jobs.

Understanding current forms of racial inequality in the labor market requires an examination of the distinct patterns in the private and public sectors. In short, the issue is not just having a job or not—or having a high-status job or not. Disparities also emerge because African Americans, including those in management and the professions, are overrepresented in government jobs. There is evidence that unique advantages flow to blacks employed in government. For example, blacks employed in the public sector face less race-based disadvantage relative to those employed in the private sector: they experience less earning and wage rate discrimination and fare better in terms of occupational placement (Asher and Popkin 1984; Beggs 1991; Blank 1985; W. Johnson 1978; Maume 1985). In short, the public sector has more egalitarian employment practices relative to the private sector. But the disproportionate concentration of minorities in government does carry its own set of disadvantages: blacks are disproportionately employed in social service bureaucracies, such as housing, education, and welfare, and during periods of economic recession and government reduction these services are often among the first to be reduced or eliminated.

In the private sector, the trends highlight that the private sector plays an important role in shaping racial disparities. Black participation in the private sector increased between 1966 and 1999, from 8.2 to 14 percent of the private sector. But at the same time, the gains made in occupations where African Americans were *under*represented in 1966 failed to erode their *over*concentration in menial and low-paid fields. For example, African Americans went from 3.6 to 9.8 percent of all skilled craft workers in the private sector and from 0.9 to 6.2 percent of officials and managers in the private sector. Although there were modest increases in the percentages of operatives, the percentages remained about the same for service workers and laborers. In other words, African Americans remained overrepresented in lower-status occupations.

A key message from the private sector highlights an important feature of contemporary patterns of racial inequality: the only job sectors to become racially equalized during this thirty-year period were the midrange and highly feminized fields of office and clerical work and sales jobs, which are on the lower rung of the white-collar job hierarchy. Other research supports this trend by indicating that the post-1960 upward mobility of African American women is a result of a shift into clerical and sales positions from domestic and personal service jobs (Freeman 1976; King 1993). In short, racial inequality persists at the top and the bottom: blacks remain overrepresented in menial work and underrepresented in the most prestigious private-sector occupations.

PERSISTENT RACIAL INEQUALITY IN THE CONTEXT OF
INCREASING DIVERSITY

As discussed elsewhere in this chapter, the population of the United States has become increasingly diverse—and this is true both overall and within various minority groups. The Latino population now roughly equals that of African Americans; the Asian American and Pacific Islander populations are on a rapid ascent; and nearly seven million Americans checked more than one racial box in the 2000 census. By the middle of this century, the United States will no longer be a majority non-Hispanic white nation, and the very concept and meaning of race will have evolved. Although researchers historically focus on economic gaps between whites and blacks, since the 1980 U.S. census, measures of race and ethnicity have been based on self-identified race and ancestry rather than on state-defined categories (Darity, Guilkey, and Winfrey 1996; Farley 1989, 1990; Harris and Farley 2000). This means that finer distinctions within and between groups are possible: economic achievement among Asians, for example, can be distinguished by Japanese, East Indian, Chinese, Vietnamese, or Korean ancestry. Similar distinctions can be made between black and white Hispanics and between blacks reporting West Indian and non–West Indian backgrounds.

But even with these more complex and detailed comparisons, it is clear that when employment, occupational attainment, and wage and salary data are examined, self-identified white and U.S.-born Asians are at the top while blacks are at the bottom (Darity, Guilkey, and Winfrey 1996). Virtually all self-identified white groups have higher per capita income than do blacks of any ethnicity (Darity, Guilkey, and Winfrey 1996; Farley 1989, 1990), and the economic profile of non-Hispanic whites was the highest among all Americans. In contrast, the economic profile of black, Hispanic, and other nonwhite groups—including large numbers of recent immigrants—fell below the national average. The exceptions are Asians of Japanese, East Indian, or

Chinese ancestry. The economic consequence of color shows up even among Hispanic workers. Hispanic black men suffer much greater proportionate losses than their Hispanic nonblack counterparts (Darity, Guilkey, and Winfrey 1996). Thus, even when racial inequality in America is no longer viewed exclusively through the black-white prism, that prism remains an essential feature for understanding U.S. systems of stratification. The meaning of race may be changing, but the relationship between economic inequality and color remains strong.

THE CAUSES OF RACIAL INEQUALITY IN THE LABOR MARKET

The effects of labor market discrimination on occupational attainment decreased dramatically in the decade between the mid-1960s and the mid-1970s, much as we saw in the case of education. But more evidence indicates that racial discrimination persists and the trend toward equity no longer holds. For example, African American males continue to suffer 12 to 15 percent losses in earning as a consequence of persistent discrimination (Darity 1998; Gottschalk 1997). This suggests that the initial impetus provided by the civil rights movement (Darity and Myers 2001; Jackson and Jones 2001) resulted in historic black attainments, but the relative position of blacks has not continued to improve. Equally disheartening is that poverty, unemployment, and non-participation rates signaled the growth of a black "underclass" in conjunction with blacks' entry into traditionally closed positions during that time period (see Farley and Bianchi 1983; Glasgow 1980; Parsons 1980; W. J. Wilson 1978). Most important is that employment conditions for blacks continue to deteriorate, although blacks attaining at least a college education appear to be better off than in decades past.

As with housing and education, the causes of these persistent patterns of inequality constitute a core part of the debate about race, ethnicity, and labor markets. This debate is likely to continue to focus on the degree to which relative labor market status is mediated by educational attainment and human capital characteristics (O'Neill 1990; Smith and Welch 1977; Smith 1984; Welch 1973) versus employment structure (Collins 1997a, 1997b) and racial discrimination (Fix and Struyk 1993; Fosu 1993; Horton 1995; F. H. Wilson 1995; G. Wilson 1997). Economists' human capital theory and sociologists' status attainment theory presume that job allocation among blacks is a color-blind function of supply-side characteristics such as education, skill, and individual preferences. The latter parallels the theory that residential segregation occurs because of racial differences in economic status. Thus, according to these perspectives, racial inequalities are not a response to race per se, in the form of discrimination by employers and structural barriers (Smith and Welch 1984, 1986; Thernstrom and Thernstrom 1997). In this view, racial discrimination is an individual anomaly rather than an entrenched feature of U.S. society. Labor market inequalities are understood to be due to the fact that African Americans, American Indians, and some Hispanic groups stand lower than whites and Asian Americans on these indicators of human capital. For example, James Smith (2001) finds that the gap in the economic status between races is influenced mostly by skill-related factors. By extension, inequality in employment, occupational, and earnings arenas will be ameliorated with increased levels of education among racial and ethnic minorities. Other research notes that unemployment gaps between whites and blacks result from educational disparity coupled with increasing demands for skilled labor (Holzer 1996).

The alternative contention is that labor market attainment is a function of social structure and demand-side characteristics. In a field experiment using job résumés, for example, Marianne Bertrand and Sendhil Mullainathan (2003) show that racial discrimination is a prominent feature in U.S. labor markets. They find that résumés with white-sounding names are about 50 percent more likely to receive callbacks from prospective employers than résumés with African American–sounding names. They find a statistically uniform amount of discrimination across all job and industrial categories contained in their experiment. Discrimination was also highlighted in a survey of Chicago employers by Jolene Kirschenman and Kathryn Neckerman (1991), who found that these employers often engaged in "statistical discrimination" by making negative assumptions about African American job candidates because of their perceptions regarding racial group membership. Survey-based research has also documented substantial reports of racial discrimination in the workplace (Bobo and Suh 2000; Forman, Williams, and Jackson 1997; Forman 2003).

Other theorists attribute people's limited progress to the characteristics of their jobs (Doeringer and Piore 1970; Thurow 1975). In this case, minorities are subjected to tokenism and tracking mechanisms that lead them to fill niches in white-collar occupations that are either in decline or do not lead to advancement (Ghiloni 1987; Kanter 1977; Reskin and Roos 1990). For example, Sharon Collins (1997a, 1997b) shows that college-educated blacks in professional and managerial positions are concentrated in niches responsible for managing blacks or delivering services and products to black people and therefore are "functionally segregated" within occupations and labor markets. Labor market inequality, then, is perpetuated in ways that are slightly more subtle than flat-out refusals to hire. Again, it is not explicit and blatant exclusion but more subtle and slippery—and equally problematic—actions that result in persistent inequalities.

A number of scholars maintain that discrimination remains an obstacle to blacks' full economic participation (Feagin and Sikes 1994; Forman 2003; Landry 1987; Zweigenhaft and Domhoff 1991). They view institutional practices and prejudice as barriers that restrict blacks' economic chances, regardless of human capital and other class-related advantages. For example, networks and mentors are important ingredients of success in the work world, yet blacks tend to be excluded from the relaxed social interactions with whites through which beneficial relationships of this kind tend to originate. In a recent study of graduates from vocational schools, Deirdre Royster (2003) illustrates how the networks that help white graduates get jobs are simply not accessible to black graduates. As the title implies, her book, *Race and the Invisible Hand: How White Networks Exclude Black Men from Blue-Collar Jobs,* is a compelling illustration of the subtle ways in which race operates in social institutions in the United States today. Blacks are not barred from entrance into vocational schools and are no less likely to complete the training, but they are shut out—in often subtle and indirect ways—of the networks necessary for securing the good jobs in the fields in which they are trained. Overall, the confluence of such barriers may help to explain why black male college graduates earned 17 percent less than their white counterparts in 1996, despite the unprecedented job advancement they experienced in the post-1960 period (Levy 1998).

THE FUTURE OF RACE, ETHNICITY, AND LABOR MARKETS

With Increasing Immigration, What Role Does the Politics of Race and Ethnicity Play in Shaping Labor Markets?   A critical question for the future is the politics of race and ethnicity and the role that immigration will play in U.S. labor markets (for a discussion, see Zhou 2001). The consensus is that the demand for low-skilled labor has been declining (Bailey 1987). Within the context of the changing terrain of race and ethnicity in the United States, this means that young black men and low-skilled, nonwhite native groups who remain concentrated in temporary, low-status, and low-paying work are placed directly into job competition with newly arriving and unskilled immigrant labor. A central question is: will the influx of ethnic immigrants lead to the displacement of nonwhite unskilled workers, particularly black workers? George Borjas (1990), for instance, argues that immigrants do little to lower earnings among blacks or to increase black underemployment and unemployment. Yet other research suggests that the impact of immigrant competition on blacks' labor market status is real and that the arrival of immigrants into urban populations lowers the earnings of high school graduates (Katz, Borjas, and Freeman 1992). Roger Waldinger (1996) and Allen Scott (1996) find that less-educated blacks in the inner city are at a competitive disadvantage for low-skilled work because jobs are monopolized by immigrant networks. In addition, Robert Cherry and William Rodgers (2000) show that discrimination against blacks and black disadvantage increase when there is strong competition for jobs.

Evidence of the possible negative effects of immigration on racial inequality in the labor market also comes indirectly from the work of Kirschenman and

Neckerman (1991). Reacting in large part to William Julius Wilson's (1978) arguments about the causes of inner-city unemployment, they found that employers have a rank order of preferred workers that favors white workers and even workers from certain Latino ethnicities over African American workers. Waldinger (1997, 366) notes this finding and suggests that employers have a hierarchy in which native white workers are at the top, followed by immigrant whites and immigrant Hispanics. Thus, although the evidence for a direct replacement hypothesis is not supported, other studies suggest that native-born blacks—directly or indirectly—lose out where immigrant labor pools are large. Given the projected trends in population dynamics, questions surrounding this issue will continue to need attention by researchers.

What Is the Fate of Affirmative Action and How Will It Affect Racial Inequality in Labor Markets?   A second area for future research lies in the impact of challenges to affirmative action on the labor market for racial minorities. General economic trends aside, occupational upgrading among African Americans in particular is tied to the impact of affirmative action (Herring and Collins 1995; Leonard 1984, 1987, 1990, 1998; Neumark and Stock 2001; Rodgers 1996). By extension, if affirmative action policy is dismantled, employer efforts to create and maintain equal employment opportunities may shrink accordingly. Despite an almost universal acceptance of affirmative action in corporate America, administrative efforts at the federal level have been severely curtailed. The Office of Federal Contract Compliance Programs (OFCCP) was gutted by the Reagan administration, and the Supreme Court has held that to prove discrimination, plaintiffs must show that numerical imbalance is not a business necessity (Anderson 1996; Leonard 1990, 1998). The OFCCP has the power to revoke federal contracts and bar firms from bidding for future contracts. Although debarment is rarely used, it is a powerful incentive nevertheless to increase minority private-sector employment. Thus, both the economic and legal incentives to enforce affirmative action and drive structural change in the private sector are removed. Moreover, in-house corporate mechanisms to protect racial minorities' access to higher-paying jobs in the private sector are also weakening (Collins 1997a). What is happening in the education realm is mirrored in the labor markets: federal actions are being taken to undermine and undo the policies and programs that were intended to increase integration, reduce inequality, and improve the living conditions of people of color—and in many cases were modestly successful in doing so.

Finally, the focus of corporate initiatives such as formal recruitment, retention, and business supplier programs, which initially worked to bring blacks into the economic mainstream, is now being shifted so that other groups are included in these programs. Typically, such programs covered two groups—women and minorities—but there is now evidence, according to *Fortune* magazine, that the number of protected groups has increased to as many as twenty-two. At the same time, charges of reverse discrimination, the inte focus on the "plight" of the white male, and the resurgence of a conservatis in the federal government raise the question of whether progress can continue in this climate. Black political pressure and affirmative action once were the key tools for creating access to management and the professions in corporations, but these forces have eroded. Whether the erosion of these and other forces will result in a retrogression, as we are seeing in the arena of education, is a subject in need of future research.

What Will Be the Impact on Racial Inequality of the Shift from "Affirmative Action" to "Diversity"? Corporate America has begun to shift its focus away from affirmative action and toward an interest in "diversity." On the one hand, this shift may signal the emergence of a more enlightened form of capitalism that values a more racially and ethnically inclusive work environment. In a highly competitive economy, for example, race and ethnicity are useful marketing tools and can be a source of greater profit for big business. Thus, the connection between color and markets for products and services may lead companies to increase their efforts to include racial and ethnic groups to enhance their market position. On the other hand, the shift to diversity may foreshadow programmatic displacement of blacks in favor of other workers. Indeed, it may be a new form of institutional racism and laissez-faire racism. Diversity means color-blindness, and it constitutes a liberal stance for the corporate world. But the "all-inclusiveness" of diversity may result in reductionism if it equates the status of blacks with every other status and equates black problems with the problems of every other worker.

RELIGION

The next social institution we consider differs in many fundamental ways from housing, education, and the labor market. As a voluntary institution, and as one outside the purview of governmental regulation, religion has a fundamentally different foundation and emphasis than these other institutions. At the same time, race is and has been central to the organization—and associated social structures—of religious institutions in the United States. Religion, as a white-dominated institution, has been a participant in the construction and perpetuation of the American racial order. In short, systems of exclusion and segregation are evident in religion just as in the institutions of housing, education, and the labor market. Within religion, this is evident in the exclusion of racial minorities from full religious participation in congregations and other religious organizations. For example, during the eighteenth century African American participation in Protestant churches was restricted to worship service attendance. Hence, opportunities for mobility within the church for African Americans were very rare (Frazier 1974). Because the Spanish had already introduced Catholicism to Latino homelands before the United States conquered Puerto Rico and Mexico, a Latino Catholicism was established before the U.S. invasion and subsequent imposition of American Catholicism. The U.S. Catholic Church, with the intent of Americanizing Latino Catholicism, used its control within the Catholic Church to inferiorize "expressions of [Latino] Catholics . . . [and] subordinate their way of expressing the faith" to that of Euro-American Catholicism (Stevens-Arroyo 1998, 29).

As with the other social institutions we have considered here, then, religion has excluded and subordinated racial and ethnic minorities in the United States. Religion differs from other institutions because it has been a source of empowerment and advancement for race-specific religious organizations that have developed. In creating their own ethnic and race-specific religious organizations, nonwhite organizations have created something of a paradox: religion in America has been a liberating force for communities of color, but it has also been employed to oppress these same communities. For example, both Latinos (Stevens-Arroyo 1998) and African Americans (Morris 1984) used their respective religions as a platform for civil rights activism. At the same time, white evangelicals have both supported racial progress (with the abolitionist movement, for instance, and the civil rights movement) and opposed it (southern pro-slavery evangelicals) (Emerson and Smith 2000). This paradox continues to be relevant and is likely to persist, particularly as the growing racial-ethnic diversity of our nation's population creates new questions about how this aspect of the changing terrain of race and ethnicity will play itself out within the paradoxical setting of religion in America. In this chapter, after a review of the recent research on race and ethnicity in religion, we focus on the response of religious institutions to segregation, efforts to dismantle segregation, and the effects on religion of increasing racial and ethnic diversity.

EFFORTS TO INTEGRATE RELIGIOUS INSTITUTIONS

Whereas local, state, and federal laws could be used first to ensure segregation in education and housing and then to break it down, clearly such governmental legislation is not applicable in the domain of religious institutions. But the governing bodies of religious institutions have nevertheless begun to pay some attention to patterns of segregation and integration among worshipers. The goal of racial integration within religious institutions has been of growing interest since the civil rights movement. Martin Luther King Jr. observed that 11:00 A.M. on Sunday mornings is the most racially segregated hour of the week. The inherent challenge in this observation—that Christians need to make strides toward racial integration—has been taken up by many Christian organizations. In evangelical circles, these attempts are commonly referred to as the racial reconciliation movement. Originated by African American evangelicals and later co-opted by white evangelicals, the movement initially sought to achieve racial reconciliation by developing interracial friendships, recognizing and resisting structures of racial subordination, having whites repent their "personal, historical, and social sins" related to racial subordination, and having African Americans forgive whites for their participation in the creation and perpetuation of the racial order (Emerson and Smith 2000, 54–55). However, this understanding of racial reconciliation shifted: "As the message of racial reconciliation spread to a white audience, it was popularized. The racial reconciliation message given to the mass audience is *individual* reconciliation" (67). Thus, while black evangelicals acknowledged both the individual *and* structural aspects of the racial reconciliation process, white evangelicals acknowledged only the individual component. In this view, the steps to racial reconciliation were: (1) *individuals* developing interracial friendships and (2) *individuals* repenting of individual prejudice. The recognition that structural or collective forces helped to shape racialization were eliminated from consideration. Thus, individualism as the problem and the solution permeates perspectives on race in religion, much as it does in some recent arguments about race in the other social institutions we have discussed in this chapter.

Although studying patterns of segregation and integration has a long history in research on housing, education, and labor markets, sociologists of religion have only recently begun to document these patterns in churches. The racial reconciliation movement endorsed and encouraged the development of interracial churches, and as recounted in Raleigh Washington and Glen Kehrein's *Breaking Down Walls: A Model for Reconciliation in an Age of Racial Strife* (1993), the leaders of this movement have faced a number of challenges to achieving interracial churches. Partly owing to the barriers described in Washington and Kehrein (1993), including racism, stereotyping, and denying that there is a race problem in America, there has been little progress in the development of interracial churches in America since King's observations some forty years ago. Today, only 10 percent of American churches are interracial (Emerson and Smith 2000). There is a significant difference, however, between Christian and non-Christian religions in the prevalence of interracial congregations: nearly three times as many (28 percent) non-Christian congregations are interracial compared to Christian congregations (Christerson and Emerson 2001). This figure includes primarily Muslim but also Buddhist, Hindu, and other non-Christian religious institutions. Within non-Christian religious institutions race is apparently not the salient dividing line that it has proven to be in Christian religious institutions—a point to which we return shortly.

The Downside of Integration While racial integration is valued among some religious organizations, it also poses a potential threat to the vitality and social organization of racial minority communities. The exclusion of racial minorities from the power centers of white-dominated religious institutions has ironically led to the formation of minority-controlled organizations and institutions. In

1787 a preacher in the white-dominated Methodist denomination, Richard Allen, and other freed blacks created the African Methodist Episcopal Church after being physically removed from an unsanctioned section of the church during a crowded worship service (Frazier 1974; Marty 1985). The formation of other black denominations under similar circumstances gave birth to the "black church," which has become one of the most central institutions in the African American community (Frazier 1974; Mays and Nicholson 1985; Morris 1984).

The vast majority of African Americans, regardless of their religious affinity, have an attachment to the African American church (Lincoln 1974; Mays and Nicholson 1985). It is a space where African Americans can freely express themselves artistically, politically, and socially (Morris 1984). In addition to church-related meetings and services, church space has been used for non-church-related activities, such as business and political contacts (Drake and Cayton 1985). Moreover, the black church provided a structural framework for the creation of the Southern Christian Leadership Conference (SCLC), a crucial player in the civil rights movement (Morris 1984). For this reason, the black church has significant influence over the religious and social construction of ideas within the black community. But more important, it is a space where African American interests have been recognized, understood, and freely pursued.[1]

IMMIGRATION AND DIVERSITY WITHIN
RELIGIOUS INSTITUTIONS

A key development in our understanding of race and religion in the United States has been the response to changes in immigration patterns over the past forty years. Immigrant groups are now coming to the United States from Latin America, Asia, and to a lesser extent eastern European countries. Because of the strong connection between race-ethnicity and religion, these demographic changes have profound implications for the landscape of religion in America. Post-1965 immigration has increased the religious diversity and representation of minority religions in America, such as Hinduism, Islam, and Buddhism. It has also brought a new face to Christianity: immigrants of color arriving on American shores are disproportionately Christian (Warner, forthcoming). The result is an emerging presence in the United States of "de-Europeanized" Christianity and non-Christian religions (Warner 1998).

Recent examinations of the process of assimilation for these more recent immigrants suggest that their experiences—within the context of religion—may not follow those of their western and northern European counterparts of the nineteenth and early twentieth centuries. On the one hand, immigrants from Asian and Latin American countries, like their predecessors from western and northern Europe, have developed ethnic-specific congregations around language needs, immigrant concerns, and homeland cultural practices. Therefore, first-generation immigrant churches are ethnically, not racially, organized. This is not new. However, the assimilation of Asian immigrants has not followed the pattern that was followed by immigrants from western and northern European countries (Jeung 2002). The latter assimilated into white-dominated American religious institutions, but the children of immigrants from Asian countries have instead formed pan-Asian religious institutions, especially on the West Coast. In other areas of the country Asians tend to form ethnic-specific churches (primarily Korean or Chinese). Nonetheless, the perpetuation of ethnic-specific churches into the second generation suggests that, at the least, Asian ethnic groups are opting not to attend white-dominant churches. At worst, they are responding to exclusion from full participation in white-controlled religious institutions.

This trend suggests that immigrants from Asian countries are recognizing and responding to racialization in America: that is, they recognize that "Asian" is a relevant and salient category in the United States. This is a dimension, then, along which they are constructing religious institutions. For example, Russell Jeung (2002) finds in his study based in the San Francisco Bay Area that pan-Asian congregations have organized around a pan-Asian identity because of dominant expectations and understanding of Asians in government, the marketplace, and religious institutions. In religious institutions an Asian or Asian American identity is imposed through religious curricula and seminary training. Asian ethnic identities are thus perceived as culturally similar and having similar interests. At the same time, ethnic-specific identities are not acknowledged, suggesting that pan-Asian, or racial group, boundaries are more salient than ethnic-specific boundaries in the United States generally and within a religious context specifically. Jeung (2002, 216) argues that unlike ethnic identities, which are rooted in specific cultural practices and linguistic commonalities, pan-Asian identity is symbolic: it binds people together through "expressive feeling and connection to a group" and is adopted by Asian ethnic groups to foster solidarity and mobilize congregations.

The dramatic increase of the number of Latinos in the United States is of particular relevance for understanding the changing terrain of race and religion in the twenty-first century because this increase affects not only the racial and ethnic landscape of the country but also the American Catholic religious landscape, since Latinos are overwhelmingly Catholic. Up until the mid-twentieth century, Latino Catholic religious expression was delegitimized by the U.S. Catholic Church (Stevens-Arroyo 1998). The experience of Latino Catholics as "conquered peoples" who already practiced a form of Catholicism that differed from Euro-American Catholicism distinguishes them from European Catholic immigrants, who easily assimilated into the North American Catholic Church. However, since the civil rights movement, Latino Catholicism has been revived, particularly after Cesar Chavez drew on Catholicism to support the farmworkers' strike in Delano, California. The farmworkers' movement not only spawned institutional changes within the Catholic Church and Latino Catholic organizations but also increased Latino representation at the national level within the American Catholic Church.[2] These organizations have developed alternative religious practices, such as culturally relevant Spanish masses, thus providing Latino Catholics with relatively autonomous religious spaces within the Catholic Church. Moreover, the recent Latino Catholic presence in America has affected American Catholicism by moving it more toward religious individualism, sacramental practices, and devotion (Warner, forthcoming).

Although Latino immigrants are largely Catholic, a disproportionate number of Protestant Latino immigrants have come to America. Over the past fifteen years, membership in Protestant churches, particularly Pentecostal and evangelical denominations, has grown to include an estimated 10 percent of the population of Latin countries (Stoll and Garrard-Burnett 1993). These Protestant Latin Americans are coming to the United States and reportedly amount to 23 percent of the Latino population (Espinosa, Elizondo, and Miranda 2003, 14–16). Hence, American Protestantism may also be changed by the increase in Latino immigration to the United States.

Finally, other immigrant groups are arriving on America's shores from such places as the Caribbean, Africa, and India. Many of these groups practice minority religions, including Hinduism, Rastafarianism, and Buddhism. In Stephen Warner and Judith Wittner's edited volume on new immigrant religious groups, *Gatherings in Diaspora: Religious Communities and the New Immigration* (1998), researchers find that religious identity for these groups (as well as larger recent immigrant groups) is of particular importance and has in some cases increased in salience after coming to America because it serves to unify them as a distinct group. Additionally, they have found that new immigrant groups are adapting to the religious structure of the United States. More specifically, they are organizing into congregations whose religious activities are governed by the local body rather than by a regional governing group or bishops. More so than with the other social institutions, a consideration of religious institutions makes salient the role of racial and ethnic identity, highlighting how these very institutions are shaped by changes in the racial and ethnic diversity of the United States. The interplay is complicated, as evidenced by the development of pan-Asian churches and the emergence of legitimate Latino Catholic institutions.

THE FUTURE OF RACE, ETHNICITY, AND RELIGION

What Methodological and Theoretical Contributions Can the Study of Race and Ethnicity in Religion Make to the Overall Study of Race and Ethnicity? The sociohistorical context of American religion and the expected demographic changes elicit new and important questions about American religion and race-ethnicity.

As we embark on the twenty-first century, our prescription for understanding American religion must accommodate the expected racial and religious changes. Scholars of American religion can contribute to understanding that is relevant and applicable across cultures by employing inclusive research methods and using them to study and recognize the impact of different historical experiences, locations in social structures, and cultural norms and values. This strategy has thus far eluded many researchers (for notable exceptions, see Ammerman 1997; Emerson and Smith 2000; Warner and Wittner 1998), and as a result we have an incomplete accounting of religion across racial-ethnic groups.

But perhaps even more important, an examination of how race and ethnicity play out in U.S. religious institutions can offer valuable insights into the construction of race-ethnicity more broadly construed. Although religion has been similar to housing, education, and labor markets in that it has been used to subordinate and exclude racial and ethnic minorities in America, unlike these other institutions, religion is a space where people voluntarily choose to interact regularly, build community, and share life. Moreover, religion is not directly subject to external demands such as social policies and financial limitations. The impact of these two factors, choice and autonomy, which are void in most other contexts (particularly for racial and ethnic minorities), can illuminate our understanding of people's willingness to cross racial and ethnic boundaries and of features of race-ethnicity that may elude us in the context of other social institutions.

Should We Care That in America 11:00 A.M. Is the Most Segregated Hour of the Week? Michael Emerson and Christian Smith (2000) have provided one of the first comprehensive and systematic analyses of religious racial segregation in the United States. Although we need even more studies of the pervasiveness of racial segregation and the prospects for integration, we must also look at a larger question about the advantages and disadvantages of such congregations. Racially subordinated groups have responded to racial exclusion from white-dominated religious institutions by creating autonomous religious spaces that have become central to their communities. Unlike white religious institutions, these religious institutions are often the only base of power and influence for these minority groups. Racial minorities therefore have the most to lose as a group if American religion becomes a more racially inclusive institution. For this reason, they may resist racial integration, more so than whites. What, then, are the benefits of racial integration? Who benefits? Are religious whites willing to relinquish racial dominance within religious institutions? If so, under what conditions? Will the burden of integration remain on racial minorities, or will whites be willing to attend traditionally black, Latino, or Asian American congregations?

What Will Be the Impact on Non-Christian Religions of the Construction of Race in America?—and Vice Versa? As noted earlier, non-Christian religious institutions are more likely to be racially integrated than Christian ones. A number of questions arise from this observation: What is it about non-Christian religious institutions in America that allows for racial integration? Do these institutions construct race differently than the broader society? If so, can this construction of race be replicated in Christian institutions? Over time, will these institutions adopt a similar kind of racialization as Christian institutions? What are the effects of the terrorist attacks of September 11, 2001, on religious institutions? Will being Muslim prevent Eastern Europeans from experiencing the advantages of whiteness in America? For example, are Muslims in fact white? If not, will whiteness expand to include Eastern European Muslims? As Americans, we have been called upon to be the eyes and ears of the government in being aware of Muslim activities and potential terrorist acts. How will this expectation shape the experiences of Eastern Europeans who have white skin color and phenotype—since physical traits are not the only criteria for possessing whiteness?

What Is the Trajectory for the Religious Experiences of Asian and Latino Immigrants?   Latinos are estimated to become 23 percent of the American population by 2050, a growth rate that would make them the largest racial minority group in the United States. The number of African Americans and Asians will also increase from 12 percent to 14 percent and from 4 percent to 10 percent, respectively, while the proportion of white people in the United States is projected to decrease by one-third, to 50 percent of the American population (Schaeffer 1998).

A disproportionate number of immigrants are Christian—some estimates suggest as many as two-thirds (Jasso 2003). The large influx of European immigrants to the United States during the nineteenth century changed the culture and religious practices of American Catholicism (Marty 1985). Will Christian culture be similarly affected by the large increase in Asian and Latino Christians in this country?

Finally, we already know that Asian and Latino immigrants are following different patterns in their religious experiences than previous immigrant groups: unlike their Western and Northern European counterparts, second-generation immigrants from these countries have formed racialized religious organizations. The existence of pan-Asian and pan-Latino religious institutions suggests a recognition of and response to the exclusion of nonwhite groups in America. Therefore, what role will pan-ethnic religious institutions play in the community life of ethnic subordinates? What does the existence of pan-Asian and pan-Latino organizations say about the power of race in the United States and its impact on the organization of incoming immigrant groups? Will these patterns persist? In the decades to come, will these institutions, in the tradition of other black and Latino churches of the past, be a source for new movements for civil rights or for struggles against racial discrimination?

THE CRIMINAL JUSTICE SYSTEM

The criminal justice system is distinct in many ways from the institutions addressed so far in this chapter. Whereas people voluntarily participate in religious and educational institutions, few people voluntarily come into contact with the criminal justice system; whether as criminal victim or offender, most people prefer not to be involved with this institution. But even for those who have no direct contact with criminal justice systems, their policies and practices can have profound consequences. The impact of this institution is evident in the tremendous growth of criminal justice systems and related industries over the past several decades. The adverse consequences of this expansion are dramatically revealed in its disproportionate impact on individuals, families, and communities of color.

In this section, we begin by reviewing the growing use of incarceration, briefly considering the causes of those increases (and whether they are linked to increases in criminal activity). We then consider how race operates to shape—sometimes subtly and other times not so subtly—the experiences of individuals at different stages of the administration of criminal justice, including policing, the courts, and sentencing. We conclude with a discussion of the collateral consequences of racialized mass criminalization and incarceration—that is, how policies and decisions in criminal justice spill beyond courtrooms and prison walls to influence individual life chances, community conditions, and other social institutions.

RACE AND THE PUNISHMENT BOOM

The criminal justice system has drawn tremendous scrutiny in recent years, especially where issues at the intersection of race, crime, and justice are concerned. And for good reason. The past quarter-century has witnessed numerous cases of race-related police brutality and misconduct; official acknowledgments of systematic racial profiling in policing; the exoneration of numerous falsely convicted persons, including many who faced capital punishment; and a tremendous increase in the number of people in U.S. prisons, jails, and detention facilities, especially persons of color.

The U.S. government confines its citizens and other residents in detention facilities, jails, and prisons at rates far exceeding that of any other industrialized nation (see Chambliss 1995; Zimring 2001). The number of inmates in state and federal prisons more than tripled between 1980 and 2000. Although the number is still increasing, the rate of increase has slowed somewhat (U.S. Department of Justice, Bureau of Justice Statistics 2002c). Nevertheless, by 2001, over 6.5 million Americans were under some form of correctional supervision (prison, jail, probation, or parole). Over 2.1 million of these were incarcerated in State or Federal prisons or local jails (U.S. Department of Justice 2002c).

The increase in the U.S. prison population is in large part due to the incarceration of black and Latino young women and men for drug-related and typically nonviolent offenses. While the number of adults of all races increased during the 1980s and 1990s, the number of blacks who were incarcerated rose much more quickly, doubling during this time period (U.S. Department of Justice 1999). In 1997, 2 percent of the white population was under some form of correctional supervision, compared to 9 percent of the black population (U.S. Department of Justice 1999). Since 1990, the number of Hispanics in jail has increased at a faster annual rate than for any other group, yet by the year 2000 blacks were still twice as likely as Hispanics, and five times more likely than whites, to be incarcerated (U.S. Department of Justice 2002b). The Bureau of Justice Statistics recently made the dire prediction that, "based on current rates of first incarceration, an estimated 28 percent of black males will enter State or Federal prison during their lifetime, compared to 16 percent of Hispanic males and 4.4 percent of white males" (U.S. Department of Justice 2003). Although the number of black women in prison is comparatively small, the increase in rates of incarceration has recently been greater among black women than black men. By 1998 the incarceration rate for black women actually exceeded that of white males in 1980 (Currie 1998, 14; Mauer and Huling 1995). Today African American men and women together represent a numerical majority of state and federal prisoners in the United States, exceeding the total number of white prisoners by more than 100,000 (Davis 2003, 20).

The sociological causes and consequences of the prison buildup, and the racial disparities therein, are complex and far-reaching. For example, increases in the U.S. prison population have coincided with dramatic increases in spending on the criminal justice system, spending that might otherwise support other social institutions, including those we have already discussed. Expenditures on different sectors of the justice system have more than tripled since the 1980s for municipal, county, state, and federal governments (U.S. Department of Justice 2002a). Direct and intergovernmental justice system expenditures in the United States totaled nearly $36 billion in 1982, and had climbed to nearly $147 billion by 1999. Over the same period, direct and intergovernmental expenditures on policing increased from nearly $20 billion in 1982 to over $65 billion by 1999. Combined federal, state, and local expenditures on corrections totaled just over $9 billion in 1982 and $49 billion in 1999 (U.S. Department of Justice 2002a).

It is beyond the scope of this chapter to provide a full elaboration of these social developments and their implications. Instead, the remainder of this section focuses on select issues related to the development of racial disparities in criminal justice, especially in terms of court processing and incarceration, and the more general consequences of racialized mass imprisonment for individuals, families, and communities.

HOW RACE OPERATES IN THE CRIMINAL JUSTICE SYSTEM

Notwithstanding important changes over the course of the twentieth century, racial discrimination and inequality continue to permeate the U.S. criminal justice system, such that criminal justice processes in the United States can be viewed as reflections and reinforcements of our larger racialized social system (Bonilla-Silva 1997). Indeed, race and crime—in the eyes of the public and many officials—remain intertwined, as is clear from sources ranging from surveys of public opinion to the campaigns of candidates for elective office. Perhaps more than for any of the institutions we have considered so far, it is difficult to discuss criminal justice in contemporary U.S. society without considering race and ethnicity or to seriously advance the cause of racial equality without confronting problems of criminal (in)justice.

Although seemingly discrete categories in the criminal justice system, policing, the courts, and corrections are more appropriately seen as the interconnected stages at which decisions about punishment and social control are initially shaped, further refined, and subsequently applied. What happens at any one of these stages can have profound consequences for what happens at another, and this spillover effect is critical to appreciating the effect of race in criminal justice processes.

Police officers are the most visible representations of the rule of law, and the first to deliberately enter the scenes of real and suspected crimes. Mandated to serve and protect the public, they are our criminal justice system's front-line service providers, its key ambassadors and gatekeepers. It is through their interactions with victims, perpetrators, suspects, and bystanders that our experiences of law and order are conditioned. Throughout history, race has shaped and strained these interactions in a number of ways, as reflected in police violence within minority communities, in resistance to racially integrating police forces, and in the recently acknowledged practice of racial profiling. Notwithstanding improvements in police and community relations and increases in police accountability, these problems persist today. In the wake of the terrorist attacks of September 11, 2001, they are likely to have an impact on new racialized groups, especially those of Middle Eastern descent.

There is substantial research and anecdotal evidence that police target minority communities for surveillance and aggressive law enforcement (Chambliss 1994). One result of targeted and aggressive tactics is that blacks and whites have very different relations with and perceptions of the police: the former trust the criminal justice system less than whites do and perceive more bias in it (Russell 1998; Tuch and Weitzer 1997; Weitzer 2000). Another result, of course, is that racial and ethnic minorities enter the formal processing stages of criminal justice administration at greater rates and are therefore subject to additional potential biases, further increasing the likelihood of criminal conviction and incarceration.

Even as the U.S. prison population has dramatically expanded, there has been general stability in crime rates, as shown by the National Crime Victimization Survey (U.S. Department of Justice 1997). This suggests that crime alone cannot fully explain either the massive growth of the U.S. prison population or its racial disproportions. Although differential offending is among the factors related to racially disproportionate incarceration, research on race and court sanctions has provided an accumulation of evidence over the past several decades that racialized disadvantage also operates across a number of decision points in criminal justice processing. Among others, these include decisions about bail, detention, plea-bargaining, sentencing, and parole. Similar to what happens in housing, education, and the labor market, these disparities often result from complex and indirect processes. For example, race can indirectly influence sentencing decisions through its relationship with other relevant variables, such as bail status, occupational status, type of offense, age, and prior incarceration (Burke and Turk 1975; LaFree 1985; Lizotte 1978).

Another prominent pattern in court processing has been the devaluation of black victims and the corresponding prioritization of white victims. That is, black (and white) offenders of black victims have historically been treated more leniently than black offenders of white victims, who received substantially harsher punishments (LaFree 1989; Myers 1979). As one author has observed, the color line of criminal justice marks a patterned underprotection and excessive punishment of racial and ethnic minorities (Kennedy 1997). However, it is no longer the case that people of color are indiscriminately and without exception subject to severe court sanctions, as was true at earlier points in the past century. It is thus critical to examine interaction effects—race of the offender with race of the victim, occupational status, age, and so on—to appreciate the nature and extent of racially disparate treatment in court processing (Zatz 1987).

The adoption of a "determinate sentencing" policy in the 1980s significantly influenced the nature of race effects in court processing. Under this policy, sentences are determined a priori, according to "legal factors," including the formal charge and the defendant's offense history. Determinate sentencing policies have thus markedly reduced judicial discretion at the sentencing stage. In addition, through the emphasis in determinate sentencing on formal charges, the role of police officers and especially prosecutors in sentencing decisions has increased substantially. This reorganization of court processing has thus altered and further complicated the scenarios by which race can influence criminal sanctions.

A key arena in which this transformation has taken place and contributed to racial disparities in criminal sanctions is in drug-related prosecutions and sentencing. Mandatory sentencing laws for drug possession, sales, and distribution have been passed in states nationwide as part of the "War on Drugs." Although advertised as an assault on drug dealers, these policies have in practice affected mainly drug users and those on the lowest rungs of illegal drug distribution. The casualties have disproportionately been young racial minorities. For example, while the number of state prison inmates incarcerated for drug-related crimes increased dramatically between 1985 and 1995, the increase was twice as great for blacks as for whites. In 1996, 62 percent of all drug offenders admitted to state prisons were African American, and in some states this disparity was much greater. In Maryland and Illinois, for example, 90 percent of state prison drug offender admissions that year were African American (Human Rights Watch 2000).

Though glaring, statistics on the disproportionate number of blacks incarcerated for drug offenses do not themselves establish race effects in case processing. Surveys on drug use and empirical research on sentencing both suggest, however, that differential offending does not explain these disproportionate sanctions. Much of the racial disparity in incarceration for drug crimes relates to patterns of arrest mandated by the "War on Drugs" and greater police surveillance and aggressive law enforcement in minority communities. These arrests subject minority offenders at greater rates to harsh determinate sentencing policies in state and federal courts, where prosecutorial charging decisions and opportunities for charge adjustment take on added significance.

There are several troubling aspects to the apparent racial disparities in drug crime charging decisions and sentencing outcomes. One concerns the jurisdiction where cases are prosecuted. Several researchers have suggested that state and federal court officials engage in "selective prosecution" of cases, particularly drug-related cases, and that those involving certain types of racial minority (especially the poor and young) defendants are aggressively prosecuted, while similar cases involving whites are diverted or never formally pursued to begin with (Tonry 1995; Petersilia 1983). Such a pattern is apparent in the vigorous pursuit against minority defendants of federal drug charges: the penalties mandated by federal sentencing guidelines for drug crimes are much more severe than at the state level. Others suggest that racially selective prosecution is evident in decisions to charge pregnant black drug abusers with exposing their unborn children to illegal drugs, an aggravation of charges less common among white offenders (Roberts 1991; but see Kennedy 1997, 360).

Plea-bargaining decisions become more important when determinate sentencing is adopted because it can influence the nature of the formal charges a defendant faces and thus the sentence received in the event of a conviction. In short, by accepting a lesser charge in exchange for a guilty plea or other assistance, an offender can avoid the more severe sanction reserved for the original charge. Research has found some evidence that race is related to the distribution of these opportunities. Cases involving black offenders are significantly less likely to be resolved through guilty pleas than cases involving white offenders (Petersilia 1983; Zatz and Lizotte 1985) and less likely to benefit from an especially subjective plea-bargain type known as "substantial assistance":

a reduction in charges in exchange for information, testimony, or other assistance to law enforcement (Maxfield and Kramer 1998). Studies in select jurisdictions have found that charges are more likely to be reduced for minorities through plea agreements, yet these researchers speculate that this may be true either because prosecutors devalue minority victims or because, in the absence of supporting evidence, they are making corrections to earlier overcharging by police (Holmes, Daudistel, and Farrell 1987).

The causes of disparities in plea-bargaining are multiple and complex. Not only are potential biases on the part of prosecutors relevant, but so too are the quality of the legal defense and the types of information or assistance that different defendants are able or willing to provide. Greater distrust of the criminal justice system among African Americans (Sherman 2002), for example, may render black defendants generally less inclined to plea-bargain. In addition, non-English-speaking individuals are disadvantaged in an era of determinate sentencing because, as one author notes, "the benefits and implications of pleading guilty rather than going to trial are communicated in subtle ways requiring knowledge of the . . . intricacies of the English language" (Zatz 1987, 81). Ultimately, a relative lack of plea-bargaining opportunities appears to make black and other minority defendants more likely to be sentenced for the originally charged offenses and is therefore an important factor among others in the pattern of racially disparate sanctions observed in this era of determinate and severe sentencing.

It is welcome news that rates of incarceration have slowed in recent years, even if that slowdown is due more to fiscal constraint than to changes in criminal justice policy. Yet even if prisons were miraculously emptied tomorrow, we would still need to understand the impact of decades of mass incarceration on U.S. society in general and on racial and ethnic minority communities in particular. The outward indicators of the punishment boom are rather apparent in such factors as levels of expenditure, the physical buildup of prisons, and the distributions of arrests, convictions, and criminal sanctions. Less visible and well understood—but potentially more profound—are the broader consequences of the punishment boom for individuals, families, and communities and for other social, cultural, political, and economic institutions. In short, what is the impact of the rise of the prison as a dominant social institution on other spheres of life—and how are race and ethnicity implicated in this process? It is to these questions that we now turn.

COLLATERAL CONSEQUENCES OF RACIALIZED
MASS INCARCERATION

Growing numbers of scholars and activists suggest that the full depth and significance of our social investment in the prison system will not become evident until we step outside the police precincts, courtrooms, and prison walls and move beyond official statistics to appreciate the impact of the overdevelopment of the prison on our social and cultural fabric—and particularly on the life experiences and opportunities of those individuals, families, and communities that occupy the older "ground zeroes" of our war against drugs and crime.

Since 600,000 individuals exit the criminal justice system each year, we need to ask what happens when they return. But there are deeper questions still. We must also ask about the disruptions and other effects of decades of mass criminalization and incarceration on those families and communities these individuals left behind, on those rather distinct neighborhoods marked by high rates of population turnover owing to incarceration, and on the more than two million children with incarcerated parents.

A growing body of literature is developing answers to these questions, and early findings related to the "collateral consequences" of mass incarceration give cause for great concern. We know, for example, that licensing restrictions (on driving licenses but also on occupational licenses) and patterns of hiring discrimination against convicted felons, especially racial and ethnic minorities, prevent many former prisoners from finding work (Pager 2003). Felony convictions can also result in deportation, as well as disqualification from public housing, welfare, and financial aid for education (Mauer and Chesney-Lind 2002). These formal and informal civil disabilities may undermine the possibility of successful societal reintegration and impose further strain not only on the individuals, families, and communities within a former prisoner's web of relations but ultimately on the resources of other societal institutions, including the criminal justice system itself.

Another collateral consequence of mass incarceration is a rising number of children with incarcerated parents. According to the Bureau of Justice Statistics, state and federal prisons in 1999 held more than 700,000 parents of children under the age of eighteen. Almost half of these parents reported living with their children prior to their incarceration, meaning that in 1999 "an estimated 336,300 U.S. households with minor children [were] affected by the imprisonment of a resident parent" (Mumola 2000, 1). The number of children with incarcerated parents grew dramatically in the 1990s. A total of 1.5 million children in the United States had a parent in prison in 1999, an increase of more than 500,000 since 1991. This increase was especially pronounced among African American (7 percent) and Hispanic (2.6 percent) children, who were nine and three times more likely, respectively, than white children (.8 percent) to have an incarcerated parent in 1999 (Mumola 2000, 2). These trends raise a number of questions about the consequences of incarceration for individual child development, family and community dynamics, and resulting strain on the relevant social institutions (such as child welfare agencies and schools). These are consequences experienced disproportionately by racial and ethnic minority communities.

There is thus a collective element to the civil penalties and collateral damages attendant to mass criminalization and incarceration. This may be most evident in the loss of voting rights for persons convicted of felonies and in the loss of proportional representation for those communities with large numbers of people removed to prisons. Disfranchisement of felons is a function of state law, and a variety of practices obtain nationwide. Forty-eight states prohibit adults in correctional facilities from voting. Most states maintain voting restrictions of varying periods of time for people with felony convictions. In more than a dozen states, ex-felons are prohibited from voting for the remainder of their lives unless they undergo a costly process of having their voting rights restored (Fellner and Mauer 1998).

Not surprisingly, felon disfranchisement has disproportionately and severely affected African American communities. As of 1999, approximately 13 percent of all adult black men were disqualified from voting owing to criminal convictions. In 1998, 4.3 million citizens—including 1.4 million black Americans— had lost the right to vote for life (Fellner and Mauer 1998). In Mississippi, Alabama, South Carolina, Texas, and other states, between one-quarter and one-fifth of all voting-age black residents have been either permanently or temporarily stripped of their access to the ballot (Fellner and Mauer 1998). An important analysis of electoral implications, based on conservative estimates of likely political participation, found that felon disfranchisement played a decisive role in several congressional and national elections, including the 2000 presidential election (Uggen and Manza 2002).

Compounding the issue of felon disfranchisement is how prisoners are counted in the U.S. census for purposes of defining legislative districts. This practice effectively dilutes the voting power of individuals in a prisoner's home district (often a segregated urban area), while inflating the influence of the voters in the typically rural districts where most prisons are based and whose political interests are likely to depart from those of the prisoners and urban dwellers whose voting power they assume (Wagner 2002). Thus, current and former prisoners, together with dependents and political allies, experience further exclusion from processes of civic engagement.

We find then that processes of formal social control in policing, the courts, and corrections are differentially experienced by racial and ethnic minorities and that much of this difference relates to direct and indirect patterns of racial discrimination. Notwithstanding important progress over the course of the twentieth century in realizing the constitutional right of equal protection under the law, the color line of criminal social control endures, and the consequence are significant. These consequences are elevated not only by the severe sanctions of our current criminal justice policies—and particularly the reliance on incarceration—but by what we are coming to appreciate as the collateral consequences of racialized mass incarceration. Through felon disfranchisement and other formal disabilities and informal practices of exclusion resulting from criminal convictions, racialized mass incarceration threatens to maintain and intensify the marginalization of affected minority individuals, families, and communities.

THE FUTURE OF RACE, ETHNICITY, AND CRIMINAL JUSTICE

Assuming Current Trends in Incarceration Cannot Continue, What Will Come Next? Given the budget crises nationwide, it seems unlikely that various governments can continue to invest in imprisonment on such a costly and escalating scale. Will public and official concerns about the rising costs of current incarceration trends, financial if not social, stall further expansion of the prison-industrial complex? And assuming our reliance on incarceration is unsustainable, what will come next? Will we simply revert to the goal of rehabilitation in a familiar cycle of prison reform, or will growing anti-prison movements effectively challenge the existence of the prison as a social institution, thus making progress in the radical project of prison abolition or otherwise shifting the debate? Future research should be proactive in anticipating future directions of criminal justice policy, especially in relation to prisons and their implications for racial and ethnic communities. This might help in evaluating various options and avoiding merely cosmetic responses to the current crisis.

How Will the "War on Terror" Reshape the Intersection of Race and Criminal Justice? Investigations of the role of race and ethnicity in the criminal justice system have overwhelmingly focused on the U.S. context, and particularly on the African American experience. Events of the day are disrupting this national focus, forcing us to consider these issues in a transnational context and in relation to other racial and ethnic group experiences. In addition to expanding our understanding of the experiences of newly arriving immigrants from Asia and Latin America, the declaration of a "War on Terror" challenges us to address its impact on the constantly changing terrain of race and social organization. Armed with lessons from old "wars" on crime and drugs, future research should examine how the "War on Terror" is expanding and otherwise altering the intersection of race-ethnicity, crime, and justice, including problems of racialized mass criminalization and incarceration and their collateral consequences for individuals, families, and communities—in particular those of Middle Eastern descent.

What Are the Collateral Consequences of Criminal Justice Policy in General, and for Racialized Groups in Particular? We have just begun to appreciate the collateral consequences of several decades of mass imprisonment. We have learned much about the implications of mass imprisonment for civil society, employment opportunity, representative government, social welfare, child welfare, and other issues. Yet more work is needed to determine the extent of the collateral damage of criminal justice policy, how best it can be repaired, and how it might be avoided. We hope that future research will shift some of the attention currently focused on the characteristics of those entering the criminal justice system to an examination of the situation faced by those coming out. This research must look not just at the circumstances of the formerly incarcerated individuals themselves but also at their families, communities, and the society of which they and we are a part.

CONCLUSION

In this chapter, we have not offered an exhaustive review of the role of race and ethnicity in all social institutions. Rather, we have tried to highlight key issues currently at play in several important arenas. The realities are telling. To be sure, much progress is evident in some arenas. But in others, there are clear signs of retrenchment, if not outright worsening, of racial disparities. Across a range of social institutions the most consistent pattern is one of both persistence and change. That is, although there is considerable evidence of steady (or increasing, but rarely decreasing) levels of racial inequality, these inequalities are often being produced through new mechanisms. Thus, shifts in the legal and cultural terrain of race have resulted less in the elimination of racism than in shifts in how it operates. As we outlined at the end of each section, these changes have clear implications for how we think about and research race and ethnic matters.

We recognize that the trends we have mapped out for the social institutions we examined in this chapter are also taking place in other arenas, such as the social welfare arena and the political arena. For example, there is much evidence that racial patterns in political participation are undergoing important transformations. This is evident in battles over felony disenfranchisement laws (which disproportionately affect blacks and Latinos), struggles around redistricting in states across the country, allegations of racism in key election outcomes in recent years (for example, the Florida presidential election), and a number of heated local elections (such as the 2003 Philadelphia mayoral election) in which race has been at play either implicitly or explicitly.

Moreover, in important ways these institutional patterns and transformations are not isolated from one another. For example, there are clear intersections between the arenas of criminal justice and education. What effect will the punishment boom have on children in public schools? In several states dollar-for-dollar divestment in public education has funded the construction of jails and prisons. And the introduction of criminal justice technologies and management strategies into schools has shaped the daily lives of the children attending these schools. "Zero tolerance" policies and policing strategies have been adopted in urban public school management, effectively criminalizing student misbehavior in otherwise severely underresourced schools. Divestment in education and the criminalization of school misconduct, combined with the disruption of social ties and mechanisms of informal social control through high levels of incarceration, have probably resulted in a direct pipeline from failing public schools to hopeless prisons. This is a conveyor belt that is almost exclusively the domain of black and Latino/a communities.

Similarly, there are clear intersections between housing segregation patterns and school segregation. Especially with the outlawing of the explicit segregation of schools, the persistently high levels of racial segregation of schoolchildren are due in large part to segregation in housing. On the other hand, there are some indicators that school demographics are one key measure that families use in making housing decisions. Thus, there is a dialectic and complicated relationship between these patterns in housing and education. More research is needed to uncover and clarify the dynamics involved.

At minimum this chapter has outlined a number of pressing research questions for scholars to pursue. These are questions that those centrally interested in race and ethnicity will have to engage, and they are questions with which scholars who are focused on any one of the social institutions discussed here will also need to grapple.

This chapter was a collaborative effort, with each co-author assuming responsibility for one of the social institutions: housing—Maria Krysan; education—Amanda Lewis; labor markets—Sharon Collins; the criminal justice system—Geoffrey Ward; and religion—Korie Edwards. Lewis and Krysan were responsible for editing the overall chapter.

NOTES

1. The African American church is not necessarily supportive of all African American interests equally. Patriarchy (Gilkes 1985; Dodson 1988) and antihomosexual teachings are prevalent in the black church (Griffin 2001).
2. In the 1960s the Catholic Church approved the use of other languages besides Latin in performing the liturgy. This change legitimized the use of Spanish by Latino Catholics and subsequently preserved an important part of Latino culture—their language (Stevens-Arroyo 1998).

REFERENCES

Ainsworth-Darnell, James, and Douglas B. Downey. 1998. "Assessing the Oppositional Culture Explanation for Racial-Ethnic Differences in School Performance." *American Sociological Review* 63(4): 536–53.

Alba, Richard D., John R. Logan, and Brian Stults. 2000. "How Segregated Are Middle-Class African Americans?" *Social Problems* 47(4): 543–58.

Allen, Walter, Marguerite Bonous-Hammarth, and Robert Ternishi. 2002. *Stony the Road We Trod . . . The Black Struggle for Higher Education in California.* San Francisco: James Irvine Foundation.

Ammerman, Nancy Tatom. 1997. *Congregation and Community.* New Brunswick, N.J.: Rutgers University Press.

Anderson, Bernard. 1996. "Ebb and Flow of Enforcing Executive Order 11246." *American Economic Review* 86(2): 298–301.

Anderson, James D. 1988. *The Education of Blacks in the South, 1860–1935.* Chapel Hill: University of North Carolina Press.

Asher, Martin and Joel Popkin. 1984. "The Effect of Gender and Race Differentials on Public-Private Wage Comparison: A Study of Postal Workers." *Industrial and Labor Relations Review* 38: 16–25.

Ayers, William, Bernardine Dohrn, and Rick Ayers. 2001. *Zero Tolerance: Resisting the Drive for Punishment in Our Schools: A Handbook for Parents, Students, Educators, and Citizens.* New York: New Press.

Bailey, Thomas. 1987 *Immigrant and Native Workers: Contrasts and Competition.* Boulder, Colo.: Westview.

Beggs, John J. 1991. "Value Structures and Economic Processes: Role of the Institutional Environment in Labor Market Outcomes." Unpublished manuscript. Chicago: University of Illinois.

Bertrand, Marianne, and Sendhil Mullainathan. 2003. "Are Emily and Greg More Employable Than Lakisha and Jamal? A Field Experiment on Labor Market Discrimination." Poverty Action Lab Paper no. 3. Cambridge, Mass.: National Bureau of Economic Research.

Blank, Rebecca. 1985. "An Analysis of Workers' Choice Between Employment in the Public and Private Sectors." *Industrial and Labor Relations Review* 27: 410–31.

Bobo, Lawrence. 1989. "Keeping the Linchpin in Place: Testing the Multiple Sources of Opposition to Residential Integration." *International Review of Social Psychology* 2: 305–23.

Bobo, Lawrence, and Susan Suh. 2000. "Surveying Racial Discrimination: Analyses from a Multi-ethnic Labor Market." In *Prismatic Metropolis: Inequality in Los Angeles,* edited by Lawrence Bobo, Melvin Oliver, James H. Johnson Jr., and Abel Valenzuela Jr. New York: Russell Sage Foundation.

Bobo, Lawrence, and Camille L. Zubrinsky. 1996. "Attitudes on Residential Integration: Perceived Status Differences, Mere In-group Preference, or Racial Prejudice?" *Social Forces* 74(3): 883–909.

Bonilla-Silva, Eduardo. 1997. "Rethinking Racism: Toward a Structural Interpretation." *American Sociological Review* 62(3): 465–80.

Borjas, George. 1990. *Friends or Strangers.* New York: Basic Books.

Burke, Peter J., and Austin T. Turk. 1975. "Factors Affecting Post-arrest Dispositions: A Model for Analysis." *Social Problems* 22: 313–32.

Card, David, and Alan B. Krueger. 1996. "School Resources and Student Outcomes: An Overview of the Literature and New Evidence from North and South Carolina." *Journal of Economic Perspectives* 10(4): 31–50.

Carter, Prudence. 2003. " 'Black,' Cultural Capital, Status Positioning, and Schooling Conflicts for Low-Income African American Youth." *Social Problems* 50(1): 136–55.

Chambliss, William J. 1994. "Policing the Ghetto Underclass: The Politics of Law and Law Enforcement." *Social Problems* 41(2): 177–94.

———. 1995. "Another Lost War: The Costs and Consequences of Drug Prohibition." *Social Justice* 22(2): 101–24.

Charles, Camille Zubrinsky. 2000. "Neighborhood Racial-Composition Preferences: Evidence from a Multi-ethnic Metropolis." *Social Problems* 47(3): 379–407.

———. 2001. "Processes of Racial Residential Segregation." In *Urban Inequality: Evidence from Four Cities,* edited by Alice O'Connor, Chris Tilly, and Lawrence D. Bobo. New York: Russell Sage Foundation.

———. 2003. "The Dynamics of Racial Residential Segregation." *Annual Review of Sociology* 29: 167–207.

Cherry, Robert, and William M. Rodgers III. 2000. *Prosperity for All? The Economic Boom and African Americans.* New York: Russell Sage Foundation.

Christerson, Brad, and Michael O. Emerson. 2001. "The Costs of Diversity in Religious Organizations: An In-depth Case Study." Paper presented to the annual meeting of the Society for the Scientific Study of Religion. Columbus, Ohio (October).

Clark, W. A. V. 1986. "Residential Segregation in American Cities: A Review and Interpretation." *Population Research and Policy Review* 5: 95–127.

———. 1992. "Residential Preferences and Residential Choices in a Multi-ethnic Context." *Demography* 29(3): 451–66.

Clark, W. A. V., and Julian Ware. 1997. "Trends in Residential Integration by Socioeconomic Status in Southern California." *Urban Affairs Review* 32(6): 825–44.

Coleman, James S., Ernest Q. Campbell, Carol F. Hobson, James M. McPartland, Alexander M. Mood, Frederic D. Weinfeld, and Robert L. York. 1966. *Equality of Educational Opportunity.* Washington: U.S. Government Printing Office.

Collins, Chiquita, and David R. Williams. 1999. "Segregation and Mortality: The Deadly Effects of Racism." *Sociological Forum* 74(3): 495–523.

Collins, Sharon M. 1997a. *Black Corporate Executives.* Philadelphia: Temple University Press.

———. 1997b. "Black Mobility in White Corporations: Up the Ladder but Out on a Limb." *Social Problems* 44(1): 55–67.

Conley, Dalton. 1999. *Being Black, Living in the Red: Race, Wealth, and Social Policy in America.* Berkeley: University of California Press.

Crowder, Kyle. 2000. "The Racial Context of White Mobility: An Individual-Level Assessment of the White Flight Hypothesis." *Social Science Research* 29(2): 223–57.

Currie, Elliot. 1998. *Crime and Punishment in America.* New York: Henry Holt.

Cutler, David M., and Edward L. Glaeser, 1997. "Are Ghettos Good or Bad?" *Quarterly Journal of Economics* 112(3): 827–72.

Darden, Joe T., and Sameh M. Kamel. 2000. "Black Residential Segregation in the City and Suburbs of Detroit: Does Socioeconomic Status Matter?" *Journal of Urban Affairs* 22(1): 1–13.

Darity, William, Jr. 1998. "Intergroup Disparity: Economic Theory and Social Science Evidence." *Southern Economic Journal* 64(4): 806–25.

Darity, William, Jr., David K. Guilkey, and William Winfrey. 1996. "Explaining Differences in Economic Performance Among Racial and Ethnic Groups in the USA: The Data Examined." *American Journal of Economic and Sociology* 55: 411–35.

Darity, William, Jr., and Samuel L. Myers. 2001. "Why Did Black Relative Earnings Surge in the Early 1990s?" *Journal of Economic Issues* 35(2): 533–42.

Darling-Hammond, Linda. 2003. " 'Colorblind' Education: Will It Help Us Leave No Child Behind?" Paper presented to the conference "Color-blind Racism?: The Politics of Controlling Racial and Ethnic Data." Center for Comparative Studies of Race and Ethnicity, Stanford University, Stanford, Calif. (October).

Davidson, Ann Locke. 1996. *Making and Molding Identity in Schools: Student Narratives on Race, Gender, and Academic Engagement.* Albany: State University of New York Press.

Davis, Angela Y. 2003. *Are Prisons Obsolete?* New York: Seven Stories Press.

Delpit, Lisa. 1990. "The Silenced Dialogue: Power and Pedagogy in Educating Other People's Children." In *Facing Racism in Education,* edited by Nitza M. Hidalgo, Ceasar L. McDowell, and Emilie V. Siddle. Cambridge, Mass.: Harvard Educational Review.

Denton, Nancy, and Douglas Massey. 1988. "Residential Segregation of Blacks, Hispanics, and Asians by Socioeconomic Status and Generation." *Social Science Quarterly* 69: 797–817.

Dodson, Jualynne E. 1988. "Power and Surrogate Leadership: Black Women and Organized Religion." *Sage* 5(2): 37–42.

Doeringer, Peter B., and Michael J. Piore. 1970. "Equal Employment Opportunity in Boston." *Industrial Relations* 9(3): 324–39.

Dolby, Nadine. 2001. *Constructing Race: Youth, Identity, and Popular Culture in South America.* Albany: State University of New York Press.

Drake, St. Clair, and Horace R. Cayton. 1985. "The Churches in Bronzeville." In *Afro-American Religious History: A Documentary Witness,* edited by Milton C. Sernett. Durham, N.C.: Duke University Press.

Ellen, Ingrid Gould. 2000. *Sharing America's Neighborhoods: The Prospects for Stable Racial Integration.* Cambridge, Mass.: Harvard University Press.

Emerson, Michael O., and Christian Smith. 2000. *Divided by Faith: Evangelical Religion and the Problem of Race in America.* New York: Oxford University Press.

Espinosa, Gastón, Virgilio Elizondo, and Jesse Miranda. 2003. *Hispanic Churches in American Public Life: Summary of Findings: Interim Report.* Notre Dame, Ind.: Notre Dame University, Institute for Latino Studies.

Farley, Reynolds. 1977a. "Trends in Racial Inequalities: Have the Gains of the 1960s Disappeared in the 1970s?" *American Sociological Review* 42(2): 189–208.

———. 1977b. "Residential Segregation in Urbanized Areas of the United States in 1970: An Analysis of Social Class and Racial Differences." *Demography* 14(4): 763–800.

———. 1989. "Race and Ethnicity in the U.S. Census: An Evaluation of the 1980 Ancestry Question." Unpublished paper. University of Michigan.

———. 1990. "Blacks, Hispanics, and White Ethnic Groups: Are Blacks Uniquely Disadvantaged?" *American Economic Review* 80(2): 237–41.

Farley, Reynolds, and Suzanne Bianchi. 1983. "The Growing Gap Between Blacks." *American Demographics* (July): 15–18.

Farley, Reynolds, and William H. Frey. 1994. "Changes in the Segregation of Whites from Blacks During the 1980s: Small Steps Toward a More Integrated Society." *American Sociological Review* 59(1): 23–45.

Feagin, Joe, and Melvin Sikes. 1994. *Living with Racism: The Black Middle-Class Experience.* Boston: Beacon Press.

Featherman, David L., and Robert M. Hauser. 1976. "Prestige or Socioeconomic Scales in the Study of Occupational Attainment." *Sociological Methods and Research* 4: 403–22.

Fellner, Jamie, and Marc Mauer. 1998. *Losing the Vote: The Impact of Felony Disenfranchisement Laws in the United States.* Washington, D.C.: Human Rights Watch and The Sentencing Project.

Ferguson, Ann A. 2000. *Bad Boys: Public Schools in the Making of Black Masculinity.* Ann Arbor: University of Michigan Press.

Ferguson, Ronald F. 1998a. "Can Schools Narrow the Black-White Test Score Gap?" In *The Black-White Test Score Gap,* edited by Christopher Jencks and Meredith Phillips. Washington, D.C.: Brookings Institution.

———. 1998b. "Teachers' Perceptions and Expectations and the Black-White Test Score Gap." In *The Black-White Test Score Gap,* edited by Christopher Jencks and Meredith Phillips. Washington, D.C.: Brookings Institution.

Fix, Michael E., and Raymond J. Struyk. 1993. *Clear and Convincing Evidence.* Washington, D.C.: Urban Institute.

Fordham, Signithia, and John Ogbu. 1986. "Black Students' School Success: Coping with the Burden of Acting White." *Urban Review* 18: 176–206.

Forman, Tyrone. 2003. "The Social Psychological Costs of Racial Segmentation in the Workplace: A Study of African American Well-being." *Journal of Health and Social Behavior* 44(3): 332–52.

Forman, Tyrone, David Williams, and James Jackson. 1997. "Race, Place, and Discrimination." *Perspectives on Social Problems* 9: 231–61.

Fosu, Augustin Kwasi. 1993. "Do Black and White Women Hold Different Jobs in the Same Occupation? A Critical Analysis of the Clerical and Service Sectors." *Review of the Black Political Economy* (Spring): 67–81.

Frankenberg, Erica, and Chungmei Lee. 2002. *Race in American Public Schools: Rapidly Resegregating School Districts.* Cambridge, Mass.: Harvard University, Civil Rights Project.

Frankenberg, Erica, Chungmei Lee, and Gary Orfield. 2003. *A Multiracial Society with Segregated Schools: Are We Losing the Dream?* Cambridge, Mass.: Harvard University, Civil Rights Project.

Franklin, John Hope. 2000. *From Slavery to Freedom: A History of African Americans,* 8th ed. New York: Alfred A. Knopf.

Frazier, E. Franklin. 1974. *The Negro Church in America.* New York: Schocken.

Freeman, Richard. 1976. *Black Elite: The New Market for Highly Educated Black Americans.* Report prepared for the Carnegie Commission on Higher Education. New York: McGraw-Hill.

Gates, Susan Wharton, Vanessa Gail Perry, and Peter M. Zorn. 2002. "Automated Underwriting in Mortgage Lending: Good News for the Underserved?" *Housing Policy Debate* 13(2): 369–91.

Ghiloni, Beth W. 1987. "The Velvet Ghetto: Women, Power, and the Corporation." *Power Elites and Organizations,* edited by G. William Donholf and Thomas R. Dye. Newbury Park, Calif.: Sage.

Gilkes, Cheryl Townsend. 1985. " 'Together in Harness': Women's Traditions in the Sanctified Church." *Signs: Journal of Women in Culture and Society* 10(4): 678–99.

Glaeser, Edward L., and Jacob L. Vigdor. 2001. "Racial Segregation in the 2000 Census: Promising News." Center on Urban and Metropolitan Policy Survey Series. Washington, D.C.: Brookings Institution (April).

Glasgow, Douglas G. 1980. *The Black Underclass: Poverty, Unemployment, and Entrapment of Ghetto Youth.* San Francisco: Jossey-Bass.

Gottschalk, Peter. 1997. "Inequality, Income Growth, and Mobility: The Basic Facts." *Journal of Economic Perspectives* 11(2): 21–40.

Griffin, Horace. 2001. "Their Own Received Them Not: African American Lesbians and Gays in Black Churches." In *The Greatest Taboo: Homosexuality in Black Communities,* edited by Delroy Constantine-Simms. Los Angeles: Alyson Books.

Hanushek, Eric. 1994. "Money Might Matter Somewhere: A Response to Hedges, Laine, and Greenwald." *Educational Researcher* 23: 5–8.

Harris, David R. 2001. "Why Are Whites and Blacks Averse to Black Neighbors?" *Social Science Research* 30(1): 100–16.

Harris, David R., and Reynolds Farley. 2000. "Demographic, Economic, and Social Trends." In *New Directions: African Americans in a Diversifying Nation*, edited by James S. Jackson. Washington, D.C.: National Policy Association.

Harris, Louis (with the Peter Harris Research Group). 2004. *Report on the Status of Public School Education in California: 2004*. Prepared for the William and Flora Hewlett Foundation. Los Angeles: UCLA/IDEA. Available at: www.idea.gseis.ucla.edu/publications/harris/index.html (accessed June 18, 2004).

Hart, Kevin D., Stephen J. Kunitz, Ralph Sell, and Dana B. Mukamel. 1998. "Metropolitan Governance, Residential Segregation, and Mortality Among African Americans." *American Journal of Public Health* 88(3): 434–38.

Hauser, Robert, and David Featherman. 1974. "White/Nonwhite Differentials in Occupational Mobility in the United States, 1962–1972." *Demography* 11(2): 247–66.

Herring, Cedric, and Sharon Collins. 1995. "Retreat from Equal Opportunity? The Case of Affirmative Action." In *The Bubbling Cauldron*, edited by Joe Feagin. New Haven, Conn.: Yale University Press.

Herrnstein, Richard J., and Charles Murray. 1994. *The Bell Curve: Intelligence and Class Structure in American Life*. New York: Free Press.

Holmes, Malcolm D., Howard Daudistel, and Ronald A. Farrell. 1987. "Determinants of Charge Reductions and Final Dispositions in Cases of Burglary and Robbery." *Journal of Research in Crime and Delinquency* 24: 233–54.

Holzer, Harry. 1996. *What Employers Want: Job Prospects for Less Educated Workers*. New York: Russell Sage Foundation.

Horton, Hayward Derrick. 1995. "Population Change and the Employment Status of College-Educated Blacks." *Race and Ethnic Relations* 8: 99–114.

Horvat, Erin, and Carla O'Connor, eds. Forthcoming. *Beyond Acting White: Reassessments and New Directions in Research on Black Students and School Success*. Boulder, Colo.: Rowman & Littlefield.

Human Rights Watch. 2000. *Punishment and Prejudice: Racial Disparities in the War on Drugs*. Vol. 12, no. 2(G) (May). Available at www.hrw.org/reports/2000/usa.

Institute for Democracy, Education, and Access (IDEA). 2004. *Separate and Unequal 50 Years After Brown: California's Racial "Opportunity Gap."* Los Angeles: UCLA, Graduate School of Education and Information Studies.

Jackson, James S., and Nicholas A. Jones. 2001. "New Directions in Thinking About Race in America: African Americans in a Diversifying Nation." *African American Research Perspectives* 7: 1–36.

Jasso, Guillermina. 2003. "Exploring the Religious Preferences of Recent Immigrants to the United States: Evidence from the New Immigrant Survey Pilot." In *Religion and Immigration: Christian, Jewish, and Muslim Experiences in the United States,* edited by Yvonne Yazbeck Haddad, Jane I. Smith, and John L. Esposito. Lanham, Md.: Altamira Press.

Jeung, Russell. 2002. "Asian American Pan-ethnic Formation and the Congregational Church." In *Religions in Asian America: Building Faith Communities,* edited by Pyong Gap Min and Jung Ha Kim. Walnut Creek, Calif.: Altamira Press.

Johnson, Devon. 2003. "Justice or 'Just Us'? Perceived Racial Bias in the Criminal Justice System." Paper presented to the annual meeting of the American Association for Public Opinion Research. Nashville (May).

Johnson, Tammy, Jennifer Emiko Boyden, and William J. Pittz. 2001. *Racial Profiling and Punishment in U.S. Public Schools.* Oakland, Calif.: Applied Research Center.

Johnson, William. 1978. "Racial Wage Discrimination and Industrial Structure." *Ball Journal of Economics* 9: 70–81.

Kanter, Rosabeth Moss. 1977. *Men and Women of the Corporation.* New York: Basic Books.

Katz, Lawrence, George Borjas, and Richard Freeman. 1992. "On the Labor Market Effects of Immigration and Trade." In *Immigration and the Work Force,* edited by Richard Freeman and George Borjas. Chicago: University of Chicago Press.

Kennedy, Randall. 1997. *Race, Crime, and the Law.* New York: Pantheon.

King, Mary C. 1993. "Black Women's Breakthrough into Clerical Work: An Occupational Tipping Model." *Journal of Economic Issues* 27(4): 1097–1127.

Kirschenman, Jolene, and Kathryn M. Neckerman. 1991. " 'We'd Love to Hire Them, but . . .': The Meaning of Race for Employers." In *The Urban Underclass,* edited by Paul E. Peterson and Christopher Jencks. Washington, D.C.: Brookings Institution.

Kozol, Jonathan. 1991. *Savage Inequalities.* New York: Harper Perennial.

Krivo, Lauren J., and Robert L. Kaufman, 1999. "How Low Can It Go? Declining Black-White Segregation in a Multi-ethnic Context." *Demography* 36(1): 93–110.

Krysan, Maria. 2002. "Community Undesirability in Black and White: Examining Racial Residential Preferences Through Community Perceptions." *Social Problems* 49(4): 421–543.

Krysan, Maria, and Nakesha Faison. 2002. "Segregated Neighborhoods in the U.S.: How Do Whites, Blacks, Latinos, and Asians Explain Them?" Paper presented to the meeting of the American Sociological Association. Chicago (August).

Krysan, Maria, and Reynolds Farley. 2002. "The Residential Preferences of Blacks: Do They Explain Persistent Segregation?" *Social Forces* 80(3): 937–80.

LaCour-Little, Michael. 2000. "The Evolving Role of Technology in Mortgage Finance." *Journal of Housing Research* 11(2): 173–205.

LaFree, Gary D. 1985. "Official Reactions to Hispanic Defendants in the Southwest." *Journal of Research in Crime and Delinquency* 22: 213–37.
————. 1989. *Rape and Criminal Justice: The Social Construction of Sexual Assault.* Belmont, Calif.: Wadsworth.
Landry, Bart. 1987. *The New Black Middle Class.* Berkeley: University of California Press.
Lareau, Annette, and Erin McNamara Horvat. 1999. "Moments of Social Inclusion and Exclusion: Race, Class, and Cultural Capital in Family-School Relationships." *Sociology of Education* 72(1): 37–53.
LaViest, Thomas A. 1989. "Linking Residential Segregation to the Infant Mortality Rate: Disparity in U.S. Cities." *Social Science Review* 73(2): 90–94.
————. 1993. "Segregation, Poverty, and Empowerment: Health Consequences for African Americans." *Milbank Quarterly* 71(1): 42–64.
Lee, Jaekyung. 2002. "Racial and Ethnic Achievement Gap Trends: Reversing the Progress Toward Equity?" *Educational Researcher* 31(1): 3–12.
Leonard, Jonathan S. 1984. "Employment and Occupational Advancement Under Affirmative Action." *Review of Economics and Statistics* 66(3): 377–85.
————. 1987. "Affirmative Action in the 1980s: With a Whimper, Not a Bang." Unpublished paper. University of California, Berkeley.
————. 1990. "The Impact of Affirmative Action Regulation and Equal Employment Law on Black Employment." *Journal of Economic Perspectives* 4(4): 47–63.
————. 1998. "Wage Disparities and Affirmative Action in the 1980s." *American Economic Review* 86(2): 285–89.
Levy, Frank. 1998. *The New Dollars and Dreams: American Incomes and Economic Change.* New York: Russell Sage Foundation.
Lewis, Amanda. 2003. *Race in the Schoolyard: Negotiating the Color Line in Classrooms and Communities.* New Brunswick, N.J.: Rutgers University Press.
Lincoln, C. Eric. 1974. *The Black Church Since Frazier.* New York: Schocken.
Lizotte, Alan J. 1978. "Extra-Legal Factors in Chicago's Criminal Courts Testing the Conflict Model of Criminal Justice." *Social Problems* 25: 564–80.
Ma, Jacinta. 2002. *What Works for the Children? What We Know and Don't Know About Bilingual Education.* Cambridge, Mass.: Harvard University, Civil Rights Project.
Marty, Martin E. 1985. *Pilgrims in Their Own Land: Five Hundred Years of Religion in America.* New York: Penguin.
Massey, Douglas S., and Nancy Denton. 1993. *American Apartheid: Segregation and the Making of the Underclass.* Cambridge, Mass.: Harvard University Press.
Massey, Douglas S., and Mary J. Fischer. 1999. "Does Rising Income Bring Integration? New Results for Blacks, Hispanics, and Asians in 1990." *Social Science Research* 28(3): 316–26.
Mauer, Marc, and Meda Chesney-Lind. 2002. *Invisible Punishment: The Collateral Consequences of Mass Imprisonment.* New York: New Press.

Mauer, Marc, and Tracy Huling. 1995. "Young Black Americans and the Criminal Justice System: Five Years Later." Washington, D.C.: The Sentencing Project.

Maume, David, Jr. 1985. "Government Participation in the Local Economy, and Race- and Sex-Based Earning Inequality." *Social Problems* 32: 285–99.

Maxfield, Linda, and John H. Kramer. 1998. *Substantial Assistance: An Empirical Yardstick Gauging Equity in Current Federal Policy and Practice.* Washington: U.S. Sentencing Commission.

Mays, Benjamin, and Joseph W. Nicholson. 1985. "The Genius of the Negro Church." In *Afro-American Religious History: A Documentary Witness,* edited by Milton C. Sernett. Durham, N.C.: Duke University Press.

McKee, James B. 1993. *Sociology and the Race Problem: The Failure of a Perspective.* Urbana: University of Illinois Press.

Meyer, Stephen Grant. 2000. *As Long as They Don't Move Next Door: Segregation and Racial Conflict in American Neighborhoods.* Lanham, Md.: Rowman & Littlefield.

Mickelson, Roslyn A. 1990. "The Attitude-Achievement Paradox Among Black Adolescents." *Sociology of Education* 63(1): 44–61.

Montejano, David. 1987. *Anglos and Mexicans in the Making of Texas, 1836–1986.* Austin: University of Texas Press.

Morris, Aldon D. 1984. *The Origins of the Civil Rights Movement: Black Communities Organizing for Change.* New York: Free Press.

Mumola, Christopher. 2000. "Incarcerated Parents and Their Children." Bureau of Justice Statistics: Special Report. Washington: U.S. Department of Justice (August). Available at http://www.ojp.usdoj.gov/bjs.

Munnell, Alicia H., Geoffrey M. B. Tootell, Lynn E. Browne, and James McEneaney. 1996. "Mortgage Lending in Boston: Interpreting HMDA Data." *American Economic Review* 86(1): 25–53.

Myers, Martha A. 1979. "Offender Parties and Official Reactions: Victims and the Sentencing of Criminal Defendants." *Sociological Quarterly* 20: 529–40.

Nettles, Michael T., and L. W. Perna. 1997. *The African American Education Data Book.* Fairfax, Va.: Frederick D. Patterson Research Institute of the College Fund.

Neumark, David, and Wendy A. Stock. 2001. "The Effects of Race and Sex Discrimination Laws." Working paper 8215. Cambridge, Mass.: National Bureau of Economic Research.

O'Connor, Carla. 2001. "Making Sense of the Complexity of Social Identity in Relation to Achievement: A Sociological Challenge in the New Millennium." *Sociology of Education* (extra issue): 159–68.

O'Connor, Carla, Amanda Lewis, and Jennifer Mueller. Forthcoming. "Researching African Americans' Educational Experiences: Theoretical and Practical Considerations." In *Research Methodology in African American*

Communities, edited by James Jackson and Cleo Caldwell. Thousand Oaks, Calif.: Sage Publications.

Ogbu, John. 1978. *Minority Education and Caste: The American System in Cross-cultural Perspective.* New York: Academic Press.

Oliver, Melvin L., and Thomas M. Shapiro. 1995. *Black Wealth/White Wealth: A New Perspective on Racial Inequality.* New York: Routledge.

O'Neill, June. 1990. "The Role of Human Capital in Earnings Differences Between Black and White Men." *Journal of Economic Perspectives* 90(4): 25–45.

Orfield, Gary, and Nora Gordon. 2001. *Schools More Separate: Consequences of a Decade of Resegregation.* Cambridge, Mass.: Harvard University, Civil Rights Project. Available at: http://www.civilrightsproject.harvard.edu/research/deseg/deseg_gen.php (accessed June 18, 2004).

Orfield, Gary, and Chungmei Lee. 2004. *Brown at Fifty: King's Dream or Plessy's Nightmare?* Cambridge, Mass.: Harvard University, Civil Rights Project. Available at: http://www.civilrightsproject.harvard.edu/research/deseg/deseg_gen.php (accessed June 18, 2004).

Orfield, Gary, and John T. Yun. 1999. *Resegregation in American Schools.* Cambridge, Mass.: Harvard University, Civil Rights Project. Available at: http://www.civilrightsproject.harvard.edu/research/deseg/reseg_schools99.php (accessed June 18, 2004).

Pager, Devah. 2003. "The Mark of a Criminal Record." *American Journal of Sociology* 108(5): 937–75.

Parsons, Donald O. 1980. "Racial Trends in Male Labor Force Participation." *American Economic Review* 70(5): 911–20.

Patterson, Orlando. 1997. *The Ordeal of Integration: Progress and Resentment in America's "Racial" Crisis.* Washington, D.C.: Civitas/Counterpoint.

Perry, Pamela. 2002. *Shades of White: White Kids and Racial Identities in High School.* Durham, N.C.: Duke University Press.

Petersilia, Joan. 1983. *Racial Disparities in the Criminal Justice System.* Santa Monica, Calif.: Rand.

Peterson, Ruth D., and Lauren J. Krivo. 1991. "Racial Segregation and Urban Black Homicide." *Social Forces* 70(4): 1001–26.

———. 1999. "Racial Segregation, the Concentration of Disadvantage, and Black and White Homicide Victimization." *Sociological Forum* 14(3): 465–93.

Pettigrew, Thomas F. 1979. "Racial Change and Social Policy." *Annals of the American Academy of Political and Social Science* 441: 114–31.

Polednak, Anthony P. 1990. "Black-White Differences in Infant Mortality in Thirty-eight Standard Metropolitan Statistical Areas." *American Journal of Public Health* 81(11): 1480–82.

Reardon, Sean F., and John T. Yun. 2002. *Private School Racial Enrollments and Segregation.* Cambridge, Mass.: Harvard University, Civil Rights Project.

Reskin, Barbara, and Patricia Roos. 1990. "Job Queues, Gender Queues: Explaining Women's Inroads into Male Occupations." In *Women in the Political Economy.* Philadelphia: Temple University Press.

Roberts, Dorothy. 1991. "Punishing Drug Addicts Who Have Babies: Women of Color, Equality, and the Right of Privacy." *Harvard Law Review* 104: 1419–54.

Rodgers, William M. 1996. "The Effect of Federal Contractor Status on Racial Differences in Establishment-Level Employment Shares: 1979–1993." *American Economic Review* 86(2): 290–93.

Ross, Stephen L., and John Yinger. 2002. *The Color of Credit: Mortgage Discrimination, Research Methodology, and Fair Lending Enforcement.* Cambridge, Mass.: MIT Press.

Royster, Deidre A. 2003. *Race and the Invisible Hand: How White Networks Exclude Black Men from Blue-Collar Jobs.* Berkeley: University of California Press.

Russell, Katheryn. 1998. *The Color of Crime.* New York: New York University Press.

Schaeffer, Richard T. 1998. *Racial and Ethnic Groups.* Reading, Mass.: Addison-Wesley Educational Publishers.

Scott, Allen. 1996. "The Manufacturing Economy: The Ethnic and Gender Division of Labor." *Ethnic Los Angeles,* edited by Roger Waldinger and Mehdi Bozorgmehr. New York: Russell Sage Foundation.

Sherman, Lawrence. 2002. "Trust and Confidence in Criminal Justice." *National Institute of Justice Journal* 248: 22–31.

Smith, James P. 1984. "Race and Human Capital." *American Economic Review* 74(4): 685–98.

———. 2001. "Race and Ethnicity in the Labor Market: Trends over the Short and Long Run." In *America Becoming: Racial Trends and Consequences in the U.S.,* Vol. II, edited by Neil Smelser, William Julius Wilson, and Faith Mitchell. Washington, D.C.: National Academy of Sciences.

Smith, James P., and Finis Welch. 1977. "Black-White Male Wage Ratios: 1960–1970." *American Economic Review* 67(3): 323–38.

———. 1978. *Race Differences in Earnings: A Survey and New Evidence.* Santa Monica, Calif.: Rand.

———. 1984. "Affirmative Action and Labor Markets." *Journal of Labor Economics* 2(2): 269–302.

———. 1986. *Closing the Gap: Forty Years of Economic Progress for Blacks.* Santa Monica, Calif.: Rand.

Smith, Robin, and Michelle DeLair. 1999. "New Evidence from Lender Testing: Discrimination at the Preapplication Stage." In *Mortgage Lending Discrimination: A Review of the Existing Evidence,* edited by Margery Austin Turner and Felicity Skidmore. Washington, D.C.: Urban Institute.

South, Scott J., and Kyle Crowder. 1998. "Leaving the 'Hood: Residential Mobility Between Black, White, and Integrated Neighborhoods." *American Sociological Review* 63(1): 17–26.

Stevens-Arroyo, Anthony M. 1998. "The Latino Religious Resurgence." *Annals of the American Academy of Political and Social Science: Americans and Religions in the Twenty-first Century* (July): 163–77.

St. John, Craig, and Robert Clymer. 1999. "Racial Residential Segregation by Level of Socioeconomic Status." *Social Science Quarterly* 81(3): 701–15.

Stoll, David, and Virginia Garrard-Burnett, eds. 1993. *Rethinking Protestantism in Latin America*. Philadelphia: Temple University Press.

Straka, John W. 2000. "A Shift in the Mortgage Landscape: The 1990s Move to Automated Credit Evaluations." *Journal of Housing Research* 11(2): 207–32.

Sugrue, Thomas J. 1996. *The Origins of the Urban Crisis: Race and Inequality in Postwar Detroit*. Princeton, N.J.: Princeton University Press.

Takaki, Ronald T. 1989. *Strangers from a Different Shore: A History of Asian Americans*. Boston: Little, Brown.

Thernstrom, Stephan, and Abigail Thernstrom. 1997. *American in Black and White: One Nation, Indivisible*. New York: Simon & Schuster.

Thurow, Lester C. 1975. *Generating Inequality: Mechanisms of Distribution in the U.S. Economy*. New York: Basic Books.

Tonry, Michael. 1995. *Malign Neglect: Race, Crime, and Punishment in America*. New York: Oxford University Press.

Tuch, Steven A., and Ronald Weitzer. 1997. "The Polls-Trends: Racial Differences in Attitudes Toward the Police." *Public Opinion Quarterly* 61: 642–63.

Turner, Margery Austin, and Ron Wienk. 1993. "The Persistence of Segregation in Urban Areas: Contributing Causes." In *Housing Markets and Residential Mobility*, edited by G. Thomas Kingley and Margery A. Turner. Washington, D.C.: Urban Institute.

Uggen, Christopher, and Jeff Manza. 2002. "Democratic Contraction? Political Consequences of Felon Disenfranchisement in the United States." *American Sociological Review* 67(6): 777–803.

U.S. Census. 2001. *Statistical Abstracts of the United States: 2001*. Washington: Government Printing Office. Available at: http://www.census.gov/prod/2002pubs/01statab/educ.pdf (accessed June 18, 2004).

U.S. Department of Justice. Bureau of Justice Statistics. 1997. *National Crime Victimization Survey: Criminal Victimization, 1974–1995*. Washington: U.S. Department of Justice.

———. 1999. *Bureau of Justice Statistics Correctional Surveys*. Washington: U.S. Department of Justice. Available at: www.ojp.usdoj.gov/bjs/glance/cprace.htm.

———. 2002a. *Justice Expenditure and Employment Extracts*. Washington: U.S. Department of Justice. Available at: www.ojp.usdoj.gov/bjs/glance/expgov.htm.

———. 2002b. *Bureau of Justice Statistics Correctional Surveys*. Washington: U.S. Department of Justice. Available at: www.ojp.usdoj.gov/bjs/glance/jailrair.htm.

———. 2002c. *Correctional Populations in the United States, 1997, and Prisoners in 2001*. Washington: U.S. Department of Justice. Available at: www.ojp.usdoj.gov/bjs/glance/incrt.htm.

———. 2003. *Criminal Offenders Statistics*. Washington: U.S. Department of Justice. Available at: www.ojp.usdoj.gov/bjs/crimoff.htm.

Van Ausdale, Debra, and Joe R. Feagin. 2001. *The First R: How Children Learn Race and Racism*. Lanham, Md.: Rowman & Littlefield.

Wagner, Peter. 2002. "Importing Constituents: Prisoners and Political Clout in New York." Springfield, Mass.: Prison Policy Initiative.

Waldinger, Roger. 1996. *Still the Promised City? African Americans and the New Immigrants in Post-industrial New York*. Cambridge, Mass.: Harvard University Press.

———. 1997. "Black-Immigrant Competition Reassessed: New Evidence from Los Angeles." *Sociological Perspectives* 40(3): 365–86.

Walters, Pamela Barnhouse. 2001. "Educational Access and the State: Historical Continuities and Discontinuities in Racial Inequality in American Education." *Sociology of Education* (extra issue): 35–49.

Warner, R. Stephen. 1998. "Immigration and Religious Communities in the United States." *Gatherings in the Diaspora: Religious Communities and New Immigration,* edited by R. Stephen Warner and Judith G. Wittner. Philadelphia: Temple University Press.

———. Forthcoming. "The De-Europeanization of American Christianity." In *A Nation of Religions: The Politics of Pluralism in the United States,* edited by Stephen Prothero.

Warner, R. Stephen, and Judith G. Wittner. 1998. *Gatherings in Diaspora: Religious Communities and the New Immigration*. Philadelphia: Temple University Press.

Washington, Raleigh, and Glen Kehrein. 1993. *Breaking Down Walls: A Model for Reconciliation in an Age of Racial Strife*. Chicago: Moody Press.

Weitzer, Ronald. 2000. "Racialized Policing: Residents' Perceptions in Three Neighborhoods." *Law and Society Review* 34(1): 129–55.

Welch, Finis. 1973. "Black-White Differences in Returns to Schooling." *American Economic Review* 63(5): 893–907.

Wilson, Frank Harold. 1995. "Rising Tide or Ebb Tide? Recent Changes in the Black Middle Class in the U.S., 1980–1990." *Research in Race and Ethnic Relations* 8: 21–55.

Wilson, George. 1997. "Payoffs to Power Among Males in the Middle Class: Has Race Declined In Its Significance?" *Sociological Quarterly* 38: 607–22.

Wilson, William Julius. 1978. *The Declining Significance of Race.* Chicago: University of Chicago Press.

Wyly, Elvin K., and Steven R. Holloway. 1999. " 'The Color of Money' Revisited: Racial Lending Patterns in Atlanta's Neighborhoods." *Housing Policy Debate* 10(3): 555–600.

Yinger, John. 1995. *Closed Doors, Opportunities Lost.* New York: Russell Sage Foundation.

Zatz, Marjorie S. 1987. "The Changing Forms of Racial-Ethnic Biases in Sentencing." *Journal of Research in Crime and Delinquency* 24(1): 69–92.

Zatz, Marjorie, and Alan J. Lizotte. 1985. "The Timing of Court Processing: Towards Linking Theory and Method." *Criminology* 23: 313–35.

Zhou, Minn. 2001. "Contemporary Immigration and the Dynamics of Race and Ethnicity." In *America Becoming: Racial Trends and Their Consequences,* edited by Neil J. Smelser, William Julius Wilson, and Faith Mitchell. Washington, D.C.: National Research Council.

Zimring, Franklin. 2001. "Imprisonment Rates and the New Politics of Criminal Punishment." *Punishment and Society* 3(1): 161–66.

Zweigenhaft, Richard L., and G. William Domhoff. 1991. *Blacks in the White Establishment?* New Haven, Conn.: Yale University Press.

PART II

Changes in Racial Categories and Boundaries

5

IDENTIFYING WITH MULTIPLE RACES: A SOCIAL MOVEMENT THAT SUCCEEDED BUT FAILED?

ᔓ

Reynolds Farley

THE CIVIL RIGHTS revolution of the 1960s fundamentally changed how racial information is used. Prior to that decade, race was used to assign students to schools, to determine where people could live, to determine which job, if any, candidates were offered, and even whom people could marry. The litigation strategy of the National Association for the Advancement of Colored People (NAACP) and their allies shifted federal courts away from their endorsement of state-imposed racial discrimination. Later, grassroots desegregation efforts led by such unlikely people as Rosa Parks in Montgomery, Alabama, and Ezell Blair, Franklin McClain, Joseph McNeil, and David Richmond in Greensboro, North Carolina, evolved into the most potent social movement of the last century.

The word "tolerance" was still frequently mentioned with regard to race relations in the 1960s, rather than "racial ratios," "quotas," or "affirmative action." Racial data were gathered and scrutinized to promote discrimination. Employers seeking white-collar workers typically asked job-seekers to include their picture with their applications, as did many colleges. This allowed both employment and admissions offices to readily limit or segregate Negroes. Using racial data from the census, lenders redlined neighborhoods, thereby perpetuating residential segregation.

In its early stages, the civil rights movement sought to terminate the collection of racial information in hopes of thereby ending discrimination. Employers and colleges dropped their demand for photographs. New Jersey stopped collecting racial data on birth and death certificates. Later in the decade the pendulum swung far in the other direction. The federal government mandated that employers and schools at every level gather racial information to demonstrate the absence of discrimination. When we fill out job applications, seek admission to schools, go to hospitals, or borrow money from fiscal institutions, we report our race because of these encompassing federal regulations. And when we die, the mortician will register our race one final time.

The social movement to allow us to identify with multiple races is the foreseeable outcome of three developments flowing from the civil rights decade. First, federal courts required racial data for the enforcement of constitutional mandates. Second, the controversy about which races would benefit from federal protection led to congressional actions and eventually a federal decree about how the population was to be classified by race. Third, after interracial marriages had produced a mixed-race population, dissatisfaction arose with the federal government's traditional rule that everyone fit into one and only one racial category. A multiracial movement developed in the 1990s and succeeded in getting the federal statistical system to permit a person to identify with several races.

FEDERALLY REQUIRED RACIAL DATA: THE 1960S

The congressional discussion that led to civil rights legislation in the 1960s focused on ending discrimination against blacks (Whalen and Whalen 1985). To do so, federal laws, agencies, and courts quickly insisted that job applicants, students, and those seeking mortgages be tabulated by race, since the most convincing evidence of nondiscrimination was an appropriate representation of minorities.

The Voting Rights Act of 1965 made the Fifteenth Amendment effective in all states by calling for federal oversight of elections in geographic areas where African Americans had not been allowed to vote. But rather than specifically mentioning race, the law required federal supervision in jurisdictions where less than 50 percent of the voting-age population was registered in November 1964 or where less than 50 percent of those registered actually cast ballots in the Johnson-Goldwater presidential election.

Federal courts simultaneously wrestled with the unwillingness of southern schools to accept the integration mandates of *Brown v. Board of Education* (1955). When faced with a court order to desegregate, numerous southern districts adopted "freedom of choice" plans that, in theory, allowed white students and black students to transfer from schools of their own race to schools where the student population was of a different race. As expected, few whites sought to do so (Klueger 1976, ch. 27). Tired of southern strategies that kept schools thoroughly segregated despite court orders, the Supreme Court, in *Green v. New Kent County* (1968), declared that the only acceptable integration plan was one that actually placed white and black children in the same schools. Quickly, federal judges issued orders requiring the assignment of black and white students and black and white teachers to the same schools. In a key and unanimous ruling, *Swann v. Charlotte Mecklenburg County* (1971), the Supreme Court called for the use of both racial ratios and busing to integrate schools in Charlotte, North Carolina. A school district could comply with these court orders only if they had classified their students and employees by race. By this time the Office for Civil Rights within the Department of Health, Education, and Welfare (HEW) was collecting information about the race of those enrolled in individual public schools using, as authority, Title IV of the Civil Rights Act of 1964.

On the employment front, Title VII of the identical law established the Equal Employment Opportunities Commission (EEOC) and gave it authority to investigate racial discrimination, a task that required data about the racial characteristics of people working at different jobs. President Johnson's Executive Order 11246 prohibited racial discrimination in all work performed by federal contractors and created the Office of Federal Contract Compliance (OFCC), which had broad powers to terminate contracts if firms practiced employment discrimination. The agency rapidly collected data about the race of employees by occupations within specific firms. The absence of black workers in a job category raised questions about the employer's hiring and promotion practices.

George Schultz, secretary of labor in the Nixon administration, sought to end the persistent exclusion of black men from skilled construction trades. He hammered out the Philadelphia Plan, which was to serve as a national model. Construction firms could retain their lucrative federal contracts and unions could avoid federal suits by demonstrating that they hired sufficient numbers of black men at all ranks, including the crafts trades. The test of compliance was to be the actual employment of black men.

The Supreme Court's key employment discrimination ruling was *Griggs v. Duke Power* (1971). While banning the use of tests that do not assess the actual skill level of the job to be performed, the decision went further and placed great importance on the classification of workers by race. The justices observed that seemingly neutral screening procedures, such as requiring a high school diploma for a laborer's job, often had a disparate impact on the employment opportunities of members of one racial group. Rather than requiring plaintiffs to prove the intent to discriminate, this Supreme Court decision opened the door for litigation based on the underrepresentation of minorities in a job classification.

To boost a sluggish economy by creating construction jobs, the Carter administration initiated, and Congress enacted, a $4 billion public works program in 1977. Congress used an innovative strategy: for the first time, it specifically set aside 10 percent of these funds for qualified minority contractors, defined as "Negroes, Spanish-speaking, Orientals, Indians, Eskimos and Aleuts" (La Noue and Sullivan 2001, 74). In *Fullilove v. Klutznik* (1980) the Supreme Court, in a six-to-three decision, upheld the specific allocation of federal spending to qualified minority firms. During President Reagan's administration this earmarking of federal spending for minorities was extended to include the Departments of Defense and Transportation. Congress assumed not only that racial data existed but that firms could be categorized by the race of their owner or top officer and that federal dollars for minority firms would break down traditional discrimination.

In 1960 many civil rights leaders opposed the collection of racial data, since historically they had been used to deny opportunities. Less than a dozen years later the federal government had firmly established the norm that racial data should be gathered from everyone. Overcoming past discrimination depended on whether sufficient numbers of minorities were hired and promoted, were admitted to universities, or received contracts from governmental agencies. In the span of just a decade and a half, racial data went from being a tool for discrimination to a strategy for proving nondiscrimination.

DEFINING RACIAL GROUPS: FROM THE SIMPLE TO THE COMPLEX IN THE 1970S AND 1980S

Discussions of race in the civil rights decade focused on African Americans. Few comments were offered about the half a million American Indians (Snipp 1989, fig. 3.1), many of whom lived in remote areas of sparsely populated states. The Asian population in 1960 numbered just 875,000—comprising primarily about 500,000 Japanese and 250,000 Chinese (Barringer, Gardner, and Levin 1993, table 2A). Asians were concentrated in Hawaii, Los Angeles, San Francisco, and New York. The 1970 census did not specifically identify the Spanish-origin population, although the census reported that there were 892,000 individuals of Puerto Rican birth or parentage, as well as 3.4 million persons with Spanish surnames living in five southwestern states (Bean and Tienda 1987, ch. 2; U.S. Department of Commerce 1963a, 1963b).

Two changes broadened the discussion of race after 1970. First, the success of the African American civil rights movement in providing new federal protections for the employment, voting, and educational rights of blacks spurred movements to extend those protections to other groups that believed they were targeted for discrimination. Among the largest were American Indians, Hispanics, Asians, the elderly, and, later, the disabled and gays and lesbians. Second, the ideology of the civil rights decade induced Congress to remove national-origin quotas from the immigration laws—the quotas that favored Western Europeans but discouraged immigration from elsewhere. After 1968 immigration from Asia, the Caribbean, Mexico, Latin America, and Africa soared, thereby increasing the size and heterogeneity of the minority population and providing a strong demographic base for new civil rights organizations.

The Spanish-origin population occupied a unique status because of the nation's victory in the war against Mexico in 1848 and against Spain a half-century later, the latter of which added the Spanish-speaking colonies of Puerto Rico, Cuba, and the Philippines. By the late 1960s Latinos were a rapidly growing minority without obvious ties to either major political party. Political campaigners cannot effectively seek the votes of a minority unless they know their location, size, and characteristics. The Census Bureau was already printing questionnaires for the 1970 count when Daniel Patrick Moynihan, then a White House domestic policy adviser to President Nixon, ordered that a question identifying Latinos be added. New forms were printed, and a 5 percent sample was asked whether their origin or descent was Mexican, Puerto Rican, Cuban, Central or South American, other Spanish, or none of the above (Choldin 1986). For the first time, a census question sought to measure the size of a specific non-European-origin ethnic group.

In the early 1970s Hispanic advocates in Washington sought to share in the legal protections and benefits flowing to African Americans from the civil rights laws and court rulings. Consideration was given to adding Spanish to the race question, but it was difficult to justify doing so since several European ancestry groups—English, German, and Irish—were much larger. And the use of "Mexican" as a race in the enumeration of 1930 had met with such virulent criticism from Mexicans who did not want to be classed with nonwhite races that the Census Bureau refused to publish information about the Mexican "race" (Jaffe, Cullen, and Boswell 1980).

The Voting Rights Act came up for renewal one decade after its passage. That law used a 50 percent voting criterion for determining where the U.S. Justice Department would superintend elections. By this time Latino advocates knew that the Voting Rights Act enhanced the election chances of black candidates through the drawing of electoral districts. A revision of that law to include areas with many Spanish-origin residents would increase the number of Latinos elected to office.

To accomplish that, Congress created the concept of a "language minority." As amended, the Voting Rights Act called for a federal pre-clearance of changes in election procedures in all counties where fewer than 50 percent of the adult population voted in 1972 or where elections were conducted in English and at least 5 percent of the voting-age population were members of a *single language minority,* as determined by the Census Bureau. Congress specified that language minorities could consist only of Asian Americans, Alaskan Natives, American Indians, and persons of Spanish heritage. Parishes in Louisiana with French-speaking minorities did not receive protection, but northern counties with large Puerto Rican and Indian populations were covered, including New York City, all of South Dakota, and much of Alaska—places that did not have a history of denying the franchise. This was a major victory for Hispanic advocacy groups, and it did not require classifying the Spanish-origin population as a race (Thernstrom 1987).

The success of Latinos prompted other groups to develop definitions so that they could become a protected category deriving federal benefits from civil rights laws and court rulings. At this time there was no federal policy about the collection of racial information, and the Census Bureau's racial categories changed from one enumeration to the next. In 1973 Caspar Weinberger, then serving as secretary of health, education, and welfare in the Nixon administration, asked the Federal Interagency Committee on Education to develop government-wide standards with regard to racial classification. For several years, representatives of federal agencies discussed this issue. In the first year of President Carter's administration, the Office of Management and the Budget (OMB), relying on the efforts of Katherine Wallman, issued Directive 15. This was extremely important since it was the first federal mandate specifying which racial categories had to be used in the national statistical system. All federal agencies gathering demographic data were required to classify persons into one of four mutually exclusive major racial categories: white, black, Asian or Pacific Islander, and American Indian or Alaskan Native.

Agencies also had to obtain information about the Hispanic origin of everyone, but the directive permitted either a distinct question about this or the use of Hispanic origin as if it were a race similar to white, black, or Asian (Spencer 1997). This directive served as the commanding word on federal racial statistics for twenty-three years but had a much greater impact since employers, schools, and firms linked in any fashion to federal spending had powerful incentives to gather data consistent with the government's requirement.

The questionnaire for the 1980 census was strongly influenced by OMB Directive 15. To avoid the possibility of minimizing the count of Hispanic persons, a special question about this ethnicity was added, and most federal offices followed this practice. All of the major racial groups in Directive 15 were listed on the census schedule, but race questions in the last three enumerations have been strongly influenced by Representative Robert Matsui (D-Calif.). Fearing that specific Asian groups might not be fully counted if the inclusive term "Asian" were used, he insisted that many specific Asian origins be listed. Thus, the 1980 census listed Japanese, Chinese, Filipino, Vietnamese, Asian Indian, Hawaiian, Guamanian, and Samoan.

Directive 15 settled the measurement of race in an official sense, but litigation continued to hash out which groups might be treated as races with regard to legal protections. In its *St. Francis College v. Al-Khazraji* (1987) decision, the Supreme Court declared that an Iraqi was entitled to sue his employer on grounds of racial discrimination. On the same day the Supreme Court ruled that a Maryland man who defaced a synagogue could be prosecuted under a state law prohibiting crimes of racial hatred; in this case, Jews were protected as if they were a race (*Shaare Tefila Congregation v. Cobb,* 1987). These simultaneous Supreme Court decisions broadened the meaning of race.

A NEW DEVELOPMENT: THE MULTIRACIAL MOVEMENT IN THE 1990S

Court decisions and congressional discussions through 1990 never challenged the principle that all persons can be classified into one and only one race, but that year's census provoked a social movement that drastically changed the nation's racial classifications. In 1988 Susan Graham developed an umbrella organization for clubs and groups representing the interests of mixed-race couples and their offspring. She was a white woman from suburban Atlanta married to Gordon Graham, a black man who was an anchorman for CNN. She knew Georgia school systems inevitably classified children as minorities if one parent was not white—hence the name of her organization, Reclassify All Children Equally (Project RACE). The arrival of her 1990 census questionnaire propelled her to a leadership position in a small but effective social movement. After examining the form, she said later, she called the Census Bureau to ask how a child's race should be reported if his or her parents differed in race. She claimed that Census Bureau personnel told her that she had to mark the mother's race for the child's.

At the same time, Carlos Fernandez, an attorney in San Francisco of Mexican and white ancestry, was upset by the federal requirement that everyone be slotted into only one race. Upon learning about the 1990 census, he considered filing a suit in federal court but did not locate a plaintiff with standing. He founded an organization called the Association of Multi-Ethnic Americans (AMEA). Shortly thereafter, local groups sprang up to represent the interests of mixed-race persons, including A Place for Us (APFU), an advocacy group founded in Los Angeles by a white man who sought to marry a black woman but was turned down by his minister; the Brick by Brick Church, created by Pastor Kenneth Simpson in Lexington, Kentucky, to minister to the spiritual needs of multiracial people; the Interracial Family Alliance, founded by parishioners at the Episcopal church in Augusta, Georgia; and the Interracial Lifestyle Connection, created as a correspondence club for persons who wished to cross racial boundaries (Skerry 2000, ch. 2). Fortunately for this movement, the Internet has allowed a rapid and low-cost exchange of information and is an effective medium for recruitment and promotion.

To give national visibility to this emerging movement, AMEA called a "Loving Conference" for June 1992 in Washington to commemorate the quarter-century anniversary of the Supreme Court's *Loving v. Virginia* (1967) decision, which overturned state laws prohibiting interracial marriage. The group invited governmental officials and succeeded in getting the attention of both Ohio Congressman Thomas Sawyer, who headed the House Subcommittee on the Census, and Nampeo McKinney, who had responsibility for racial statistics at the Census Bureau. When Congressman Sawyer held hearings in 1993 about the 2000 census, he invited representatives of the multiracial movement to speak, giving them a more prominent platform then they ever had before. Susan Graham and her collaborators, in the meantime, worked at the state level to raise awareness of the psychological damage that is done to multiracial children when they are forced to identify with only their mother's or only their father's race. They persuaded legislatures in Ohio, Illinois, and Georgia to add "multiracial" as a category in state-mandated data collections (Spencer 1997).

By late 1993, traditional civil rights organizations recognized a threat in the addition of a multiracial category on the census. If the multiracial movement convinced many people to mark it rather than one of the traditional races, the demographic foundation for racial advocacy groups would shrink. Billy Tidwell, director of research for the Urban League, relied on Roderick Harrison of the Census Bureau to argue that black civil rights organizations could find themselves representing a much smaller African American population if persons were allowed to identify as multiracial (Williams 2000).

With planning for the 2000 census speeding along, OMB in 1994 declared that the racial categories delineated in Directive 15 were of decreasing value and that a revision of that directive would be considered. With the issue of deciding which racial categories should be used by the government in play, the multiracial movement gained new opportunities for congressional testimony and lobbying. The OMB declaration about revising Directive 15 stimulated three major Census Bureau surveys that used a variety of new questions to gather racial data: the 1995 Supplement on Race and Ethnicity to the Current Population Survey, the 1996 National Content Test, and the 1996 Race and Ethnic Targeted Test (Hirschman, Alba, and Farley 2000).

As hearings were held in Washington and governmental agencies developed recommendations, advocacy organizations succeeded in bringing attention to their cause. Susan Graham lived in Congressman Newt Gingrich's (R-Ga.) district, and after the Republican victory in the 1996 congressional election, he gave his boisterous support to the multiracial movement. AMEA spokespersons called attention to the large number of prominent multiracial Americans, including persons often considered to be black, such as W. E. B. DuBois, Langston Hughes, Alex Haley, Malcolm X, and General Colin Powell. Lani Grenier came in for special criticism for emphasizing her black rather than her Jewish background in order to get a federal appointment. A Multiracial Solidarity March was called for Washington in July 1996, with the specific aim of adding "multiracial" to the list of racial groups on the 2000 census (Williams 2000, ch. 6). Tiger Woods declared on *The Oprah Winfrey Show* in 1997 that he was neither black nor Thai, but rather Cablinasian (Caucasian, black, American Indian, and Asian). Representative Thomas Petri (R-Wisc.) introduced House Bill 830. Known as the "Tiger Woods bill," it called for the addition of "multiracial" or "multi-ethnic" as a racial category on the 2000 census, but was never enacted.

By the late 1990s the multiracial movement was supported by individuals with very different but compatible aims: parents who wanted to identify their children as multiracial and politicians who presumed that Democrats benefited from the way racial data were gathered and used, especially in redrawing congressional districts.

As pressures for a multiracial category increased, Katherine Wallman and others at OMB considered an alternative strategy: letting respondents identify with as many races as they wished. When spokespeople for the multiracial movement were asked their opinions about this—additional congressional hearings were held in 1997—they were unenthusiastic. No one would be able to identify themselves as multiracial. Furthermore, this option would produce unwieldy data, since there would be dozens of combinations of races and no unambiguous count of multiracial persons or any one race.

By 1997 the most powerful civil rights lobbyists in Washington, especially the Leadership Conference on Civil Rights representing the interests of African Americans, came to support OMB's "check all that apply" idea. Census Bureau studies suggested that a relatively small proportion of people, perhaps 1.5 percent, would identify with a multiracial category or mark a second race if given the option, so a multiracial option would not seriously reduce the counts of minorities. Indeed, the size of a minority race might increase a bit if some who first marked a different race checked that race as a second or third racial identity.

On October 30, 1997, OMB officials announced their authoritative decision. It had its most immediate and greatest impact on the 2000 census. All persons were to be given the option to identify with as many racial groups as they wished, starting with the decennial enumeration and extending to all federal data systems by 2003. OMB announced that five major racial groups were to be used in the federal system: American Indian and Alaskan Native; Asian; black or African American; Native Hawaiian or Other Pacific Islander (NHOPI); and white.

This OMB directive also mandated the gathering of data about the Spanish origin of each person. It recommended a distinct question about race and another dichotomous question about whether the individual's origin was or was not Hispanic or Latino. Native Hawaiians and other Pacific Islanders were separated from Asians and designated as one of the five major racial groups, primarily because of the effective lobbying of Senator Daniel Akaka (D-Hawaii). This October 1997 decision settled the issue of measuring race for the 2000 census, and perhaps for the next few censuses.

The multiracial movement of the 1990s can be easily summarized:

- Frequently spokespeople for this movement and those for the traditional civil rights movement traded heated and ad hominem charges. Civil rights leaders asserted that the multiracial movement intended to turn back the clock and eliminate the racial progress of the last three decades, progress that depended on a simple and clear system for classifying race. The multiracialists were described as stalking horses for the growing anti–affirmative action movement. For their part, the multiracialists charged that traditional civil rights leaders were denying the multiracial reality of the nation and trying to force outdated racial concepts on everybody for their own gains.

- Participants in this contentious debate seldom called on experts, and they seldom, if ever, cited scholarly studies concerning the measurement of race and ethnicity.

- While gaining considerable attention in the press and on Capitol Hill, the multiracial groups had few members, were not well financed, and did not establish lobbying offices in Washington. Nor did they have the statistical capability to conduct surveys or analyze the substantial flow of findings from the Census Bureau tests of racial queries.

- Nevertheless, there were good reasons to think that the multiracial population grew rapidly in the 1990s, since an increasing number of marriages were between spouses who reported different races (Farley 1999).

- The grassroots multiracial movement of the 1990s did not succeed in getting its favored term, "multiracial," added to the government's list of races. But it did win a major battle when the decision was made to have the 2000 census allow all people to identify with more than one race. Never again will we assume that everyone fits neatly into one and only one racial group.

QUESTIONS AND STRATEGIES USED TO IDENTIFY THE MULTIPLE-RACE POPULATION

You might think that the 2000 census questions would have made it very easy for people to identify with two or more races. It was certainly possible for a person to do so, but the count of the multiracial population depends as much on the coding rules developed at the Census Bureau as it does on the intentions and pencil marks of respondents. Figure 5.1 presents the race and Spanish-origin questions asked of all persons in the last two censuses. At first glance, the race options on the 2000 census seem hardly consistent with OMB specifications: respondents could check as many of the race boxes as they wished. They were given the choice of white, black, American Indian, or Alaska Native, and then they could identify with as many as seven different Asian origins (one a write-in) or with any or all of four Pacific Island origins (one a write-in). Finally, they could fill in the box for "some other race" and write in a term if they felt that none of the eighteen racial designations printed on the census form applied to them.

Coding rules were extremely influential. If an immigrant from Bangkok filled in the box for "Chinese" and the box for "some other race" and wrote "Thai," he was classified as a monoracial Asian, since Thais and Chinese were both considered component parts of the Asian major racial group. If a Honolulu resident marked "Samoan" and "Native Hawaiian," she too was classified as monoracial, since she identified with two different components of the NHOPI major racial group. If a person marked "White" and "some other race" and then wrote "Italian" or "Irish," he was assumed to be a monoracial white. But

FIGURE 5.1   RACE AND SPANISH-ORIGIN QUESTIONS ASKED IN THE CENSUSES OF 1990 AND 2000

Census of 1990, Questions 4 and 7

4. Race

Fill ONE circle for the race that the person considers himself/herself to be.
If Indian (Amer.) print the name of the enrolled or principal tribe. →

- ○ White
- ○ Black or Negro
- ○ Indian (Amer.) (Print the name of the enrolled or principal tribe)

If other Asian or Pacific Islander (API), print one group, for example: Hmong, Fijian, Laotian, Thai, Tongen, Pakistani, Cambodian, and so on. →

- ○ Chinese
- ○ Filipino
- ○ Hawaiian
- ○ Korean
- ○ Vietnamese
- ○ Japanese
- ○ Asian Indian
- ○ Samoan
- ○ Guamanian
- ○ Other API

If other race, print race. →

Other race (print race)

7. Is this person of Spanish/Hispanic origin? Fill ONE circle for each person.

- ○ No (not Spanish/Hispanic)
- ○ Yes, Mexican, Mexican Amer., Chicano
- ○ Yes, Puerto Rican
- ○ Yes, Cuban
- ○ Yes, other Spanish/Hispanic. Print one group, for example, Argentinean, Colombian, Dominican, Nicaraguan, Salvadoran, Spaniard, and so on.

Census of 2000, Questions 5 and 6

→ NOTE: Please answer BOTH Questions 5 and 6.

5. Is this person Spanish/Hispanic/Latino?   Mark ☒ the "No" box if not Spanish/Hispanic/Latino.

- ☐ No, not Spanish/Hispanic/Latino
- ☐ Yes, Mexican, Mexican Amer., Chicano
- ☐ Yes, Puerto Rican
- ☐ Yes, Cuban
- ☐ Yes, other Spanish/Hispanic/Latino—print group

6. What is this person's race?   Mark ☒ one or more races *to indicate what this person considers himself/herself to be*

- ☐ White
- ☐ Black, African Amer., or Negro
- ☐ American Indian or Alaska Native—print name of enrolled or principal tribe.

- ☐ Asian Indian
- ☐ Chinese
- ☐ Filipino
- ☐ Japanese
- ☐ Korean
- ☐ Vietnamese
- ☐ Other Asian—print race
- ☐ Native Hawaiian
- ☐ Guamanian or Chamorro
- ☐ Samoan
- ☐ Other Pacific Islander—print race

- ☐ Some other race—print race

Source: Author's compilation.

Note: Major Changes in the Race and Spanish-Origin Questions

- The Spanish-origin question in 2000 preceded the race question. In 1990 the race question came first.
- In 1990 the Spanish-origin questions gave six examples of specific Spanish origins for those who identified with another Spanish or Hispanic origin. In 2000 no examples of other Spanish origins were given.
- The race question in 2000 used "African American" in addition to "black" and "Negro."
- "Eskimo" and "Aleut" were used in 1990, but in 2000 "Alaska Natives" was included with "American Indian."
- "Hawaiian" in 1990 was changed to "Native Hawaiian" in 2000.
- "Or Chamorro" was added to "Guamanian."
- "Other API" was changed to "Other Asian."
- "Other race" was changed to "some other race."

The six major races used in the census of 2000 were: white; black or African American; American Indian or Alaska Native; Asian; Native Hawaiian and Other Pacific Islander (NHOPI); and some other race.

if a person marked "White" and "some other race" and wrote "Mexican" or "Spanish," she was classified as multiracial.

The key to this procedure involves the coding responses written by those who marked "some other race." The OMB requirement did not permit the use of the "some other race" category, but the Census Bureau obtained an exemption for the 2000 census and included this category, primarily because the bureau knew that many Spanish-origin respondents would mark "some other race" as their identity.

If a person marked "some other race" and wrote a term indicating a Spanish origin, he was automatically assigned to the "other race" category. Many people identified with "some other race" alone, and so they were monoracials. Others identified with "Black" or "White," then with "some other race" and wrote a Spanish term; they were classified as multiple in race. If a person wrote a term for "some other race" other than a Spanish-origin group, the Census Bureau checked the 1990 census data to investigate the racial reports of people who used that term for their ancestry. If 70 percent or more of the people using that ancestry term in 1990 identified with a specific race, those people using that term for their "other race" in 2000 were placed into a specific racial category. For example, in the 1990 census, 99.5 percent of those who marked "Irish" as their ancestry, marked "White" for their race. This meant that someone writing in "Irish" for his only race or for his second race in the 2000 census was a monoracial white. Of those who marked "Surinamese" for their ancestry in 1990, 25 percent had identified themselves as white, 46 percent as black, and the remainder as Asian or Indian. Thus, a person writing "Surinamese" for their "other race" in 2000 was left in the "other race" category.

Figure 5.1 also shows another major change from 1990: the Spanish-origin question came prior to, not after, the race question. Census Bureau pretests suggested that if the race question came first, many respondents would feel that they had already identified their origin and would leave the Spanish-origin question blank. To prevent this, the Spanish-Hispanic-Latino query preceded the race question in 2000, with a reminder to answer the following race question as well. We do not yet know what impact this had on responses to the race question (Martin, Demaio, and Campanelli 1990). In two-thirds of the households enumerated in 2000, someone filled out the census form and mailed it back. That person presumably answered the race and Spanish-origin questions for all residents. The other one-third of households provided information to a census-taker who visited their home. We do not know how the mode of data gathering influenced the results.

2000 CENSUS RESULTS

About one American in forty, a total of 6.7 million, reported multiple races in 2000 according to the coding procedures used by the Census Bureau. This is

2.4 percent of the population. If we exclude those persons who were multiple in race because they marked one of the five major racial groups, also marked "other race," and then wrote in a Spanish term, the count of multiple races falls to 1.6 percent, or 4.4 million. This is very close to the percentage of multiracial hinted at in the Census Bureau pretest.

Because the census questionnaire listed the five major racial groups called for by OMB and "some other race," there are sixty-three different racial groups from which data are now available: six single races and fifty-seven combinations of two to six races. The top panel of table 5.1 shows the frequency of identifying with two or more racial groups. Very few individuals—fewer than one in one thousand—went on to identify with a third or fourth race. The middle panel of table 5.1 shows the most and least popular race combinations.

TABLE 5.1   POPULATION INFORMATION FROM THE REPORTING OF RACE, CENSUS OF 2000

	Number	Percentage of Total Population
Population by number of races reported		
One	274,595,678	97.4%
Two	6,368,075	2.3
Three	410,285	0.1
Four	38,408	<0.1
Five	8,637	<0.1
Six	823	<0.1
Total	281,421,905	100.0

		Percentage of Two-or-More-Races Population
Most frequently reported combination of two or more races		
White and some other race	2,206,251	32.30%
White and Indian	1,082,683	15.9
White and Asian	868,395	12.7
White and black	784,764	11.5
Black and some other race	417,249	6.1
Asian and some other race	249,108	3.6
Black and Indian	182,494	2.7
Asian and NHOPI	138,802	2.0
White and NHOPI	112,964	1.7
White, black, and Indian	106,782	1.6

(*Table continues on p. 136.*)

TABLE 5.1   CONTINUED

Least frequently reported combination of
two or more races

White, black, Indian, NHOPI, and other	68	<0.1
Black, Indian, NHOPI, and other	111	<0.1
Indian, Asian, NHOPI, and other	207	<0.1
Black, Indian, Asian, NHOPI, and other	216	<0.1
White, Indian, NHOPI, and other	309	<0.1
White, black, NHOPI, and other	325	<0.1
Black, Indian, Asian, and other	334	<0.1
White, black, Asian, NHOPI, and other	379	<0.1
Indian, NHOPI, and other	586	<0.1
White, Indian, Asian, NHOPI, and other	639	<0.1

Major Race	One Race Alone	Alone and in Combination	Maximum as Percentage of Minimum
Maximum and minimum counts of the five major races			
White	211,460,626	216,930,975	102.6%
Black or African American	34,658,190	36,658,190	105.1
Asian	10,242,998	11,898,828	116.2
American Indian	2,476,956	4,119,301	166.3
NHOPI	398,836	874,414	219.2

Source: U.S. Bureau of the Census, *Census of 2000,* "Overview of Race and Hispanic Origin," C2KBR/01-1; summary file 1, table P-4; Census 2000 supplemental survey, public use microdata sample.
Note: These data include information for those who identified with two races because they wrote in a Spanish term for their second race.

"White and some other race" tops the list because many Americans marked "White" and "some other race," then wrote in a Spanish term. These respondents amount to more than one-third of the multiple-race population. Next in popularity—with a count of 1.1 million—was the "White–American Indian" combination, reflecting the long history of marriage between European settlers and their descendants and American Indians. "White-Asian," "White-Black," and "Black-other" (that is, "Black-Spanish") ranked third, fourth, and fifth.

Some people identified with each of the 57 racial combinations, although many combinations were rarely reported: for 30 of the 57, the actual count was under 10,000. The five-race combination of "White-Black-Indian-NHOPI-other" was the least frequently reported—just 68 persons—followed by "Black-Indian-NHOPI-other." Only 823 of the 281.4 million Americans counted in 2000 identified with all six races.

The single-race count of some races differs greatly from the maximum count, but for others it does not. The final panel in table 5.1 shows the maximum count of each of the five major racial groups as a percentage of the minimum. At one extreme are the NHOPIs. Most of those who checked "Native Hawaiian," "Guamanian or Chamorro," or "Samoan" or wrote in an NHOPI term such as "Polynesian" or "Micronesian" went on to identify with a second race, typically "White" or "Asian." Consequently, the maximum count of NHOPIs is more than twice the minimum count.

Whites were distinguished by how seldom they reported a second race. Of all who marked the "White" box, no more than one in forty marked a second race. "Some other race" (Spanish origin), "American Indian," and "Asian" were the most popular choices used in combination with "White." Although few whites identified with a second race, the dominating size of the white population means that most multiple-race persons identified themselves as white. We stress that individuals did not rank-order their races. They merely filled in a box on the census schedule, so we do not know which was their primary or preferred racial identity.

WHO IDENTIFIED WITH TWO OR MORE RACES IN 2000?

The opportunity to identify with several racial groups was an abrupt change in conceptualizing and measuring race. Although the Census Bureau tested multiple race questions in the 1990s, it did not pretest the "Mark all that apply" question that was used.

Several characteristics of individuals seem likely to influence whether they would identify with one race or with more than one race. The multiracial movement emphasized the desire of parents in a mixed-race marriage to list their children as members of two races. Thus, we expect that many children whose parents differ in race would report themselves or be reported as members of two races.

Second, place of residence makes a difference. For more than a century, Hawaii has had a racially diverse population—the migrants from the Marqueses Islands who settled there; the British colonialists who preceded the Americans; Filipinos and Puerto Ricans imported to work the plantations; the Japanese who dominated the economy; and the many white and black military personnel assigned there since the U.S. war with Spain. We expect much intermarriage in Hawaii and a large multiracial population. At the other extreme, some states, such as Vermont and New Hampshire, have had a largely white population since the earliest days of European migration, and others, like North Dakota, have never had a minority population. So we expect that few residents of these states would identify with two races. In the American South, a firm color line emerged from the imposition of the "one drop" rule after the Civil War, so we also expect that most people there would identify with only one race.

Third, we expect age to be related to the number of races reported because of an increase over time in interracial marriages. Apparently fewer than 2 percent of black husbands marrying in the Depression decade or before had a white wife, but among African American men marrying in the 1990s, more than one in ten had a white wife. There was a similar increase over time in the frequency with which whites and native-born Asians married outside their own racial group (Farley 1999, fig. 5.7; 2002, table 1.1). If the offspring of mixed marriages identify with two races, then age should be strongly linked to such reporting.

Fourth, educational attainment should have an influence on the identification with more than one race. Those who complete college presumably have studied American history and social science, so they may be more likely to be aware of the complicated racial issues in the United States and the frequency with which whites, African Americans, and Indians have married outside their own race.

Finally, it is likely that racial groups differ in their propensity to identify with a second race. Since the arrival of the early settlers from the British Isles, whites and American Indians have been marrying each other, so much so that most people who identify as American Indian today have one or more white ancestors. As Randall Kennedy (2003) stresses, during the centuries of slavery interracial sex between blacks and whites occurred frequently, producing a large mulatto population in the colonies and the United States. On the eve of the Civil War, the 1860 census reported that 13 percent of the Negro population was mulatto (U.S. Department of Commerce 1918, table 1). The Census Bureau continued to classify Negroes by degree of blackness through 1890, using the terms "quadroon" and "octoroon," but then recognized the folly of doing so. Despite interracial parenting, customs and legal rulings in the South mandated that all persons be classified on one or the other side of a firmly drawn black-white dividing line. Thus, we expect that African Americans would identify with a second race much less frequently than American Indians. Because they are numerically dominant, whites should be least likely to identify with a second race. Even if race made no difference at all in the selection of a spouse, most whites would marry other whites because of the dominating size of the white population, so today's whites should be least likely to identify with several races.

To analyze patterns of multiple-race identification, the 5 percent microdata from the 2000 census were analyzed. These provide information about the reporting of race and all other characteristics for a sample of 14 million persons.[1] Because of the confounding way in which the writing of a Spanish term for "some other race" turned 1.6 million into multiple-race people, this analysis is restricted to the non-Hispanic population.

CHILDREN IN MIXED-RACE MARRIAGES: THEIR REPORTED RACES

A primary motivation for many of those who advocated a new race question was to allow parents in racially mixed marriages some flexibility in identifying their children. Did they make use of the multiple-race question? Yes, they did.

Householders were asked to list the relationship of all who lived in their home or apartment and provide racial information for each person. Using those responses, the Census Bureau identified "own children"—that is, the children of the household head or the spouse of the head. "Own children" included children related to the parents by blood, marriage, or adoption. These children were not necessarily, however, the biological offspring of one or both of the parents. In this analysis, we consider non-Hispanic children under age eighteen who lived in two-parent, married-couple households in which both parents were non-Hispanic.

There were 36.9 million "own children" under age eighteen for whom both parents identified with the same major racial group: white, black, Indian, Asian, or NHOPI. In these racially homogeneous marriages, only 0.2 percent of the children—or 2 per 1,000—were identified with two or more races. We conclude that almost all children in racially homogeneous married were single-race children. Approximately 1.4 million children were counted in husband-wife families in which the spouses differed in their reported races. Fifty-one percent of these children were marked as identifying with two or more races.

This is strong evidence of the effectiveness of the new race question, which has shown that many parents in racially mixed marriages think of their children as members of two or more racial groups. Table 5.2 reports that just over 1.0 million "own children" under age eighteen lived in two-parent households in which the races of the partners differed. Forty-four percent of those children were identified with two or more racial groups. Quite clearly, many parents in racially mixed marriages think of their children as multiracial.

Table 5.2 provides additional information about the reporting of children's races by focusing on racially mixed marriages involving whites, blacks, Asians, or American Indians. Not all interracial marriages are included here.

The first panel of table 5.2 reports that 994 per 1,000 of children in white-white marriages were identified as white only and that just 2 per 1,000 were multiracial. Similarly, 995 per 1,000 children in black-black marriages were black only. Among those couples comprising a white husband and an African American wife, 467 per 1,000 children were identified with two racial groups.

TABLE 5.2   RACE OF CHILDREN UNDER AGE EIGHTEEN IN TWO-PARENT,
NON-HISPANIC HOUSEHOLDS, BY RACE OF PARENTS

White-Only, White-Black, and Black-Only Married Couples			
Race of Husband:	White Only	White Only	Black Only	Black Only
Race of Wife:	White Only	Black Only	White Only	Black Only
Race of child				
White only	99%	15%	17%	<1%
Black only	<1	43	24	99
Multiracial	<1	30	58	<1
Another race	<1	12	1	<1
Total	100	100	100	100
Number of children	34,691,122	100,937	237,383	3,282,213

White-Only, White-Asian, and Asian-Only Married Couples			
Race of Husband:	White Only	White Only	Asian Only	Asian Only
Race of Wife:	White Only	Asian Only	White Only	Asian Only
Race of child				
White only	99%	26%	21%	<1%
Asian only	<1	21	19	99
Multiracial	<1	51	59	<1
Another race	<1	2	<1	<1
Total	100	100	100	100
Number of children	34,691,122	328,448	165,177	1,969,688

White-Only, White-Indian, and Indian-Only Married Couples			
Race of Husband:	White Only	White Only	Indian Only	Indian Only
Race of Wife:	White Only	Indian Only	White Only	Indian Only
Race of child				
White only	99%	32%	30%	3%
Indian only	<1	50	34	95
Multiracial	<1	17	33	1
Another race	<1	<1	3	1
Total	100	100	100	100
Number of children	34,691,122	105,395	112,107	134,607

(continued)

TABLE 5.2   CONTINUED

White-Only, White-Multiracial, and Multiracial Married Couples

Race of Husband: Race of Wife:	White Only White Only	White Only Multiracial	Multiracial White Only	Multiracial Multiracial
Race of child				
White only	99%	48%	50%	8%
Multiracial	<1	51	46	90
Another race	<1	<1	4	2
Total	100	100	100	100
Number of children	34,691,122	217,154	214,350	161,842

Source: U.S. Bureau of the Census, Census 2000 supplemental survey.
Note: These data refer to non-Hispanic "own" children under age eighteen who were enumerated in a married household in which both the husband and wife were non-Hispanic. "Own children" includes those related to either the husband or wife by blood, marriage, or adoption, so these children are not necessarily the biological offspring of both parents.

But among couples comprising a white wife and a black husband (see the second panel), an even higher percentage of children—529 per 1,000—were identified with two racial groups. Because black husband–white wife couples are much more numerous than the reverse, we conclude that the majority of children in black-white married couples were identified with two racial groups.

In Asian-only two-parent families, 989 per 1,000 children were identified as Asian only. Among those couples comprising a white husband and an Asian wife, 522 per 1,000 children were identified with at least two racial groups, while 518 per 1,000 children in Asian husband–white wife families were identified with two racial groups.

PLACE OF RESIDENCE AND IDENTIFICATION WITH
TWO OR MORE RACES

Figure 5.2 reports the percentage of non-Hispanic persons who identified with more than one race by state. This ranged from a low of just 0.6 percent in West Virginia to a high of 18.2 percent in Hawaii identifying with two races. Asian-NHOPI, Asian-white, and white-NHOPI were the most common dual races reported there. Hawaii was also the only state where many identified with three or more races: almost 7 percent of Hawaiian residents marked three or more races, with white-Asian-NHOPI the most popular combination.

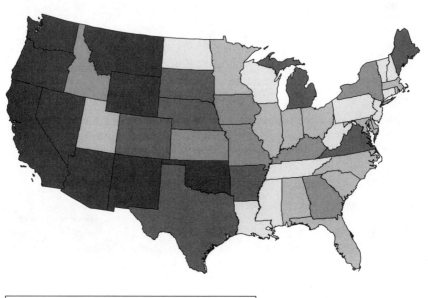

0 to 1.0 Percent
1.0 to 1.3 Percent
1.3 to 1.5 Percent
1.5 to 1.9 Percent
1.9 to 18.4 Percent

Highest Percentage		Lowest Percentage	
Washington	3.33	West Virginia	0.62
California	3.43	Washington, D.C.	0.75
Oklahoma	5.78	Mississippi	0.76
Alaska	6.54	North Dakota	0.83
Hawaii	18.14	Pennsylvania	0.86

United States: 1.6

Source: Author's compilation.

Identification with two races was most common in the Pacific Rim states and in states with large American Indian populations, such as New Mexico, Arizona, and Oklahoma, reflecting the historic experience of frequent intermarriage between Indians and whites. At the other extreme were states that have never had substantial minority populations: New Hampshire, Vermont, and North Dakota, as well as states in the Deep South, including Louisiana and Mississippi.

Examining data for metropolises reveals that Honolulu had the highest frequency of identification with two races at 20 percent. Indeed, it was the only metropolis where more than 6 percent did so. Anchorage, Alaska, came after Honolulu in density of multiracial population. In the conterminous United States, three heterogeneous California cities topped the list: Stockton, Vallejo, and Merced.

At the other extreme were metropolises where very few identified with more than one race—just over 0.5 percent of their residents. Multiple-race reporting was most rare in three Appalachian areas in Pennsylvania that have never had minority populations: Altoona, Johnstown, and Wilkes-Barre. Jackson, Mississippi, and Monroe, Louisiana, also had extremely low rates of two-race identification, but they were metropolises with large white and African American populations.

When counties are considered, the distinctive racial history of Hawaii is again evident. Four of the five counties with the highest rates of multiple-race identification were Hawaiian counties. Indeed, on the Big Island—Hawaii County—almost three residents in ten identified with two or more racial groups. In the conterminous United States, Craig County in northeastern Oklahoma had the highest rate of identification with two or more races. In that county, two-thirds of the population identified themselves as white only, about one-sixth as American Indian only, and one in nine as both white and American Indian. Four of the five counties where identification with two races was least frequent were in North Dakota. In the northern reaches of the grain belt, about one person in one thousand used the new census options to identify with two or more racial groups.

BIRTH COHORTS AND IDENTIFICATION WITH TWO OR MORE RACES

The four largest major racial groups were sorted into birth cohorts, and the percentage identifying with a second race is shown in figure 5.3. This figure lucidly indicates the substantial racial difference in the propensity of non-Hispanics to identify with a second race. In 1980 the percentages identifying with one race and then one or more other races were as follows: American Indians—43.1 percent; Asians—13.0 percent; African Americans—4.3 percent; and whites—2.0 percent. More than four of ten of those who marked

FIGURE 5.3   PERCENTAGE OF NON-HISPANIC WHITES, BLACKS, AMERICAN
INDIANS, AND ASIANS IDENTIFYING WITH TWO OR MORE RACES, BY
BIRTH COHORT: CENSUS 2000

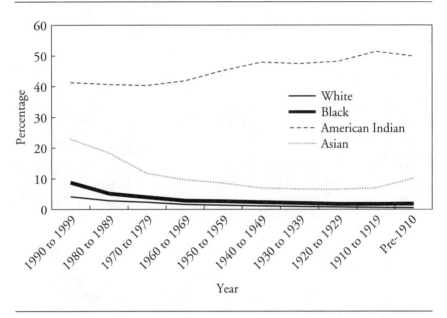

Source: U.S. Bureau of the Census, Public Use 5 Percent Sample, Microdata Sample.

"American Indian" went on to identify with a second racial group, presumably because of the centuries-old tradition of Indians marrying and bearing children with whites. The racial homogeny of white marriages helps to explain the infrequency with which whites opted to also identify with black, Asian, or Indian—just 2 percent.

Birth cohort differences in identification with two or more races are generally consistent with the hypothesis and finding that interracial marriage has increased in recent decades. Asians, blacks, and whites under age twenty in 2000 were much more likely than older members of the same racial group to be identified with two or more races. Many fewer than 1 percent of whites and African Americans over age sixty identified with two or more racial groups, but 5 percent of whites and 10 percent of blacks under age ten were multiracial. American Indians were the exception to the generalization about the effects of age on identification with two or more races: in every birth cohort, almost one-half of those who identified with Indian also identified with a second racial group. Indeed, the percentage of American Indians who identified with a second race was greater for persons over fifty than for those under twenty.

EDUCATIONAL ATTAINMENT AND IDENTIFICATION WITH TWO OR MORE RACES

We presumed that educational attainment would be linked to identification with two or more racial groups. Figure 5.4 presents findings for the non-Hispanic population age twenty-five and over. For American Indians and blacks, the link between schooling completed and the reporting of multiple races was in the expected direction. Perhaps as members of these racial groups complete college, they learn more about the nation's complex history and realize that some of their ancestors were whites. However, for both Asians and whites, educational attainment appeared unrelated to identifying with a second race.

It is quite likely that the effects of birth cohort and nativity confound the link between educational attainment and the reporting of race.

FIGURE 5.4 PERCENTAGE OF NON-HISPANIC WHITES, BLACKS, AMERICAN INDIANS, AND ASIANS AGE TWENTY-FIVE AND OVER IDENTIFYING WITH TWO OR MORE RACES, BY EDUCATIONAL ATTAINMENT: CENSUS 2000

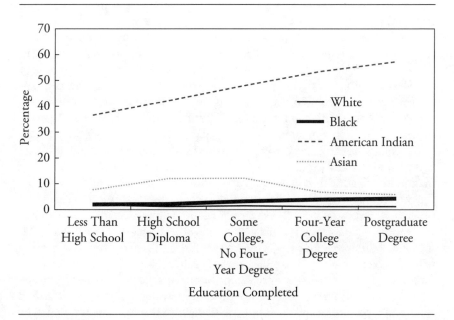

Source: U.S. Bureau of the Census, Public Use Microdata Sample.

CONCLUSION

As recently as five decades ago, racial data were used to maintain segregation, but in the 1960s the civil rights movement ended governmental support for discrimination. By the early 1970s, federal courts, agencies, and employers were using an effective and unambiguous test to demonstrate the elimination of racial discrimination: Did employers hire African Americans and promote them to all occupations? Did black workers earn as much as whites? Did school systems enroll blacks, hire African American teachers, and assign both students and employees without regard to race? Were election districts drawn so that minorities had opportunities to win? Congress also directed federal spending toward firms owned by minorities. To demonstrate that blacks were represented appropriately, racial data were needed. Instead of being an instrument of segregation, racial data were used to help overcome traditional practices of discrimination.

The success of the African American civil rights movement led other minorities to seek the benefits that they perceived as flowing from the use of goals, quotas, and affirmative action and from the delineation of districts with the electability of minorities in mind. Because the large and rapidly growing Hispanic population succeeded in gaining a special status in the federal statistical system, all federal agencies must now ask everyone whether their origin is Spanish. The tireless efforts of Representative Robert Matsui made certain that many specific Asian racial groups were listed on the census schedule, and Senator Daniel Akaka raised Native Hawaiians and other Pacific Islanders to the status of a major race equivalent to whites and African Americans.

The multiracial movement in the 1990s provoked a fundamental change in the way racial data are collected. With interests that briefly overlapped those of a powerful Speaker of the House, they succeeded in overturning the idea that the government can classify everyone into one and only one race. They failed to win their major goal of making "multiracial" the equivalent of "White," "Black," or "Asian," but they fundamentally changed the rules so that when we fill out a governmental form we now have the opportunity to identify simultaneously with up to five racial groups. In the 2000 census, about 1.6 percent of the population identified with two or more of the five racial groups, and an additional 0.8 percent marked one of the five major racial groups, then also checked "some other race" and wrote in a Spanish term for their identity. The multiracial movement succeeded in giving parents whose races differed new options for identifying their children. The majority of the 1.4 million children in racially heterogeneous, two-parent families were identified with two or more races.

Although the multiracial movement has been successful in changing the federal statistical system, at this point there is no strong evidence that it shifted how people think about race or how racial data from the census are used. The redrawing of congressional and state legislative districts was accomplished without controversy or litigation concerning those with two or more racial identities. As of now, no plaintiffs have prominently litigated the rights or legal prerogatives of two-race persons.

The multiracial population will undoubtedly grow rapidly in the future as the number of interracial marriages increases. I doubt, however, that "multiracial" will be commonly used as if it were a race, either when people identify themselves or when agencies and courts wrestle with equal opportunities for all races. Giving people an opportunity to identify with two racial groups may remind individuals that they have racial options and can use one or another, or both, of their races, as the circumstances dictate. The child of an Asian parent and a white parent might mark "White" when applying to an engineering or computer science program at a California university, but mark "Asian" when applying to study European history in North Carolina. A woman with one African American parent and one white parent might identify as "Black" if she wishes to secure a highway paving contract for her construction company but mark "White" when seeking a mortgage for a new home. Popularizing the multiracial concept may be a challenge.

By 2003 the census-oriented multiracial movement had faded into oblivion. The website of Susan Graham's Project RACE is no longer accessible. Carlos Fernandez's AMEA website has not been updated since March 2001, and its spanner announces the cancellation of the AMEA 2001 convention.

NOTE

1.   Available at: www.pdq.com and www.census.gov.

REFERENCES

Barringer, Herbert, Robert W. Gardner, and Michael J. Levin. 1993. *Asians and Pacific Islanders in the United States.* New York: Russell Sage Foundation.

Bean, Frank D., and Marta Tienda. 1987. *The Hispanic Population of the United States.* New York: Russell Sage Foundation.

Choldin, Harvey M. 1986. "Statistics and Politics: The 'Hispanic Issue' in the 1980 Census." *Demography* 23(3): 403–18.

Farley, Reynolds. 1999. "Racial Issues: Recent Trends in Residential Patterns and Intermarriage." In *Diversity and Its Discontents: Cultural Conflict and Common Ground in Contemporary American Society,* edited by Neil J. Smelser and Jeffrey C. Alexander. Princeton, N.J.: Princeton University Press.

———. 2002. "Racial Identities in 2000: The Response to the Multiple Race Option." In *The New Race Question: How the Census Counts Multiracial Individuals,* edited by Joel Perlmann and Mary C. Waters. New York: Russell Sage Foundation.

Hirschman, Charles, Richard Alba, and Reynolds Farley. 2000. "The Meaning and Measurement of Race in the U.S. Census: Glimpses into the Future." *Demography* 37(3): 381–94.

Jaffe, A. J., Ruth M. Cullen, and Thomas D. Boswell. 1980. *The Changing Demography of Spanish Americans.* New York: Academic Press.

Kennedy, Randall. 2003. *Interracial Intimacies: Sex, Marriage, Identity, and Adoption.* New York: Pantheon Books.

Klueger, Richard. 1976. *Simple Justice: The History of* Brown v. Board of Education *and Black America's Struggle for Equality.* New York: Alfred A. Knopf.

La Noue, George R., and John C. Sullivan. 2001. "Deconstructing Affirmative Action Categories." In *Color Lines: Affirmative Action, Immigration, and Civil Rights Options for America,* edited by John David Skrentny. Chicago: University of Chicago Press.

Martin, Elizabeth, Theresa J. Demaio, and Pamela C. Campanelli. 1990. "Context Effects for Census Measures of Race and Hispanic Origin." *Public Opinion Quarterly* 54: 551–66.

Skerry, Peter. 2000. *Counting on the Census.* Washington, D.C.: Brookings Institution.

Snipp, C. Matthew. 1989. *American Indians: The First of This Land.* New York: Russell Sage Foundation.

Spencer, John Michael. 1997. *The New Colored People: The Mixed Race Movement in America.* New York: New York University Press.

Thernstrom, Abigail M. 1987. *Whose Votes Count? Affirmative Action and Minority Voting Rights.* Cambridge, Mass.: Harvard University Press.

U.S. Department of Commerce. U.S. Bureau of the Census. 1918. *Negro Population in the United States 1790–1915.* Washington: U.S. Government Printing Office.

———. 1963a. *Census of Population: 1960.* PC (2)-1D. Washington: U.S. Government Printing Office.

———. 1963b. *Census of Population: 1960.* PC (2)-1B. Washington: U.S. Government Printing Office.

Whalen, Charles, and Barbara Whalen. 1985. *The Longest Debate: A Legislative History of the 1964 Civil Rights Act.* New York: New American Library.

Williams, Kim. 2000. "Changing Race as We Know It? The Political Location of the Multiracial Movement." Unpublished paper. Harvard University, John F. Kennedy School of Government, Taubman Center for State and Local Government, Cambridge, Mass.

6

"WE ARE ALL AMERICANS":
THE LATIN AMERICANIZATION OF
RACE RELATIONS IN THE UNITED STATES

℘

Eduardo Bonilla-Silva and Karen S. Glover

We need to speak about the impossible because we know too much about the possible.
—Silvio Rodríguez, Cuban New Song
Movement singer and composer

"WE ARE ALL Americans!" This, we contend, will be the racial mantra of the United States in years to come. Although for many analysts, because of this country's deep history of racial divisions, this prospect seems implausible, nationalist statements denying the salience of race are the norm throughout the world.[1] Countries such as Malaysia and Indonesia, Trinidad and Belize, and, more significantly for our discussion, Iberian countries such as Puerto Rico, Cuba, Brazil, and Mexico, all exhibit this ostrichlike approach to racial matters. That is, they all stick their heads deep into the social ground and say, "We don't have races here. We don't have racism here. Races and racism exist in the United States and South Africa. We are all Mexicans (Cubans, Brazilians, or Puerto Ricans)!"

Despite these claims, racial minorities in these self-styled racial democracies tend to be worse off, comparatively speaking, than racial minorities in Western nations. In Brazil, for example, blacks and "pardos" (tan or brown) earn 40 to 45 percent as much as whites. In the United States blacks earn 55 to 60 percent as much as whites. In Brazil blacks are half as likely as blacks in the United States to be employed in professional jobs, and about one-third as less likely to attend college; they have a life expectancy, controlling for education and income, between five and six years shorter than that of white Brazilians. This last statistic is similar in size to the black-white difference in the United States (Andrews

1991; Silva do Valle 1985; Hasenbalg 1985; Lovell and Wood 1998; Telles 1999; Hasenbalg and Silva 1999; do Nascimento and Larkin-Nascimento 2001).

In this chapter, we contend that racial stratification and the rules of racial (re)cognition in the United States are becoming Latin America–like. We suggest that the biracial system typical of the United States, which was the exception in the world racial system, is becoming the "norm" (for the racialization of the world system, see Balibar and Wallerstein 1991; Goldberg 1993, 2002; Mills 1997; Winant 2001). That is, the U.S. system is evolving into a complex racial stratification system.[2] Specifically, we argue that the United States is developing a tri-racial system with "whites" at the top, an intermediary group of "honorary whites" (similar to the coloreds in South Africa during formal apartheid), and a nonwhite group or the "collective black" at the bottom.[3] We predict that the "white" group will include "traditional" whites, new "white" immigrants, and, in the near future, assimilated Latinos, some (light-skinned) multiracials, and other subgroups. The intermediate racial group, or "honorary whites," will comprise most light-skinned Latinos (most Cubans, for instance, and segments of the Mexican and Puerto Rican communities; Rodríguez 1998), Japanese Americans, Korean Americans, Asian Indians, Chinese Americans, the bulk of multiracials (Rockquemore and Arend, forthcoming), and most Middle Eastern Americans.[4] Finally, the "collective black" will include blacks, dark-skinned Latinos, Vietnamese, Cambodians, Laotians, and maybe Filipinos.

PRELIMINARY MAP OF TRI-RACIAL SYSTEM IN THE UNITED STATES

"Whites"

- Whites
- New whites (Russians, Albanians, and so on)
- Assimilated white Latinos
- Some (white-looking) multiracials
- Assimilated (urban) Native Americans
- A few Asian-origin people

"Honorary Whites"

- Light-skinned Latinos
- Japanese Americans
- Korean Americans
- Asian Indians
- Chinese Americans
- Middle Eastern Americans
- Most multiracials

"Collective Black"

- Filipinos
- Vietnamese
- Hmong
- Laotians
- Dark-skinned Latinos
- Blacks
- New West Indian and African immigrants
- Reservation-bound Native Americans

This map is heuristic, however, rather than definitive. It is included as a guide for how we think various ethnic groups will line up in the new emerging racial order. We acknowledge several caveats: the position of some groups may change (for example, Chinese Americans, Asian Indians, or Arab Americans); the map does not include all groups in the United States (Samoans and Micronesians, for instance, do not appear); and at this early stage, owing in part to data limitations, some groups may end up in a different racial stratum altogether. For example, Filipinos may become "honorary whites" rather than another group in the "collective black" stratum. More significantly, if our Latin Americanization thesis is accurate, the categories will be porous and a "pigmentocracy" will make the map useful for group-level rather than individual-level predictions. (By porous we mean that individual members of a racial stratum can move up [or down] the stratification system, as might happen when a light-skinned middle-class black person marries a white woman and moves to the "honorary white" stratum. Pigmentocracy refers to the rank ordering of groups and members of groups according to phenotype and cultural characteristics, such as may happen when Filipinos move to the top of the "collective black" stratum because of their high level of education and income and a high rate of interracial marriage with whites.)

We recognize that our thesis is broad (attempting as it does to classify where everyone will fit in the racial order) and difficult to verify empirically with the existing data (there are no systematic data on the skin tone of all Americans). Nevertheless, we believe it is paramount to begin working toward a paradigm shift in the field of race relations. We consider our efforts here a preliminary push in that direction.

In the remainder of the chapter, we have four aims. First, we draw on research on race in Latin American and Caribbean societies to provide insight into the key features of their racial stratification systems. Second, we outline five reasons why Latin Americanization will occur at this historical juncture in the United States. Third, we examine various objective (income, education, occupation), subjective (racial views and racial self-classification), and social interaction indicators (residential preferences and interracial marriage) to assess whether the data point in the direction predicted by the Latin American-ization thesis. Finally, we discuss the likely implications of Latin American-ization for the future of race relations in the United States.

HOW RACE WORKS IN THE AMERICAS

> *To advocate transculturation without attempting to change the systems and insti-tutions that breed the power differential would simply help to perpetuate the utopian vision that constructs Latin America . . . as the continent of hope.*
> —Lourdes Martínez-Echazabal (1998, 32)

One of the authors has argued elsewhere that racial stratification systems oper-ate in most societies without races being officially acknowledged (Bonilla-Silva 1999). For example, although racial inequality is more pronounced in Latin America than in the United States, racial data in Latin America are gathered inconsistently or not at all. Yet most Latin Americans, including those most af-fected by racial stratification, do not recognize the inequality between "whites" and "nonwhites" in their countries as racial. "Prejudice" (Latin Americans do not talk about "racism") is viewed as a legacy from slavery and colonialism, and inequality is regarded as the product of class dynamics (Wagley 1952; for a critique, see Skidmore 1990). Therein lies the secret of race in Latin America and a suggestion as to why racial protest is so sporadic. An examina-tion of the long history that produced this state of affairs is beyond the scope of this chapter, and thus we sketch only the six central features of Latin American (and Caribbean) racial stratification.

MISCEGENATION OR "MESTIZAJE"

Latin American nation-states, with the exceptions of Argentina, Chile, Uruguay, and Costa Rica, are thoroughly racially mixed. This mixture has led many ob-servers to follow the historian Gilberto Freyre (1959, 7)—who described Brazil as having "almost perfect equality of opportunity for all men regardless of race and color"—and label them "racial democracies." However, all con-tacts between Europeans and the various peoples of the world have involved racial mixing. The important difference is that the mixing in Latin America led to a socially and sometimes legally recognized intermediate racial stratum of mestizos, browns, or "trigueños."[5]

However, racial mixing in no way challenged white supremacy in colonial or postcolonial Latin America. Four pieces of evidence support this claim: the mixing was between white men and Indian or black women, thus maintain-ing the race-gender order; the men were fundamentally poor or working-class, which helped maintain the race-class order; the mixing followed a racially hierarchical pattern in which "whitening" was the goal; and marriages among people in the three main racial groups were (and still are) mostly homogamous (Hoetink 1967, 1971; Morner 1967; Martínez-Alier 1974; for Puerto Ricans, see Fitzpatrick 1971). The last point requires qualification: although most marriages have been within-stratum, they have produced phenotypical variation because members of all racial strata have variations in phenotype. This means that members of any stratum can try to "marry up" by choosing a light-skinned partner *within* their stratum.

THE TRI-RACIAL STRATIFICATION SYSTEM

Although Portuguese and Spanish colonial states wanted to create "two societies," the demographic realities of colonial life superseded their wishes.[6] Because most colonial outposts were scarcely populated by Europeans, all these societies developed an intermediate group of "browns," "pardos," or "mestizos" who buffered sociopolitical conflicts. Even though this group did not achieve the status of "white," it nonetheless had a better status than the Indian or black masses and therefore developed its own distinct interest. As many commentators have observed, without this intermediate group, Latin American countries would have followed the path of Haiti (us versus them). The similarities between a tri-racial stratification system and a complex class stratification system are clear: whereas class *polarization* leads to rebellion, a *multiplicity* of classes and strata leads to diffused social conflict (for an early summary on classes in modern industrial societies, see Bottomore 1968).

COLORISM OR PIGMENTOCRACY

There is yet another layer of complexity in Latin American racial stratification systems: the three racial strata are also internally stratified by "color." By color we mean skin tone, but also phenotype, hair texture, eye color, culture and education, and class. All of these features matter in the Latin American system of racial stratification, and this further stratification by "color" is referred to as pigmentocracy or colorism (Kinsbrunner 1996). Pigmentocracy has been central to the maintenance of white power in Latin America because it has fostered: (1) divisions among all those in secondary racial strata; (2) divisions *within* racial strata that limit the likelihood of *within*-strata unity; (3) the view that mobility is *individual* and conditional on "whitening"; and (4) the belief that white elites should be regarded as legitimate representatives of the "nation" even though they do not look like the average member of the nation.[7]

BLANQUEAMIENTO: WHITENING AS IDEOLOGY
AND PRACTICE

"Blanqueamiento" (whitening) has been treated in research on Latin America as an ideology (Degler 1986). However, blanqueamiento is not simply an ideology: it is an economic, political, and personal process. It is a "dynamic that involves culture, identity and values" (Wade 1997, 341). At the personal level, members of families can be color-divided or even racially divided and treat their dark-skinned members differently (Kasper 2000). The material origin of "whitening" was the 1783 Cédulas de Gracias al Sacar (petitions to "cleanse" persons of "impure origins"), which allowed mulattoes to buy certificates that officially declared them to be white (Guerra 1998). With this certificate, they were allowed to work in the military and colonial administrative posts. It was also a ticket to mobility for their offspring (Kinsbrunner 1996).

As a social practice, whitening "is not just neutral mixture but hierarchical movement . . . and the most valuable movement is upward" (Wade 1997, 342). Thus, whitening does not reveal a Latin American racial flexibility but instead demonstrates the effectiveness of the logic of white supremacy. This practice also works in apparently homogeneous societies such as Haiti (Trouillot 1990) and even Japan (Weiner 1997), where slight variations in skin tone (lighter shade) and cultural affectations (being more French in Haiti or Western-oriented in Japan) are regarded as valuable assets in the marriage market.

THE NATIONAL IDEOLOGY OF MESTIZAJE

National independence in Latin America meant, among other things, the silencing of discussions about race and the forging of a myth of national unity (Morner 1993; Marx 1998). After years of attempting to unite Latin American nations under the banner of "Hispanidad" (Martínez-Echazabal 1998; de la Fuente 2001), a more formidable ideology crystallized: the ideology of "mestizaje" (racial mixing) and "mulataje"—or in the words of José Vasconcelos, "la raza cósmica."[8] Fathers of the homeland such as Hostos and Betances in Puerto Rico, Martí in Cuba, Bolivar in Venezuela, and San Martín and Artigas in southern South America preached national unity and mestizaje, despite the fact that none of them had clean records on racial matters (Martínez-Echazabal 1998).

The mestizaje ideology hides the salience of race and the existence of a "racial structure" (Bonilla-Silva 1997, 2001), unites the "nation," and safeguards white power more effectively than "Hispanidad" (regarding oneself or one's country as Spanish). "The Hispanidad ideology" persists among white elites in Latin America and causes problems for the maintenance of non-racialism (for Puerto Rico, see Negrón-Muntaner 1997 and Torres-Saillant 1998; for Venezuela, see Wright 1990).

"WE ARE ALL LATINOAMERICANOS":
RACE AS NATIONALITY AND CULTURE

Most Latin Americans, even those who are obviously "black" or "Indian," refuse to identify themselves in racial terms. Instead, they prefer to use national (or cultural) descriptors, such as "I am Puerto Rican" or "I am Brazilian."[9] This behavior has been the subject of much confusion and described as an example of the fluidity of race in Latin America (for examples, see the otherwise superb work of Clara Rodríguez [1991, 2000]). However, defining the nation and the "people" as the "fusion of cultures" (even though the fusion is viewed in a Eurocentric manner) is the logical outcome of all of the factors mentioned here. Rather than evidence of nonracialism, nationalist statements such as "We are all Puerto Ricans" are a direct manifestation of the racial stratification peculiar to Latin America. These statements, which are taught to "Latinoamericanos" in schools and at home as historical truths, represent the agency of nonwhites to carve a space in the nation.[10] But they also help maintain the traditional racial hierarchy by hiding racial division and racial rule (Goldberg 2002).

WHY LATIN AMERICANIZATION NOW?

Why are race relations in the United States becoming Latin America–like at this point in our history? The reasons are multiple. First, the demography of the nation is changing. Racial minorities make up 30 percent of the population today. Population projections suggest that minorities as a group may become a numeric majority in the year 2050 (U.S. Department of Commerce 1996). More recent data from the census of 2000 suggest that these projections may be an underestimate, since the Latino population exceeded expectations and the proportion white was lower than expected (Grieco and Cassidy 2001).

The rapid darkening of America is creating a situation similar to that of Puerto Rico, Cuba, and Venezuela in the sixteenth and seventeenth centuries, or Argentina, Chile, and Uruguay in the late eighteenth and early nineteenth centuries. In both historical periods, the elites realized that their countries were becoming "black" (or "nonwhite"), and they devised a number of strategies (unsuccessful in the former and successful in the latter) to whiten their population (Helg 1990). Although whitening the population through immigration or by classifying many newcomers as white (Gans 1999; Warren and Twine 1997) is one possible outcome of the new American demography, for reasons discussed later in the chapter, we do not think it is likely that these strategies will be implemented. Rather, we argue that a more plausible response to the new racial reality will be to (1) create an intermediate racial group to buffer racial conflict; (2) allow some newcomers into the white racial stratum; and (3) incorporate most immigrants into the collective black stratum.

The second reason we believe Latin Americanization will occur now is because of the tremendous reorganization that has transpired in America in the post–civil rights era. Specifically, a kinder and gentler white supremacy has emerged. Elsewhere, Bonilla-Silva has labeled this the "new racism" (Bonilla-Silva and Lewis 1999; Bonilla-Silva 2001; see also Smith 1995). In post–civil rights America, systemic white privilege is maintained socially, economically, and politically through institutional, covert, and apparently nonracial practices. Whether in banks or universities, in stores or housing markets, "smiling discrimination" (Brooks 1990) tends to be the order of the day. This new white supremacy has produced the accompanying Latin America–like ideology: color-blind racism. This ideology, the norm throughout Latin America, denies the salience of race, scorns those who talk about race, and increasingly proclaims that "We are all Americans" (for a detailed analysis of color-blind racism, see Bonilla-Silva 2001, ch. 5).

A third reason for Latin Americanization is that race relations have become globalized (Lusane 1997). The once almost all-white Western nations have now "interiorized the other" (Miles 1993). The new world systemic need for capital accumulation has led to the incorporation of "dark" foreigners as "guest workers" and even as permanent workers (Schoenbaum and Pond 1996). Thus, European nations today have in their midst racial minorities who are progressively becoming an underclass (Castles and Miller 1993; Cohen 1997; Spoonley 1996). In addition, they have developed an internal "racial structure" (Bonilla-Silva 1997) that maintains white power, as well as a curious combination of ethno-nationalism and a race-blind ideology similar to the color-blind racism of the contemporary United States (for more on this, see Bonilla-Silva 2000).

This new global racial reality, we believe, will reinforce the Latin Americanization trend in the United States while versions of color-blind racism will become prevalent in most Western nations. Furthermore, as many formerly almost-all-white Western countries (for example, Germany, France, England) become more and more diverse, the Latin American model of racial stratification may surface in these societies as well.

A fourth reason for the emergence of Latin Americanization in the United States is the convergence of the political and ideological actions of the Republican Party, conservative commentators and activists, and the so-called multiracial movement (Rockquemore and Brunsma 2002). This has created the space for a radical transformation of the way in which racial data are gathered in America. One possible outcome of the Census Bureau's changes in racial and ethnic classifications is either the dilution of racial data or the elimination of race as an official category (for more on the multiracial movement and its implications, see Farley, this volume). At this point, chair of the campaign for Racial Privacy Initiative (RPI) and UC Regent Ward Connerly and the American Civil Rights Coalition (ACRC) lost the first round in their move to establish "California Racial Privacy," which would prohibit collecting data on race, but we believe that they may be successful in other rounds of this battle.

Finally, the attack on affirmative action, which is part of what Stephen Steinberg (1995) has labeled the "racial retreat," is the clarion call signaling the end of race-based social policy in the United States. The recent Supreme Court *Grutter v. Bollinger* decision, hailed by some observers as a victory, is at best a weak victory because it allows for a "narrowly tailored" use of race in college admissions, imposes an artificial twenty-five-year deadline for the program, and encourages a monumental case-by-case analysis for student admissions. The last provision is likely to create chaos and push institutions to make admissions decisions based on test scores. This trend reinforces the Latin Americanization thesis because the elimination of race-based social policy is, among other things, predicated on the notion that race no longer affects minorities' status. As in Latin America, we may succeed in eliminating race by decree but nevertheless maintain—or even increase—levels of racial inequality.

A LOOK AT THE DATA

To recapitulate, we contend that because of a number of important demographic, sociopolitical, and international changes, the United States is developing a more complex system of racial stratification. This system resembles those typical of Latin American societies. We suggest that three racial strata will develop: whites, honorary whites, and the collective black. And we argue that a central factor determining where groups and members of racial and ethnic groups will fit into the strata will be "phenotype"—lighter people at the top, medium in the middle, and dark at the bottom.[11] Although we posit that Latin Americanization will not fully materialize for several more decades, in the sections that follow we examine various objective, subjective, and social interaction indicators to see whether the trends support our thesis.

OBJECTIVE STANDING OF "WHITES," "HONORARY WHITES," AND "BLACKS"

If Latin Americanization is happening in the United States, gaps in income, poverty rates, education, and occupational standing between whites, honorary whites, and the collective black should be evident. The available data suggest this is the case. In terms of income, as table 6.1 shows, "white" Latinos (Argentines, Chileans, Costa Ricans, and Cubans) are doing much better than dark-skinned Latinos (Mexicans, Puerto Ricans). The apparent exceptions in table 6.1—Bolivians and Panamanians—are examples of the effect of self-selection among these immigrant groups.[12] Table 6.1 also shows that Asians exhibit a pattern similar to that of Latinos. Hence, a severe income gap exists between honorary white Asians (Japanese, Koreans, Filipinos, and Chinese)

Table 6.1   Mean Per Capita Income of Selected Asian and Latino Ethnic Groups, 2000

Latinos	Mean Income (U.S. Dollars)	Asian Americans	Mean Income (U.S. Dollars)
Mexicans	9,467.30	Chinese	20,728.54
Puerto Ricans	11,314.95	Japanese	23,786.13
Cubans	16,741.89	Koreans	16,976.19
Guatemalans	11,178.60	Asian Indians	25,682.15
Salvadorans	11,371.92	Filipinos	19,051.53
Costa Ricans	14,226.92	Taiwanese	22,998.05
Panamanians	16,181.20	Hmong	5,175.34
Argentines	23,589.99	Vietnamese	14,306.74
Chileans	18,272.04	Cambodians	8,680.48
Bolivians	16,322.53	Laotians	10,375.57
Whites	17,968.87	Whites	17,968.87
Blacks	11,366.74	Blacks	11,366.74

Source: 2000 Public Use Microdata Sample, 5 Percent Sample.
Note: We use per capita income because family income distorts the status of some groups (particularly Asians and whites), since some groups have more people in the household who are contributing toward the family income.

and those Asians we contend belong to the collective black (Vietnamese, Cambodian, Hmong, and Laotians).

Tables 6.2, 6.3, and 6.4 exhibit similar patterns in terms of education. Table 6.2 shows that light-skinned Latinos have between three and four years of educational advantage over dark-skinned Latinos. The same table indicates that elite Asians have up to eight years more education than most of the Asian groups we classify as belonging to the collective black. A more significant fact, given that the American job market is becoming bifurcated such that good jobs go to the educated and bad jobs to the undereducated, is that the proportion of white Latinos with "some college" is equal to or higher than the proportion of the white population with the same level of education. Hence, as table 6.3 shows, 35 percent of Cubans, 37 percent of Costa Ricans, 48 percent of Argentines, and 44 percent of Chileans have attained "some college" or higher levels of education, proportions that compare very favorably with the 38 percent of whites with this level of education. In contrast, the bulk of Mexican Americans, Salvadorans, Puerto Ricans, and Guatemalans (70 percent) have attained twelve or fewer years of education. Table 6.4 shows a similar pattern among Asians: elite Asians substantially outperform their brethren (and even whites) in the "some college" and higher categories. It is worth pointing out that the distance in educational attainment between elite and "collective black" Asians is larger than that between white and dark-skinned Latinos. For exam-

TABLE 6.2   MEDIAN YEARS OF SCHOOLING OF SELECTED ASIAN AND LATINO
ETHNIC GROUPS, 2000

Latinos	Median Years of Education	Asian Americans	Median Years of Education
Mexicans	9.00	Chinese	12.00
Puerto Ricans	11.00	Japanese	14.00
Cubans	12.00	Koreans	12.00
Guatemalans	7.50	Asian Indians	14.00
Salvadorans	9.00	Filipinos	14.00
Costa Ricans	12.00	Taiwanese	14.00
Panamanians	12.00	Hmong	5.50
Argentines	12.00	Vietnamese	11.00
Chileans	12.00	Cambodians	9.00
Bolivians	12.00	Laotians	10.00
Whites	12.00	Whites	12.00
Blacks	12.00	Blacks	12.00

Source: 2000 Public Use Microdata Sample, 5 Percent Sample.

ple, whereas 50 percent of Chinese, Japanese, and Koreans have "some college" or higher levels of education, in excess of 80 percent of Hmong, Laotians, and Cambodians have attained a high school diploma or less.

Substantial group differences are also evident in occupational status. The light-skinned Latino groups have achieved parity with whites in their proportional representation in the top jobs in the economy. Thus, the share of Argentines, Chileans, and Cubans in the top two occupational categories ("managers and professional related occupations" and "sales and office") is 55 percent or higher, a figure similar to whites' 59 percent (see table 6.5). In contrast, dark-skinned Latino groups such as Mexicans, Puerto Ricans, and Central Americans are concentrated in the four lower occupational categories.[13] Along the same lines, the Asian groups we classify as "honorary whites" are more likely to be well represented in the top occupational categories than those we classify as the "collective black." For instance, whereas 61 percent of Taiwanese and 56 percent of Asian Indians are in the top occupational category, only 15 percent of Hmong, 13 percent of Laotians, 17 percent of Cambodians, and 25 percent of Vietnamese are in that category (see table 6.6).[14]

SUBJECTIVE STANDING OF WHITES, HONORARY WHITES,
AND THE COLLECTIVE BLACK

Social psychologists have demonstrated that it takes very little for groups to form, to develop a common view, and to create status positions based on nominal characteristics (Tajfel 1970; Ridgeway 1991). Thus, it should not be surprising if

TABLE 6.3 EDUCATIONAL ATTAINMENT OF SELECTED LATINO ETHNIC GROUPS, 2000

Ethnic Groups (N)	Less Than High School Diploma	High School Diploma	Some College	College Degree	Advanced Degree
Mexicans (1,005,506)	71.21%	13.93%	9.19%	4.50%	1.16%
Puerto Ricans (153,838)	58.69	17.76	12.96	8.30	2.28
Cubans (58,538)	48.08	16.91	14.14	13.68	7.20
Guatemalans (18,765)	71.22	13.42	8.84	5.09	1.43
Salvadorans (33,391)	72.43	13.44	8.90	4.21	1.02
Costa Ricans (3,403)	44.43	18.63	18.31	13.99	4.64
Panamanians (4,414)	36.34	17.56	22.50	17.74	5.87
Argentines (4,857)	34.67	17.21	17.77	16.92	13.42
Chileans (3,375)	37.75	17.81	18.55	17.33	8.56
Bolivians (1,894)	36.43	19.48	20.01	17.42	6.65
Whites (11,018,124)	37.69	23.19	17.33	15.75	6.04
Blacks (1,649,132)	52.45	20.45	15.42	8.97	2.71

Source: 2000 Public Use Microdata Sample, 5 Percent Sample.

gaps in income, occupational status, and education contribute to group formation and consciousness. That is, honorary whites may classify themselves as "white" and believe they are different (better) than those in the collective black category. If this is happening, this group should also be in the process of developing whitelike racial attitudes befitting their new social position and also differentiating themselves from the collective black.

In line with our thesis, we also expect whites to make distinctions between honorary whites and the collective black by exhibiting a more positive outlook toward honorary whites than toward members of the collective black. Finally, if Latin Americanization is occurring, we speculate that the collective black

TABLE 6.4   EDUCATIONAL ATTAINMENT OF SELECTED ASIAN ETHNIC GROUPS, 2000

Ethnic Groups (N)	Less Than High School Diploma	High School Diploma	Some College	College Degree	Advanced Degree
Chinese (105,975)	39.29%	11.06%	11.25%	22.51%	15.89%
Japanese (37,765)	20.53	20.03	17.80	31.33	10.31
Koreans (48,992)	35.05	15.99	15.13	24.44	9.40
Asian Indians (73,500)	35.48	8.57	9.44	24.46	22.05
Filipinos (88,191)	33.16	12.70	18.19	30.77	5.18
Taiwanese (5,654)	25.65	9.13	12.43	28.26	24.53
Hmong (7,523)	79.42	9.08	7.01	4.07	0.43
Vietnamese (51,572)	53.19	14.29	14.06	15.32	3.13
Cambodians (8,435)	69.45	12.69	10.48	6.30	1.09
Laotians (7,811)	66.10	16.45	10.40	6.40	0.65
Whites (11,018,124)	37.69	23.19	17.33	15.75	6.04
Blacks (1,649,132)	52.45	20.45	15.42	8.97	2.71

Source: 2000 Public Use Microdata Sample, 5 Percent Sample.

should exhibit a diffused and contradictory racial consciousness similar to what occurs among blacks and Indians throughout Latin America and the Caribbean (Hanchard 1994). The following sections examine these possibilities.

SOCIAL IDENTITY OF HONORARY WHITES

Self-Reports on Race: Latinos   Historically, most Latinos have classified themselves as "white," but the proportion who do so varies tremendously by group. As table 6.7 shows, whereas 60 percent or more of the members of the Latino honorary white groups classify themselves as "white," about 50 percent—or

TABLE 6.5   OCCUPATIONAL STATUS OF SELECTED LATINO GROUPS, 2000

Ethnic Groups	Managers and Professional Related Occupations	Sales and Office	Services	Construction, Extraction, and Maintenance	Production, Transportation, and Materials Moving	Farming, Forestry, and Fishing
Mexicans	13.18%	20.62%	22.49%	14.41%	23.76%	5.54%
Puerto Ricans	21.14	29.46	21.40	8.34	19.01	0.66
Cubans	27.84	28.65	16.09	10.21	16.68	0.53
Guatemalans	9.49	16.13	29.73	14.59	27.55	2.51
Salvadorans	8.96	17.29	32.11	15.44	24.84	1.37
Costa Ricans	23.35	22.76	25.46	11.61	16.27	0.55
Panamanians	31.07	32.82	20.27	5.61	9.94	0.29
Argentines	39.77	24.68	14.84	9.24	10.96	0.51
Chileans	32.12	23.92	20.05	10.32	13.13	0.46
Bolivians	27.20	25.80	23.85	11.19	11.73	0.23
Whites	32.07	27.03	15.02	10.12	14.77	1.00
Blacks	21.48	26.48	23.96	7.57	19.84	0.65

Source: 2000 Public Use Microdata Sample, 5 Percent Sample.

TABLE 6.6 OCCUPATIONAL STATUS OF SELECTED ASIAN ETHNIC GROUPS, 2000

Ethnic Groups	Managers and Professional Related Occupations	Sales and Office	Services	Construction, Extraction, and Maintenance	Production, Transportation, and Materials Moving	Farming, Forestry, and Fishing
Chinese	47.79%	22.83%	15.04%	2.77%	11.42%	0.15%
Japanese	46.90	28.05	13.24	4.50	6.70	0.60
Koreans	36.51	31.26	15.65	3.97	12.38	0.23
Asian Indians	55.89	23.39	8.07	2.25	10.03	0.37
Filipinos	34.87	28.70	18.49	4.62	12.35	0.98
Taiwanese	60.95	24.78	8.44	1.34	4.43	0.06
Hmong	14.67	24.14	17.33	4.51	38.57	0.77
Vietnamese	25.21	19.92	19.64	6.02	28.50	0.71
Cambodians	16.66	25.37	17.26	5.45	34.67	0.59
Laotians	12.55	20.60	15.02	6.07	44.96	0.81
Whites	32.07	27.03	15.02	10.12	14.77	1.00
Blacks	21.48	26.48	23.96	7.57	19.84	0.65

Source: 2000 Public Use Microdata Sample, 5 Percent Sample.

TABLE 6.7   RACIAL SELF-CLASSIFICATION BY SELECTED LATIN AMERICA–
ORIGIN LATINO ETHNIC GROUPS, 2000

Ethnic Groups	White	Black	Other	Native American	Asian
Dominicans	28.21%	10.93%	59.21%	1.07%	0.57%
Salvadorans	41.01	0.82	56.95	0.81	0.41
Guatemalans	42.95	1.24	53.43	2.09	0.28
Hondurans	48.51	6.56	43.41	1.24	0.29
Mexicans	50.47	0.92	46.73	1.42	0.45
Puerto Ricans	52.42	7.32	38.85	0.64	0.77
Costa Ricans	64.83	5.91	28.18	0.56	0.53
Bolivians	65.52	0.32	32.79	1.32	0.05
Colombians	69.01	1.53	28.54	0.49	0.44
Venezuelans	75.89	2.58	20.56	0.36	0.60
Chileans	77.04	0.68	21.27	0.44	0.56
Cubans	88.26	4.02	7.26	0.17	0.29
Argentines	88.70	0.33	10.54	0.08	0.35

Source: 2000 Public Use Microdata Sample, 5 Percent Sample.

fewer—of the members of the groups we regard as belonging to the collective black do so. As a case in point, Mexicans, Dominicans, and Central Americans are very likely to report "other" as their preferred racial classification, while most Costa Ricans, Cubans, Chileans, and Argentines choose the "white" descriptor. The 2000 census data mirror the results of the 1988 Latino National Political Survey (de la Garza et al. 1992).[15]

"Racial" Distinctions Among Asians   Although on political matters Asians tend to vote pan-ethnically (Espiritu 1992), distinctions between native-born and foreign-born (for example, American-born Chinese and foreign-born Chinese) and between economically successful and unsuccessful Asians are developing. In fact, many analysts have argued that, given the tremendous diversity of experiences among Asian Americans, "all talk of Asian pan-ethnicity should now be abandoned as useless speculation" (San Juan 2000, 10). Leland Saito (1998) points out in *Race and Politics* that many Asians are fleeing the cities of immigration, disidentifying from new Asians, and invoking the image of the "good immigrant" as a way to escape the "Asian flack." In some communities this trend has led older, assimilated segments of a community to dissociate from recent migrants. For example, a Nisei returning to his community after years of overseas military service had this to say to his father: "Goddamn dad, where the hell did all these Chinese came from? Shit, this isn't even our town anymore" (Saito 1998, 59).

To be sure, Asian Americans have engaged in coalition politics and, in various locations, in concerted efforts to elect Asian American candidates (Saito 1998). However, we argue that it is also important to bear in mind that the group labeled "Asian Americans" is profoundly divided along many axes. We further suggest that many of those already existing divisions will be racialized by whites. As examples, there is the sexploitation of Asian women by lonely white men in the "Oriental bride" market (Kitano and Daniels 1995) and the intra-Asian preferences that follow a racialized hierarchy of desire (Tuan 1998).

RACIAL ATTITUDES OF VARIOUS RACIAL STRATA

Another way of assessing if Latin Americanization is taking place is examining the racial consciousness of the various racial strata to see if their views correspond to our predictions. In what follows, we attempt to assess the racial consciousness of Latinos, Asians, and whites with attitudinal data.

Latinos' Racial Attitudes   Although researchers have shown that Latinos tend to hold negative views of blacks and positive views of whites (Lambert and Taylor 1990; Mindiola, Rodríguez, and Niemann 1996; Niemann et al. 1994; Yoon 1995), the picture is more complex. For example, a study of Latinos in Houston, Texas, found differences between native-born and immigrant Latinos: 38 percent of native-born Latinos, compared to 47 percent of foreign-born Latinos, held negative stereotypes of blacks (Mindiola, Rodríguez, and Niemann 1996). This may explain why 63 percent of native-born Latinos versus 34 percent of foreign-born Latinos report frequent contact with blacks.

The incorporation of the majority of Latinos as "colonial subjects" (Puerto Ricans), refugees from wars (Central Americans), or illegal migrant workers (Mexicans) has foreshadowed subsequent patterns of integration into the racial order. In a similar vein, the incorporation of a minority of Latinos as "political refugees" (Cubans, Chileans, and Argentines) or as "neutral" immigrants trying to better their economic situation (Costa Rica, Colombia) has provided them with a more comfortable ride in America's racial boat (Pedraza 1985). Therefore, whereas the incorporation of most Latinos into the United States has meant becoming "nonwhite," for a few it has meant becoming "almost white."

Nevertheless, given that most Latinos experience discrimination in labor and housing markets as well as in schools, they quickly realize their nonwhite status. This leads them, as Nilda Flores-Gonzáles (1999) and Suzanne Oboler (1995) have shown, to adopt a plurality of identities that signify "otherness." Thus, dark-skinned Latinos are calling themselves "black," "Afro-Dominican" or "Afro-Puerto Rican" (Howard 2001). For example, José Ali, a Latino interviewed by Clara Rodríguez (2000, 56), stated: "By inheritance I am Hispanic. However, I identify more with blacks because to white America, if you are my

color, you are a nigger. I can't change my color, and I do not wish to do to."
When asked, "Why do you see yourself as black?" he said, "Because when I
was jumped by whites, I was not called 'spic,' but I was called a 'nigger.'"

The identification of most Latinos as racial "others" has led them to be more
pro-black than pro-white. Table 6.8, for example, indicates that the proportion
of Mexicans and Puerto Ricans who feel very warm toward blacks is much
higher than the proportion who feel very warm toward Asians. (The readings
in the "thermometer" range from 0 to 100, and the higher the "temperature,"
the more positive are the feelings toward the group in question.) In contrast,
the proportion of Cubans who feel very warm toward blacks is ten to fourteen
percentage points *lower* than their feelings toward Mexicans and Puerto Ricans.
Cubans are also more likely to feel very warm toward Asians than toward blacks.
More fitting with our thesis, table 6.9 shows that although Latinos who identify as white express similar empathy toward blacks and Asians, those who identify as black express the most positive affect toward blacks (about twenty degrees
warmer toward blacks than toward Asians).

Asians' Racial Attitudes Various studies have documented that Asians tend to
hold anti-black and anti-Latino attitudes. For instance, Lawrence Bobo and his
colleagues (1995) found that Chinese residents of Los Angeles expressed negative racial attitudes toward blacks. One Chinese resident stated, "Blacks in
general seem to be overly lazy," and another asserted, "Blacks have a definite
attitude problem" (Bobo et al. 1995, 78; see also Bobo and Johnson 2000).
Studies of Korean shopkeepers in various locales have found that over 70 percent of them hold anti-black attitudes (Weitzer 1997; Yoon 1997; Min 1996).

TABLE 6.8   PROPORTION OF LATINOS WHO EXPRESS HIGH AFFECT TOWARD
            BLACKS AND ASIANS

Degrees of Feeling Thermometer	Toward Blacks	Toward Asians
Mexicans' feelings		
51–74 (less positive)	11.9	11.8
75–100 (more positive)	34.3	22.2
Puerto Ricans' feelings		
51–74 (less positive)	11.8	9.0
75–100 (more positive)	39.5	25.3
Cubans' feelings		
51–74 (less positive)	14.5	9.9
75–100 (more positive)	25.1	29.9

Source: Forman, Martínez, and Bonilla-Silva (forthcoming).

TABLE 6.9   LATINOS' AFFECT TOWARD BLACKS AND ASIANS, BY
LATINO ETHNICITY AND RACIAL SELF-CLASSIFICATION

	Toward Blacks	Toward Asians
Latino ethnicity		
Mexicans	60.07	52.88
Puerto Ricans	60.24	50.81
Cubans	56.36	56.99
Racial self-classification		
White	57.71	53.49
Black	69.62	48.83
Latino self-referent	61.01	53.10

Source: Forman, Martínez, and Bonilla-Silva (forthcoming).
Note: See table 6.8 for "degrees of feeling."

These general findings are confirmed in table 6.10, which contains data on the degree (in a scale running from 1 to 7) to which various racial groups subscribe to stereotypes about the intelligence and welfare dependency of other groups. The table clearly shows that Asians (in this study, Koreans, Chinese, and Japanese) are more likely than even whites to hold anti-black and anti-Latino views. For example, whereas whites score 3.79 and 3.96 for blacks and Latinos, Asians score 4.39 and 4.46. Asians also hold, comparatively speaking, more positive views about whites than about Latinos and blacks (for a more thorough analysis, see Bobo and Johnson 2000). Thus, as in many Latin American and Caribbean societies, members of the intermediate racial stratum buffer racial matters by holding more pro-white attitudes than do whites themselves.

The Collective Black and Whites' Racial Attitudes   After a protracted conflict over the meaning of whites' racial attitudes (for a discussion, see Bonilla-Silva and Lewis 1999), survey researchers seem to have reached an agreement: "A hierarchical racial order continues to shape all aspects of American life" (Dawson 2000, 344). Whites express and defend their social position on issues such as affirmative action and reparations, school integration and busing, neighborhood integration, welfare reform, and even the death penalty (see Sears, Sidanius, and Bobo 2000; Tuch and Martin 1997; Bonilla-Silva 2001). Regarding how whites think about Latinos and Asians, not many researchers have separated the groups that make up "Latinos" and "Asians" to assess whether whites make distinctions among them. However, the available evidence suggests that whites hold Asians in high regard but are significantly less likely to hold Latinos in high regard (Bobo and Johnson 2000). Thus, when judged on a host of racial stereotypes, whites rate themselves and Asians almost identically (and positively) but negatively rate both blacks and Latinos (at about the same level).

TABLE 6.10   RELATIONSHIP BETWEEN RACE–ETHNICITY AND RACIAL
STEREOTYPES OF INTELLIGENCE AND WELFARE DEPENDENCY OF
BLACKS, LATINOS, ASIANS, AND WHITES IN LOS ANGELES,
1993 TO 1994

| Group | Group Stereotyped | | | |
Stereotyping	Blacks	Latinos	Asians	Whites
Unintelligent?				
White	3.79***	3.96***	2.90***	3.09***
Asians	4.39***	4.46***	2.90***	3.25***
Latinos	3.93***	3.57***	2.74***	2.87***
Blacks	3.31***	3.96***	3.21***	3.32***
Prefer Welfare?				
White	4.22***	4.08***	2.30***	2.48***
Asians	5.10***	5.08***	2.52***	2.93***
Latinos	5.57***	4.49***	2.77***	2.77***
Blacks	4.12***	4.29***	2.67***	2.77***

Source: Los Angeles Study of Urban Inequality, 1993 to 1994.
*** $p < .001$.

Lawrence Bobo and Devon Johnson (2000) also show that Latinos tend to rate blacks negatively and that blacks tend to do the same regarding Latinos. They also found that Latinos, irrespective of national ancestry, self-rate lower than whites and Asians. (Blacks, however, self-rate at the same level as whites, and higher than Asians.) This pattern seems to confirm Latin Americanization: those at the bottom in Latin America tend to have a diffused racial consciousness. Our contention seems further bolstered by the finding that "blacks give themselves ratings that tilt in an unfavorable dimension on the traits of welfare dependency and involvement with gangs" and that "for Latinos, three of the dimensions [involvement with drugs, poor English ability, and welfare dependency] tilt in the direction of negative in-group ratings" (Bobo and Johnson 2000, 103).

SOCIAL INTERACTION AMONG MEMBERS OF THE
THREE RACIAL STRATA

If Latin Americanization is happening in the United States, we would expect to see more social contact (such as friendships and associations as neighbors) and intimate contact (marriage, for instance) between whites and honorary whites than between whites and members of the collective black. A cursory analysis of the data support this expectation.

Interracial Marriage   Although most marriages in America are still intraracial, the rates vary substantially by group. Whereas 93 percent of whites and blacks marry within-group, 70 percent of Latinos and Asians do so, and only 33 percent of Native Americans marry other Native Americans (Moran 2001, 103). More significantly, when we disentangle the generic terms "Asian" and "Latino," the data fit even more closely the Latin Americanization thesis. For example, among Latinos, Cubans, Mexicans, Central Americans, and South Americans have higher rates of out-marriage than Puerto Ricans and Dominicans (Gilbertson, Fitzpatrick, and Yang 1996). Although interpreting the Asian American out-marriage pattern is very complex (groups such as Filipinos and Vietnamese have higher than expected rates owing in part to the Vietnam War and the military bases in the Philippines), it is worth pointing out that the highest rate belongs to Japanese Americans and Chinese (Kitano and Daniels 1995) and the lowest to Southeast Asians.

Furthermore, racial assimilation through marriage ("whitening") is significantly more likely for the children of Asian-white and Latino-white unions than for those of black-white unions, a fact that bolsters our Latin Americanization thesis. Hence, whereas only 22 percent of the children of black fathers and white mothers are classified as white, the children of similar unions among Asians are twice as likely to be classified as white (Waters 1999). For Latinos, the data fit the thesis even more closely: Latinos of Cuban, Mexican, and South American origin have high rates of exogamy compared to Puerto Ricans and Dominicans (Gilbertson et al. 1996). We concur with Rachel Moran's (2001) speculation that the high percentage of dark-skinned Puerto Ricans and Dominicans (see table 6.7) results in restricted chances for out-marriage to whites in a highly racialized marriage market.

Residential Segregation Among Racial Strata   An imperfect measure of interracial interaction is the level of neighborhood "integration" (for some of the limitations of this index, see Bonilla-Silva and Baiocchi 2001). Nevertheless, the various segregation indices devised by demographers allow us to gauge in general terms the level of interracial contact in various cities. In this section, we focus on the segregation of Latinos and Asians, since the extreme segregation of blacks is well known (Massey and Denton 1993; Yinger 1995).

Latinos are less segregated from and more exposed to whites than blacks (Massey and Denton 1987; Charles 2003). Yet it is also true that dark-skinned Latinos experience blacklike rates of residential segregation from whites. Early research on Latino immigrant settlement patterns in Chicago, for example, showed that Mexicans and Puerto Ricans were relegated to spaces largely occupied by blacks, in part because of skin color discrimination (Betancur 1996). More contemporary studies also demonstrate the race effect on Latino residential segregation patterns. Latinos who identify as white, primarily Cubans and South Americans, are considerably more likely to reside in areas with non-Latino whites than are Latinos who identify as black, mainly Dominicans and Puerto Ricans (Logan 2001; Alba and Logan 1993; Massey and Bitterman 1985).

Asian Americans are the least segregated of all the minority groups. However, they have experienced an increase in residential segregation in recent years (Frey and Farley 1996; White, Biddlecom, and Guo 1993). In a recent review, Camille Charles (2003) finds that from 1980 to 2000 the index of dissimilarity for Asians had increased three points (from 37 to 40) while the exposure to whites had declined sixteen points (from 88 to 62).[16] Part of the increase in segregation (and the concomitant decrease in exposure) may be the result of the arrival of newer immigrants from Southeast Asia (Vietnam, Cambodia, and Laos) over the last two decades (Frey and Farley 1996). For example, the Vietnamese—who, we theorize, will be considered part of the collective black during the Latin Americanization process—have almost doubled their U.S. presence during the 1990 to 2000 period (Logan 2001). The majority of residential segregation studies are based on black-Latino-Asian proximity to whites and thus limit an examination of intragroup differences among Asians (and Latinos). Nevertheless, the totality of the lower dissimilarity indexes and higher exposure indexes for Asians to whites vis-à-vis Latinos—and particularly blacks—to whites tends to fit our prediction that the bulk of Asians belong to the honorary white category. Phenotype research on blacks, Latinos, and Asians, based on subgroup research within each category, is needed in order for studies on the effect of skin color to fully develop.

CONCLUSION

We have presented a broad and bold thesis about the future of racial stratification in the United States.[17] However, at this early stage of the analysis, and given the serious limitations of the data on "Latinos" and "Asians" (the data are not generally parceled out by subgroups and little is separated by skin tone), it is hard to make a conclusive case. It is possible that factors such as nativity or socioeconomic characteristics explain some of the patterns we documented.[18] Nevertheless, almost all of the objective, subjective, and social interaction indicators we reviewed go in the direction of Latin Americanization. For example, the objective data clearly show substantial gaps between the groups we labeled "white," "honorary white," and "collective black." In terms of income and education, whites tend to be slightly better off than honorary whites, who are in turn significantly better off than the collective black. Not surprisingly, a variety of subjective indicators signal the emergence of *internal* stratification among racial minorities. For example, whereas some Latinos (such as Cubans, Argentines, and Chileans) are very likely to self-classify as whites, others do not (for example, Dominicans and Puerto Ricans living in the United States). This has resulted in a racial attitudinal profile—at least in terms of subscription to stereotypical views about groups—similar to that of whites. Finally, the objective and subjective indicators have a behavioral correlate. Data on interracial marriage and residential segregation show that whites are significantly more likely to live near and intermarry with honorary whites than with members of the collective black.

If our predictions are right, what will be the consequences of Latin Americanization for race relations in the United States? First, racial politics will change dramatically. The "us-versus-them" racial dynamic will lessen as honorary whites grow in size and social importance. They are likely to buffer racial conflict—or derail it—as intermediate groups do in many Latin American countries. Second, the ideology of color-blind racism will become even more salient among whites and honorary whites and will also have an impact on members of the collective black. Color-blind racism (Bonilla-Silva 2001), similar to the ideology prevalent in Latin American societies, will help glue the new social system and further buffer racial conflict.

Third, if the state decides to stop gathering racial statistics, the struggle to document the impact of race in a variety of social venues will become monumental. More significantly, because state actions always have an impact on civil society, if the state decides to erase race from above, the *social* recognition of "races" in the polity may become harder. We may develop a Latin American–like "disgust" for even mentioning anything that is race-related.

Fourth, the deep history of black-white divisions in the United States has been such that the centrality of the black identity will not dissipate. Even the research on the "black elite" shows that this group exhibits racial attitudes in line with their racial group (Dawson 1994). That identity, as we argue in this chapter, may be taken up by dark-skinned Latinos, as it is being rapidly taken up by most West Indians. For example, Al, a fifty-three-year-old Jamaican engineer interviewed by Milton Vickerman (1999, 199), stated:

I have nothing against Haitians; I have nothing against black Americans. . . . If you're a nigger, you're a nigger, regardless of whether you are from Timbuktu. . . . There isn't the unity that one would like to see. . . . Blacks have to appreciate blacks, no matter where they are from. Just look at it the way I look at it: That you're the same.

However, even among blacks, we predict some important changes. Namely, blacks' racial consciousness will become more diffused. For example, blacks will be more likely to accept many stereotypes about themselves (for example, "We are lazier than whites") and to have a "blunted oppositional consciousness" (see Bonilla-Silva 2001, ch. 6). Furthermore, the external pressure of "multiracials" in white contexts (Rockquemore and Brunsma 2002) and the internal pressure of "ethnic" blacks may change the notion of "blackness" and even the position of some "blacks" in the system. Colorism may become an even more important factor as a way of making social distinctions among "blacks" (Keith and Herring 1991).

Fifth, the new racial stratification system will be more effective in maintaining "white supremacy" (Mills 1997). Whites will still be at the top of the social structure but will face fewer race-based challenges. As an aside, to avoid confusion about our claim about "honorary whites," it is important to note that their standing and status will be subject to whites' wishes and practices. "Honorary" means that they will remain secondary, will still face discrimination, and will not receive equal treatment in society. For example, although Arab Americans should be regarded as honorary whites, their treatment in the post–September 11 era suggests that their status as "white" and "American" is very tenuous.

Although some analysts and commentators may welcome Latin Americanization as a positive trend in American race relations, those at the bottom of the racial hierarchy will discover that behind the statement, "We are all Americans," hides a deeper, hegemonic way of maintaining white supremacy. As a Latin America–*like* society, the United States will become a society with more rather than less racial inequality, but with a reduced forum for racial contestation.[19] The apparent blessing of "not seeing race" will become a curse for those struggling for racial justice in the years to come. We may become "all Americans," as television commercials in recent times suggest. But to paraphrase George Orwell, "some will be more American than others."

NOTES

1. Since September 11, 2001, the United States has embarked on what we regard as temporary "social peace." Hence, in post–September 11 America the motto "We are all Americans" is commonplace. This new attitude can be seen in pronouncements by politicians and television commercials parading the multiracial nature of the country. Notably, however, there are no commercials presenting interracial unions, which suggests that we may all be Americans, but we still have our own subnational or primary racial associations. Moreover, this new attitude has not changed the status differences between minorities and whites, between men and women, or between workers and capitalists. Lastly, this new nationalism excludes "foreigners," dark people, those who are not Christian, and those with unfashionable accents (German and French accents are acceptable). In short, this new Americanism, like the old Americanism, is a *herrenvolk* nationalism (Lipsitz 1998; Winant 1994).

2. To be clear, our contention is not that the black-white dynamic has ordained race relations throughout the United States, but that at the national macro level, race relations have been organized along a white-nonwhite divide. This large divide, depending on context, has included various racial

groups (whites, blacks, and Indians or whites, Mexicans, Indians, and blacks or other combinations). However, under the white-nonwhite racial order, "whites" have often been treated as superior and "nonwhites" as inferior. For a few exceptions to this pattern, see Reginald Daniels's (2002) discussion of "tri-racial isolates."

3. We are adapting Antonio Negri's (1984) idea of the "collective worker" to the situation of all those at the bottom of the racial stratification system.

4. Kerry Ann Rockquemore and Patricia Arend (forthcoming) have predicted, based on data from a mixed-race (one black parent and one white parent) student sample, that most mixed-race people will be honorary whites, a significant component will belong to the collective black, and a few will move into the white strata.

5. A middle racial stratum emerged in the United States in South Carolina and Louisiana and in eighteenth- and nineteenth-century South Africa (Fredrickson 1981). However, in both cases the status of the intermediate stratum later changed because of political necessities (South Africa) or because it was a peculiar situation that could not affect the larger, national pattern (United States). In South Africa the "colored" group was reintroduced at a later point, and in South Carolina and Louisiana those in the intermediate stratum to this day maintain a sense of *difference* from their black brethren.

6. This challenges the romantic view that Latin American states and societies were more pluralist than Great Britain or France because of their Catholic religion or their supposedly less prejudicial attitudes toward Africans; see Marx (1998) and Morner (1993).

7. Few Latin Americans object to the fact that most politicians in their societies are "white" (by Latin American standards). Yet it is interesting to point out that Latin American elites always object to the few "minority" politicians on *racial* grounds. Two recent cases are the racist opposition in the Dominican Republic to the election of the black candidate José Peña Gómez (Howard 2001) and the opposition by the business elite to the mulatto president Hugo Cesar Chávez in Venezuela.

8. At the core of this ideology is the presentation of the black and Indian in Latin America as "folklore" and as "exotic" (Radcliffe and Westwood 1996). For example, the "indigenista" cult has glorified the past and separated it from present-day indigenous groups. For indigenistas, the Indian question was a matter "of exotic and romantic symbolism, based more on the glorification of the pre-Columbian Indian ancestry of the nation than on respect for the contemporary Indian population" (Wade 1997, 32). For a list of Vasconcelos-like Latin American intellectuals in the early twentieth century, see de la Cadena (2000).

9. When pushed to choose a racial descriptor, many Latin Americans self-describe as white or highlight their white heritage, regardless of how remote or minimal it is. For example, according to a recent study in a community in Brazil, one-third of the Afro-Brazilians were registered as whites, and a large proportion of the remainder were registered as pardos (Twine 1998, 114). For a similar discussion on Puerto Ricans, see Torres (1998).

10. Sarah Chambers (2003) discusses how mestizos in eighteenth- and nineteenth-century Arequipa, Peru, had to adopt an ideology of whitening to gain resources or avoid paying taxes. For example, they occasionally claimed Indianness to get access to land. Thus, their agency was at best a bounded agency, since they could not challenge white supremacy.

11. However, as discussed in a previous section, phenotype in Latin America can be "lightened" (or "darkened") by nonphenotypical characteristics such as education, language, culture, class, and occupational background. Thus, for example, although Asian Indians are quite dark, they are likely to be viewed as honorary whites because of their mastery of the English language, high level of education, and other factors.

12. Specifically, whereas the Bolivian census of 2001 reports that 71 percent of Bolivians self-identify as Indian, fewer than 20 percent have more than a high school diploma, and 58.6 percent live below the poverty line. By contrast, 66 percent of Bolivians in the United States self-identify as white, 64 percent have twelve or more years of education, and they enjoy a per capita income comparable to that of whites (Censo Nacional de Población y Vivienda 2002). In short, Bolivians in the United States do not represent Bolivians in Bolivia. Instead, they are a self-selected group.

13. The concentration of Puerto Ricans in the lower occupational categories is slightly below 50 percent. However, looking specifically at the category "sales and office," where 20.46 percent of Puerto Ricans are located, Puerto Ricans are more likely to be in the lower-paying jobs within this broad category.

14. It is important to point out that occupational representation in a category does not mean equality. The work of Sucheng Chan (1991) shows that many Asians are pushed into self-employment after suffering occupational sedimentation in professional jobs; see also Takaki (1993).

15. Survey experiments have shown that if the question on Hispanic origin is asked first, the proportion of Latinos who report being white increases from 25 to 39 percent (Martin, Demaio, and Campanelli 1990). The same research also shows that when Latinos report belonging to the "other" category, they are not mistaken. That is, they do want to signify that they are neither black nor white. Unfortunately, we do not have results by national

groups. Are Cubans more likely to claim to be white if the order of the questions is changed? Or is the finding symmetrical for all groups? However these questions may be answered, we think this finding does not alter the direction of the overall findings on the self-identification of various Latino groups.

16. The dissimilarity index expresses the percentage of a minority population that would have to move to result in a perfectly even distribution of the population across census tracts. This index runs from 0 (no segregation) to 100 (total segregation), and it is symmetrical (not affected by population size). The exposure index measures the degree of potential contact between two populations (majority and minority) and expresses the probability of a member of a minority group meeting a member of the majority group. Like the dissimilarity index, it runs from 1 to 100, but unlike that index, it is asymmetrical (it is affected by the population size).

17. We are not alone in making this kind of prediction. Arthur K. Spears (1999), Suzanne Oboler (2000), Gary Okihiro (1994), and Mari Matsuda (1996) have made similar claims recently.

18. An important matter to disentangle empirically is whether it is color, nativity, education, or class that determines where groups fit in our scheme. A powerful alternative explanation for many of our preliminary findings is that the groups we label "honorary whites" come with high levels of human capital *before* they achieve honorary white status in the United States. That is, they fit this intermediate position not because of their color or race but because of their class background. Although this is a plausible alternative explanation that we hope to examine in the future, some available data suggest that race-color has something to do with the success of immigrants in the United States. For example, the experience of West Indians—who come to the United States with class advantages (educational and otherwise) and yet "fade to black" in a few generations— suggests that the "racial" status of the group has an independent effect in the process (Model 1991; Kasinitz, Battle, and Miyares 2001). It is also important to point out that even when some of these groups do well objectively, an examination of their returns to their characteristics, such as the monetary "return" on their education investment, when compared to whites, reveals how little they get for what they bring (Butcher 1994). And as Mary Waters and Karl Eschbach (1995, 442) stated in a review of the literature on immigration, "the evidence indicates that direct discrimination is still an important factor for all minority subgroups except very highly educated Asians." Even highly educated and acculturated Asians, such as Filipinos, report high levels of racial discrimination in the labor market. Not surprisingly, second- and third-generation Filipinos self-identity as Filipino American rather than as white or "American"

(Espiritu and Wolf 2001). For a similar finding on Vietnamese, see Zhou (2001), and for a discussion of the indeterminate relation between education and income among many other groups, see Portes and Rumbaut (1990).

19. "Latin America–like" does not mean exactly "like Latin America." The four-hundred-year history of American "racial formation" (Omi and Winant 1994) has stained the racial stratification order forever. Thus, we expect some important differences in this new American racial stratification system compared to that of Latin American societies. First, "shade discrimination" (Kinsbrunner 1996) will not work perfectly. Hence, for example, although Asian Indians are dark-skinned, they will still be higher in the stratification system than, for example, Mexican American mestizos. Second, Arabs, Asian Indians, and other non-Christian groups will not be allowed complete upward mobility. Third, because of the three hundred years of dramatic racialization and group formation, most members of the nonwhite group will maintain ethnic (Puerto Ricans) or racial (blacks) claims and demand group-based rights.

References

Alba, Richard D., and John R. Logan. 1993. "Minority Proximity to Whites in Suburbs: An Individual-Level Analysis of Segregation." *American Journal of Sociology* 98(6): 1388–1427.

Andrews, George R. 1991. *Blacks and Whites in São Paulo, Brazil, 1888–1988.* Madison: University of Wisconsin Press.

Balibar, Etienne, and Immanuel Wallerstein. 1991. *Race, Nation, and Class: Ambiguous Identities.* London: Verso.

Betancur, John J. 1996. "The Settlement Experience of Latinos in Chicago: Segregation, Speculation, and the Ecology Model." *Social Forces* 74(4): 1299–1324.

Bobo, Lawrence, and Devon Johnson. 2000. "Racial Attitudes in a Prismatic Metropolis: Mapping Identity, Stereotypes, Competition, and Views on Affirmative Action." In *Prismatic Metropolis,* edited by Lawrence Bobo, Melvin Oliver, James Johnson Jr., and Abel Valenzuela Jr. New York: Russell Sage Foundation.

Bobo, Lawrence, Camille Zubrinksy, James Johnson Jr., and Melvin Oliver. 1995. "Work Orientation, Job Discrimination, and Ethnicity." *Research in the Sociology of Work* 5: 45–85.

Bonilla-Silva, Eduardo. 1997. "Rethinking Racism: Toward a Structural Interpretation." *American Sociological Review* 62(3): 465–80.

———. 1999. "The Essential Social Fact of Race: A Reply to Loveman." *American Sociological Review* 64(6): 899–906.

————. 2000. "This Is a White Country": The Racial Ideology of the Western Nations of the World-System." *Sociological Inquiry* 70(3): 188–214.

————. 2001. *White Supremacy and Racism in the Post–Civil Rights Era.* Boulder, Colo.: Lynne Rienner.

Bonilla-Silva, Eduardo, and Gianpaolo Baiocchi. 2001. "Anything but Racism: How Sociologists Limit the Significance of Racism." *Race and Society* 4(2001): 117–31.

Bonilla-Silva, Eduardo, and Amanda E. Lewis. 1999. "The New Racism: Toward an Analysis of the U.S. Racial Structure, 1960s to 1990s." In *Race, Nation, and Citizenship,* edited by Paul Wong. Boulder, Colo.: Westview Press.

Bottomore, Thomas B. 1968. *Classes in Modern Society.* New York: Vintage Books.

Brooks, Roy L. 1990. *Rethinking the American Race Problem.* Berkeley: University of California Press.

Butcher, Kristin F. 1994. "Black Immigrants in the United States: A Comparison with Native Blacks and Other Immigrants." *Industrial and Labor Relations Review* 47: 265–84.

Castles, Stephen, and Mark Miller. 1993. *The Age of Migration: International Population Movements in the Modern World.* Hong Kong: Macmillan.

Censo Nacional de Población y Vivienda. 2002. *Bolivia: Caraterísticas de la Población.* Serie Resultados, vol. 4. La Paz: Ministerio de Hacienda.

Chambers, Sarah C. 2003. "Little Middle Ground: The Instability of a Mestizo Identity in the Andes, Eighteenth and Nineteenth Centuries." In *Race and Nation in Modern Latin America,* edited by Nancy P. Applebaum et al. Chapel Hill: University of North Carolina Press.

Chan, Sucheng. 1991. *Asian Americans: An Interpretive History.* Boston: Twayne.

Charles, Camille Zubrinsky. 2003. "The Dynamics of Racial Residential Segregation." *Annual Review of Sociology* 29: 167–207.

Cohen, Robin. 1997. *Global Diasporas: An Introduction.* Seattle: University of Washington Press.

Daniels, Reginald G. 2002. *More Than Black? Multiracial Identity and the New Racial Order.* Philadelphia: Temple University Press.

Dawson, Michael C. 1994. *Behind the Mule: Race and Class in African American Politics.* Princeton, N.J.: Princeton University Press.

————. 2000. "Slowly Coming to Grips with the Effects of the American Racial Order on American Policy Preferences." In *Racialized Politics,* edited by David O. Sears, Jim Sidanius, and Lawrence Bobo. Chicago: University of Chicago Press.

Degler, Carl N. 1986. *Neither Black nor White: Slavery and Race Relations in Brazil and the United States.* Madison: University of Wisconsin Press.

De la Cadena, Marisol. 2000. *Indigenous Mestizos: The Politics of Race and Culture in Cuzco, Peru, 1919–1991.* Durham, N.C.: Duke University Press.

De la Fuente, Alejandro. 1998. "Race, National Discourse, and Politics in Cuba: An Overview." *Latin American Perspectives* 25(3): 43–69.

———. 2001. *A Nation for All: Race Inequality, and Politics in Twentieth-Century Cuba.* Chapel Hill: University of North Carolina Press.

De la Garza, Rodolfo O., Louis DeSipio, F. Chris Garcia, John Garcia, and Angelo Falcon, eds. 1992. *Latino Voices: Mexican, Puerto Rican, and Cuban Perspectives on American Politics.* Boulder, Colo.: Westview Press.

Do Nascimento, Abdias, and Elisa Larkin-Nascimento. 2001. "Dance of Deception: A Reading of Race Relations in Brazil." In *Beyond Racism,* edited by Charles Hamilton et al. Boulder: Lynne Rienner.

Espiritu, Yen Le. 1992. *Asian American Pan-ethnicity: Bridging Institutions and Identities.* Philadelphia: Temple University Press.

Espiritu, Yen Le, and Diane L. Wolf. 2001. "The Paradox of Assimilation: Children of Filipino Immigrants in San Diego." In *Ethnicities: Children of Immigrants in America,* edited by Rubén G. Rumbaut and Alejandro Portes. Berkeley: University of California Press.

Fitzpatrick, Joseph. 1971. *Puerto Rican Americans.* Englewood Cliffs, N.J.: Prentice-Hall.

Flores-Gonzáles, Nilda. 1999. "The Racialization of Latinos: The Meaning of Latino Identity for the Second Generation." *Latino Studies Journal* 10(3): 3–31.

Forman, Tyrone A., Gloria Martínez, and Eduardo Bonilla-Silva. Forthcoming. "Latinos' Perceptions of Blacks and Asians: Testing the Immigrant Hypothesis." Unpublished manuscript.

Fredrickson, George M. 1981. *White Supremacy.* Oxford: Oxford University Press.

Frey, William H., and Reynolds Farley. 1996. "Latino, Asian, and Black Segregation in U.S. Metropolitan Areas: Are Multi-ethnic Metros Different?" *Demography* 33(1): 35–50.

Freyre, Gilberto. 1959. *New World in the Tropics: The Culture of Modern Brazil.* New York: Alfred A. Knopf.

Gans, Herbert J. 1999. *The Possibility of a New Racial Hierarchy in the Twenty-first-Century United States,* edited by Michele Lamont. Chicago: University of Chicago Press.

Gilbertson, Greta A., Joseph P. Fitzpatrick, and Lijun Yang. 1996. "Hispanic Intermarriage in New York City: New Evidence from 1991." *International Migration Review* 30(2): 445–59.

Goldberg, David T. 1993. *Racist Culture: Philosophy and the Politics of Meaning.* Cambridge, Mass.: Blackwell.

———. 2002. *The Racial State.* Malden, Mass.: Blackwell.

Grieco, Elizabeth M., and Rachel C. Cassidy. 2001. *Overview of Race and Hispanic Origin 2000.* Washington: U.S. Government Printing Office.

Guerra, Lillian. 1998. *Popular Expression and National Identity in Puerto Rico: The Struggle for Self, Community, and Nation.* Gainesville: University Press of Florida.

Hanchard, Michael. 1994. *Orpheus and Power: The Movimiento Negro of Rio de Janeiro and São Paulo, Brazil, 1945–1988.* Princeton, N.J.: Princeton University Press.

Hasenbalg, Carlos A. 1985. "Race and Socioeconomic Inequalities in Brazil." In *Race, Class, and Power in Brazil,* edited by Pierre-Michel Fontaine. Los Angeles: University of California Press and Center for African American Studies.

Hasenbalg, Carlos A., and Nelson do Valle Silva. 1999. "Notes on Racial and Political Inequality in Brazil." In *Racial Politics in Contemporary Brazil,* edited by Michael George Hanchard. Durham, N.C.: Duke University Press.

Helg, Aline. 1990. "Race in Argentina and Cuba, 1880–1930: Theory, Policies, and Popular Reaction." In *The Idea of Race in Latin America, 1870–1940,* edited by Richard Graham. Austin: University of Texas Press.

Hoetink, Harry. 1967. *The Two Variants in Caribbean Race Relations: A Contribution to the Sociology of Segmented Societies.* Oxford: Oxford University Press.

———. 1971. *Caribbean Race Relations: A Study of Two Variants.* London: Oxford University Press.

Howard, David. 2001. *Coloring the Nation: Race and Ethnicity in the Dominican Republic.* Boulder, Colo.: Lynne Rienner.

Kasinitz, Philip, Juan Battle, and Ines Miyares. 2001. "Fade to Black? The Children of West Indian Immigrants in Southern Florida." In *Ethnicities: Children of Immigrants in America,* edited by Rubén G. Rumbaut and Alejandro Portes. Berkeley: University of California Press.

Kasper, Deana. 2000. " 'Y tu abuela donde está' (And your grandmother, where is she?)." Ph.D. diss., Texas A&M University.

Keith, Verna M., and Cedric Herring. 1991. "Skin Tone and Stratification in the Black Community." *American Journal of Sociology* 97(3): 760–78.

Kinsbrunner, Jay. 1996. *Not of Pure Blood: The Free People of Color and Racial Prejudice in Nineteenth-Century Puerto Rico.* Durham, N.C.: Duke University Press.

Kitano, Harry H. L., and Roger Daniels. 1995. *Asian Americans: Emerging Minorities,* 2nd ed. Englewood Cliffs, N.J.: Prentice-Hall.

Lambert, Wallace, and Donald Taylor. 1990. *Coping with Cultural and Racial Diversity in Urban America.* Westport, Conn.: Praeger.

Lipsitz, George. 1998. *The Possessive Investment in Whiteness: How White People Profit from Identity Politics.* Philadelphia: Temple University Press.

Logan, John R. 2001. *From Many Shores: Asians in Census 2000.* Report by the Lewis Mumford Center for Comparative Urban and Regional Research. Albany, N.Y.: University of Albany.

Lovell, Peggy A., and Charles H. Wood. 1998. "Skin Color, Racial Identity, and Life Chances in Brazil." *Latin American Perspectives* 25(3): 90–109.

Lusane, Clarence. 1997. *Race in the Global Era: African Americans at the Millennium.* Boston: South End Press.

Martin, Elizabeth, Theresa J. Demaio, and Pamela C. Campanelli. 1990. "Context Effects for Census Measures of Race and Hispanic Origin." *Public Opinion Quarterly* 54(4): 551–66.

Martínez-Alier, Verena. 1974. *Marriage, Class and Color in Nineteenth-Century Cuba: A Study of Racial Attitudes and Sexual Values in a Slave Society.* London: Cambridge University Press.

Martínez-Echazabal, Lourdes. 1998. "Mestizaje and the Discourse of National/ Cultural Identity in Latin America, 1845–1959." *Latin American Perspectives* 25(3): 21–42.

Marx, Anthony W. 1998. *Making Race and Nation.* Cambridge: Cambridge University Press.

Massey, Douglas S., and Brooks Bitterman. 1985. "Explaining the Paradox of Puerto Rican Segregation." *Social Forces* 64(2): 306–31.

Massey, Douglas S., and Nancy A. Denton. 1987. "Trends in the Residential Segregation of Blacks, Hispanics, and Asians: 1970–1980." *American Sociological Review* 52(6): 802–25.

———. 1993. *American Apartheid.* Cambridge, Mass.: Harvard University Press.

Matsuda, Mari J. 1996. *Where Is Your Body? and Other Essays on Race, Gender, and the Law.* Boston: Beacon Press.

Miles, Robert. 1993. *Racism After Race Relations.* London: Routledge.

Mills, Charles W. 1997. *The Racial Contract.* Ithaca, N.Y.: Cornell University Press.

Min, Pyong Gap. 1996. *Caught in the Middle: Korean Communities in New York and Los Angeles.* Berkeley, Calif.: University of California Press.

Mindiola, Tatcho, Nestor Rodríguez, and Yolanda Flores Niemann. 1996. *Intergroup Relations Between Hispanics and Blacks in Harris County.* Houston: University of Houston, Center for Mexican American Studies.

Model, Suzanne. 1991. "Caribbean Immigrants: A Black Success Story?" *International Migration Review* 25(2): 248–76.

Moran, Rachel. 2001. *Interracial Intimacy: The Regulation of Race and Romance.* Chicago: University of Chicago Press.

Morner, Magnus. 1967. *Race Mixture in the History of Latin America.* Boston: Little, Brown.

———. 1993. *Region and State in Latin America.* Baltimore: Johns Hopkins University Press.

Negri, Antonio. 1984. *Marx Beyond Marx: Lessons on the Grundrisse*, edited by Jim Fleming. South Hadley, Mass.: Bergin & Garvey.

Negrón-Muntaner, Frances. 1997. "English Only Jamas but Spanish Only Cuidado: Language and Nationalism in Contemporary Puerto Rico." In *Puerto Rico Jam: Essays on Culture and Politics*, edited by Frances Negrón-Muntaner and Ramón Grosfoguel. Minneapolis: University of Minnesota Press.

Niemann, Yolanda, Leilani Jennings, Richard Rozelle, James Baxter, and Elroy Sullivan. 1994. "Use of Free Response and Cluster Analysis to Determine Stereotypes of Eight Groups." *Personality and Social Psychology Bulletin* 20(4): 379–90.

Oboler, Suzanne. 1995. *Ethnic Labels, Latino Lives: Identity and the Politics of (Re)Presentation in the United States*. Minneapolis: University of Minnesota Press.

———. 2000. "It Must Be a Fake!" Racial Ideologies, Identities, and the Question of Rights in Hispanics-Latinos." In *The United States: Ethnicity, Race, and Rights*, edited by Jorge J. E. Gracia and Pablo de Greiff. New York: Routledge.

Okihiro, Gary. 1994. *Margins and Mainstreams: Asians in American History and Culture*. Seattle: University of Washington Press.

Omi, Michael, and Howard Winant. 1994. *Racial Formation in the United States from the 1960s to the 1990s*. New York: Routledge.

Pedraza, Silvia. 1985. *Political and Economic Migrants in America: Cubans and Mexicans*. Austin: University of Texas Press.

Portes, Alejandro, and Rubén Rumbaut. 1990. *Immigrant America: A Portrait*. Berkeley: University of California Press.

Radcliffe, Sarah, and Sallie Westwood. 1996. *Remaking the Nation: Place, Identity, and Politics in Latin America*. London: Routledge.

Ridgeway, Cecilia L. 1991. "The Social Construction of Status Value: Gender and Other Nominal Characteristics." *Social Forces* 70(2): 367–86.

Rockquemore, Kerry Ann, and Patricia Arend. Forthcoming. "Opting for White: Choice, Fluidity, and Black Identity Construction in Post–Civil Rights America." *Race and Society*.

Rockquemore, Kerry Ann, and David L. Brunsma. 2002. *Beyond Black: Biracial Identity in America*. Thousand Oaks, Calif.: Sage Publications.

Rodríguez, Clara E. 1991. *Puerto Ricans Born in the U.S.A.* Boulder, Colo.: Westview Press.

———. 2000. *Changing Race: Latinos, the Census, and the History of Ethnicity in the United States*. New York: New York University Press.

Rodríguez, Victor M. 1998. "Boricuas, African Americans, and Chicanos in the 'Far West': Notes on the Puerto Rican Pro Independence Movement in California, 1960s–1980s." *New Political Science* 20(4, December): 421–39.

Saito, Leland T. 1998. *Race and Politics: Asian Americans, Latinos, and Whites in a Los Angeles Suburb.* Urbana: University of Illinois Press.

San Juan, Epifanio, Jr. 2000. "The Limits of Ethnicity and the Horizon of Historical Materialism." In *Asian American Studies: Identity, Images, Issues Past and Present,* edited by Esther Mikyung Ghymn. New York: Peter Lang.

Schoenbaum, David, and Elizabeth Pond. 1996. *The German Question and Other German Questions.* New York: St. Martin's Press.

Sears, David O., Jim Sidanius, and Lawrence Bobo. 2000. "Race and Beliefs About Affirmative Action." In *Racialized Politics: The Debate About Racism in America,* edited by David O. Sears, Jim Sidanius, and Lawrence Bobo. Chicago: University of Chicago Press.

Silva do Valle, Nelson. 1985. "Updating the Cost of Not Being White in Brazil." In *Race, Class, and Power in Brazil,* edited by Pierre-Michel Fontaine. Los Angeles: University of California Press and Center for Afro-American Studies.

Skidmore, Thomas E. 1990. "Racial Ideas and Social Policy in Brazil, 1870–1940." In *The Idea of Race in Latin America, 1870–1940,* edited by Richard Graham. Austin: University of Texas Press.

Smith, Robert C. 1995. *Racism in the Post–Civil Rights Era: Now You See It, Now You Don't.* Albany: State University of New York Press.

Spears, Arthur K. 1999. *Race and Ideology: Language, Symbolism, and Popular Culture.* Detroit: Wayne State University Press.

Spoonley, Paul. 1996. "Mahi Awatea? The Racialization of Work in Aotearoa/New Zealand." In *Nga Patai: Racism and Ethnic Relations in Aotearoa/New Zealand,* edited by Paul Spoonley, David Pearson, and Cluny Macpherson. Palmerston North, N.Z.: Dunmore Press.

Steinberg, Stephen. 1995. *Turning Back: The Retreat from Racial Justice in American Thought and Policy.* Boston: Beacon Press.

Tajfel, Henri. 1970. "Experiments in Intergroup Discrimination." *Scientific American* 223: 96–102.

Takaki, Ronald. 1993. *A Different Mirror: A History of Multicultural America.* Boston: Little, Brown.

Telles, Edward E. 1999. "Ethnic Boundaries and Political Mobilization Among African Brazilians: Comparisons with the U.S. Case." In *Racial Politics in Contemporary Brazil,* edited by Michael Hanchard. Durham, N.C.: Duke University Press.

Torres, Arlene. 1998. "La gran familia Puertorriqueña 'Ej Prieta de Beldá' " (The Great Puerto Rican Family Is Really Really Black). In *Blackness in Latin America and the Caribbean,* vol. 2. Bloomington: Indiana University Press.

Torres-Saillant, Silvio. 1998. "The Tribulations of Blackness: Stages in Dominican Racial Identity." *Latin American Perspectives* 25(3): 126–46.

Trouillot, Michel-Rolph. 1990. *Haiti, State Against Nation: Origins and Legacy of Duvalierism.* New York: Monthly Review Press.

Tuan, Mia. 1998. *Forever Foreigners or Honorary Whites? The Asian Ethnic Experience Today*. New Brunswick, N.J.: Rutgers University Press.

Tuch, Steven A., and Jack K. Martin. 1997. *Racial Attitudes in the 1990s*. Westport, Conn.: Praeger.

Twine, France Winddance. 1998. *Racism in a Racial Democracy*. New Brunswick, N.J.: Rutgers University Press.

U.S. Department of Commerce. U.S. Bureau of the Census. 1996. *Population Projections of the United States by Age, Sex, Race, and Hispanic Origin: 1995 to 2050*. Washington: U.S. Government Printing Office.

Vickerman, Milton. 1999. *Crosscurrents: West Indian Immigrants and Race*. New York: Oxford University Press.

Wade, Peter. 1997. *Race and Ethnicity in Latin America*. London: Pluto Press.

Wagley, Charles. 1952. *Race and Class in Rural Brazil*. Paris: UNESCO.

Warren, Jonathan W., and France Winddance Twine. 1997. "White Americans, the New Minority? Nonblacks and the Ever-Expanding Boundaries of Whiteness." *Journal of Black Studies* 28(2): 200–18.

Waters, Mary C. 1999. *Black Identities: West Indian Immigrant Dreams and American Realities*. New York and Cambridge, Mass.: Russell Sage Foundation and Harvard University Press.

Waters, Mary C., and Karl Eschbach. 1995. "Immigration and Ethnic and Racial Inequality in the United States." *Annual Review of Sociology* 21: 419–46.

Weiner, Michael. 1997. *Japan's Minorities: The Illusion of Homogeneity*. London: Routledge.

Weitzer, Ronald. 1997. "Racial Prejudice Among Korean Merchants in African American Neighborhoods." *Sociological Quarterly* 38(4): 587–606.

White, Michael J., Ann E. Biddlecom, and Shenyang Guo. 1993. "Immigration, Naturalization, and Residential Assimilation Among Asian Americans in 1980." *Social Forces* 72(1): 93–117.

Winant, Howard. 1994. *Racial Conditions: Politics, Theory, Comparisons*. Minneapolis: University of Minnesota Press.

———. 2001. *The World Is a Ghetto*. New York: Basic Books.

Wright, Winthrop R. 1990. *Café con Leche: Race, Class, and National Image in Venezuela*. Austin: University of Texas Press.

Yinger, John. 1995. *Closed Doors, Opportunities Lost: The Continuing Costs of Housing Discrimination*. New York: Russell Sage Foundation.

Yoon, In-jin. 1995. "Attitudes, Social Distance, and Perceptions of Influence and Discrimination Among Minorities." *International Journal of Group Tensions* 25(1): 35–56.

———. 1997. *On My Own: Korean Businesses and Race Relations in America*. Chicago: University of Chicago Press.

Zhou, Min. 2001. "Straddling Different Worlds: The Acculturation of Vietnamese Refugee Children." In *Ethnicities: Children of Immigrants in America*, edited by Rubén G. Rumbaut and Alejandro Portes. Berkeley: University of California Press.

PART III

Theoretical Considerations in the
Changing Terrain of Race and Ethnicity

7

RACE, GENDER, AND UNEQUAL CITIZENSHIP IN THE UNITED STATES

ॐ

Evelyn Nakano Glenn

IN ITS FOUNDING documents, the United States declared its dedication to ideals of universal freedom and equality. Today, after more than two centuries of struggle to realize these ideals, race, gender, and class inequality remain pervasive and deeply entrenched in American society. Their very persistence indicates that rather than being either surface imperfections or deviations from the principles of American society, they are inherent and deeply embedded in our philosophical traditions and institutions.

In this chapter, I examine citizenship as one of the principal institutions through which unequal race and gender relations have been constituted and also contested in the United States. Citizenship has been key to inequality because it has been used to draw boundaries between those included as members of the community and entitled to respect, protection, and rights and those who are excluded and thus denied recognition and rights.

First, I examine the ideological and material roots of exclusion in Western concepts of citizenship. I then explore shifting boundaries of exclusion, showing that there has not been a linear process of increasing inclusiveness, but rather a much more uneven and contested process. Third, I examine various approaches to understanding and explaining race and gender exclusion in American citizenship despite its framing in the rhetoric of universal rights. I argue for an approach that views ascriptive exclusion and stratification as central to, rather than a deviation from, American conceptions of citizenship. Finally, I develop a concept of citizenship that considers not only the definitions inscribed in the U.S. Constitution, laws, and court decisions, and other formal documents but also localized practices in which local officials as well as members of the public enforce and challenge the boundaries of citizenship and the rights associated with it.

Roots of Exclusion: Independence–Dependence and Public–Private Divides

Since the earliest days of the nation, the idea of whiteness has been closely tied to the notions of independence and self-control necessary for republican government. This conception of white masculine citizenship was rooted in the history of the United States as a white settler nation that grew out of the conquest and seizure of territory from indigenous peoples. Its economy was developed to provide raw materials for the European market and relied on various forms of coercive labor, including chattel slavery. Imagining non-European "others" as dependent and lacking the capacity for self-governance helped rationalize the takeover of their lands, resources, and labor. The extermination and forced removal of Indians and the enslavement of blacks by European settlers therefore seemed justified (Horsman 1981). This formulation was transferred to other racialized groups, such as the Chinese, Japanese, and Filipinos, who were brought to the United States in the late nineteenth and early twentieth centuries as low-wage laborers. Often working under coercive conditions of indenture or contract labor, they were treated as "unfree labor" and denied the right to become naturalized citizens (Cheng and Bonacich 1984, chs. 1 and 2; Lopez 1996, 44; Salyer 1995; Melendy 1977, ch. 2).

It was not just whiteness but masculine whiteness that was being constructed in the discourse on citizenship. Indeed, the association of republican citizenship with masculinity had even more ancient roots than race. As the American colonists struggled to articulate their cause in the struggle for independence from England, they harked back to classical conceptions that associated patriotism and public virtue with masculinity. As Rogers Smith (1989, 244) argues, "American republicans identified citizenship with material self-reliance, participation in public life, and martial virtue. The very words 'public' and 'virtue' derived from Latin terms signifying manhood." The equation of masculinity with activity in the public domain of the economy, politics, and the military was drawn in explicit contrast to the equation of femininity with the activities of daily maintenance carried out in the private domestic sphere. Those immured in the domestic sphere—women, children, servants, and other dependents— were not considered full members of the political community.

Given these discourses, it is perhaps not surprising that until the late nineteenth century full citizenship—legal adulthood, suffrage, and participation in governance—was restricted to "free white males." How did citizenship come to be constructed as a white masculine category? To what extent have movements for inclusion succeeded in transforming the race and gender meaning of citizenship? And finally, how do we best describe and account for the raced and gendered nature of citizenship?

The modern Western notion of citizenship emerged out of the political and intellectual revolutions of the seventeenth and eighteenth centuries, which overthrew the old dynastic orders. While the traditional dynastic realms were populated by *subjects,* the new nation-states that emerged were seen as consisting of *citizens.* The earlier concept of society organized as a hierarchy of status and expressed by differential legal and customary rights among subjects, was replaced by the idea of a political order established through a social contract among citizens. A social contract implied free and equal status among those party to it. Citizenship came to be conceived as a universal status—that is, all who are included in the status supposedly have identical rights and duties, irrespective of their individual characteristics (Anderson 1991, 19–22; Kettner 1978, 3). Equality of citizenship did not, of course, rule out economic and other forms of inequality. Moreover, and importantly, equality among citizens existed alongside the inequality of others living within the boundaries of the community who were defined as noncitizens.

If there is a consistent underpinning to American citizenship it consists of two conceptual dichotomies that have permeated the discourse on citizenship since the beginning: the public-private divide and the independence-dependence opposition (Gunderson 1987; Fraser and Gordon 1994). These dichotomies have long roots in Western political philosophy and have been central elements in the conception of the "ideal citizen" since classical times. The Aristotelian tradition posed a strict separation between "polis," the public realm of abstract reason, and "oikos," the private material realm of people and things. Citizens, free from their individual, concrete, material interests, came together in the public realm to make decisions on behalf of the general welfare. In contrast to the Aristotelian ideal of leaving the world of things behind, the Roman-Gaian formulation made the capacity to act on things the central attribute of human beings. The possession of property was evidence of this capacity. The citizen was one who was free to act by law and to ask and expect the law's protection. Citizenship meant membership in a community of shared or common law; thus, to be a citizen of Rome was to be a person entitled to the rights and protection of Roman law. Although differing in their stances toward mastery of the physical world, both Greek and Roman formulations viewed independence as a necessary condition for exercising citizenship. Independence was established by family headship, ownership of property, and control over wives, slaves, and other dependents. Also, in both traditions the public realm of citizenship was defined by bracketing the household, domesticity, and the "civil society" as outside the domain of equality and rights (Pocock 1995).

The public-private distinction and the independent-dependent dichotomy were also central in the writings of Locke, Rousseau, and the other Enlightenment philosophers who shaped American political thought. Carol Pateman (1988, 1989) has noted that in the liberal tradition the "public" and the "private" are constructed in opposition: the public is the realm of citizenship, rights, and generality, while sexuality, feeling, and specificity—and women—are relegated to the "private." Citizenship was essentially defined in opposition to womanhood. Another influential writer, Uday Mehta (1990), argues that in Locke's account, though rationality was potentially reachable by all, it required extensive social inscription; those viewed as naturally irrational, less civilized, uneducated, or otherwise inadequately socially inscripted were unable to exercise reasoned choice. Thus, the notion of natural hierarchy was inherent in Lockean liberalism (see also Okin 1979; Young 1995).

As the American colonists tried to articulate their cause in the struggle for independence from England, they harked back to these earlier conceptions. Historians have documented the colonists' anxiety about dependency, an anxiety intensified by the proximity of chattel slavery. Revolutionary rhetoric constructed a fundamental opposition between independence and dependence, associating independence with liberty and dependence with slavery. Independence was what distinguished the colonists from the despised slaves and protected them from the possibility of "white enslavement." Economic independence and political freedom were linked in the minds of republican artisans. The imposition of duties by the British Parliament was nothing less than the confiscation of property necessary to "Man's Preservation," the deprivation of which would reduce Americans to a state of feudal dependency or slavery (Roediger 1991, 28–29; Jordan 1968, 291–92; Shklar 1991, 39–42). Simultaneously, as Linda Kerber (1998, 11) has noted, the political founders manifested an anxiety about the stability of their new construction that "led them, in emphasizing its reasonableness, its solidity, its link to classical models, also to emphasize its manliness and to equate unreliability, unpredictability, and lust with effeminacy. Women's weakness became a rhetorical foil for republican manliness." Rogers Smith (1997, 112) also notes the connections that republicans made between masculinity and civic virtue and their rhetorical linking of effeminacy with the "ultimate republican evils of corruption and ignorance. It was hard for them to conceive that women might have the qualities that public-spirited, virtuous republican citizenship demanded."

THE SHIFTING SANDS OF EXCLUSION

At its most general level, citizenship refers to full membership in the community in which one lives. Membership in turn implies certain rights in and reciprocal duties toward the community (Hall and Held 1989). In his influential account of the growth of citizenship in Britain, T. H. Marshall (1964, 78) distinguished between three kinds of rights—civil, political, and social. Civil citizenship consists of "the rights necessary for individual freedom—liberty of the person, freedom of speech, thought, and faith, the right to own property and to conclude valid contracts, and the right to justice"; political citizenship refers to "the right to participate in the exercise of political power, as a member of a body invested with political authority, or as an elector of the members of such a body"; and social citizenship is composed of "the whole range from the right to a modicum of economic welfare and security to the right to share to the full in the social heritage and to live the life of a civilized being according to the standards prevailing in the society." Social citizenship is necessary to transform formal rights into substantive ones; only with adequate economic and social resources can individuals exercise civil and political rights.

There is nothing in this general definition to preclude exclusion on the basis of ascriptive or achieved status, but what has made the U.S. case notable is its philosophical grounding in the doctrine of natural rights and principles of equality. American citizenship has been defined, by those who have it and therefore speak for all citizens, as universal and inclusive (the so-called American Creed), yet it has been highly exclusionary in practice. While republican rhetoric declared that individuals have inherent human rights that transcend specific attributes, whole categories of people were excluded from citizenship and denied fundamental civil, political, and social rights. The major groups left out by the nation's founders were the poor, women, slaves, and Native Americans.

The first three of these groups—the poor, women, and slaves—were each deemed to lack the independence needed to exercise free choice and the moral and intellectual qualities needed to practice civic virtue. Paupers were disqualified because their neediness and dependence rendered them unable to know and act for the common good. Women of all strata were presumed to be members of a dependent class. Under the common law doctrine of coverture, a married woman's legal identity was subsumed by her husband's. Enslaved blacks occupied the status of commodity or property. As chattel, they did not have any independent legal identity and could not own property, even their own persons. Native American peoples were considered uncivilized and conceived as members of separate nations and thus as external to the U.S. polity. Exclusion of racialized minorities was made explicit national policy by the Naturalization Act of 1790, which limited the right to become a naturalized citizen to "free white persons" (Kettner 1978, 301).

A standard historical view has been that liberal egalitarianism eventually prevailed and that "defects" in the American Creed were gradually repaired over the course of the nineteenth and twentieth centuries as formal civil and political rights were extended to each of the excluded groups. However, a closer examination of historical changes shows that the course of American citizenship has been jagged at best.

There are numerous examples of the tortuous paths that various groups have trod. More generally, blacks, especially free blacks, had fewer explicit restrictions on their rights at the beginning of the nineteenth century than they had fifty years later. Indeed, there was a brief period after the American Revolution when some blacks were able to realize in a small way the status and rights of citizens. Requirements for private manumission were liberalized in the Upper South, resulting in a sizable growth in the free black population. New state constitutions written in the Revolutionary period in the North and in some Upper

South states allowed free black men who could meet general property qualifications to vote, serve on juries, and hold office.

Starting in 1819, however, in concert with the expansion of voting rights for propertyless white men, African American men were increasingly disfranchised. Proponents of universal white manhood suffrage successfully argued for suffrage for all white men on the grounds that they were "free, productive, independent" workers and heads of households, in contrast to men of color, who were "unfree, unproductive, dependent" labor, and white women, who were dependent nonworkers. From 1819, when Maine was admitted to the Union, until the end of the Civil War, all new states guaranteed suffrage to white males irrespective of property and denied the vote to blacks. Legislatures in several states lacking such provisions in their original constitutions passed restrictive legislation. By the late 1850s, most free blacks were barred by their states from voting, and they were ruled by the Supreme Court in the *Dred Scott* decision not to be citizens. After the Civil War, with the passage of the Fourteenth Amendment, blacks for the first time were recognized by the federal government as citizens entitled to civil rights and protections. The Fourteenth Amendment inserted into the Constitution for the first time the principle of equality before the law and created national citizenship rights separate from state citizenship. It also defined a new role for the federal government as guarantor of citizen rights. These rights were once again lost with so-called Redemption and the imposition of Jim Crow segregation and systematic disfranchisement in the South and the spread of de facto segregation and discrimination in the North. Not until the second civil rights revolution of the 1950s and 1960s did significant numbers of African Americans regain civil rights protections and the franchise, at least formally.

The history of Native American citizenship is also checkered. In the 1780s Native Americans had more recognition of their independence than was later the case. For several decades they were still accorded recognition as members of separate, quasi-sovereign nations with which matters of land and trade were to be regulated by treaty with the U.S. government. By the 1850s, after years of encroachment on native lands, the taking of native lands, and finally forced removal of Native Americans from "civilized" areas, Native American nations were reduced to the status of "domestic dependent nations" and declared wards of the federal government. After the Civil War, the U.S. government phased out recognition of Native American nationhood, including communal land rights, without, however, giving Native Americans citizenship rights. Native Americans were specifically excluded from birthright citizenship in the Fourteenth Amendment while continuing to be denied the right to become naturalized on the basis of race under the 1790 Naturalization Act. This double exclusion was not redressed until Congress passed the Indian Citizenship Act in 1924 (Ringer 1983, 127–48).

With regard to the nation to which a woman owed her citizenship, before 1855 women had citizenship independent of their husbands. After that, an alien woman marrying an American citizen was automatically naturalized, regardless of her preference. Between 1907 and 1922 an American woman marrying an alien was automatically expatriated (Kerber 1998, 41–44). Passage of the Nineteenth Amendment in 1920, after more than seventy years of struggle, finally granted women suffrage. However, it did little to alter the common law of coverture and myriad statutes that circumscribed women's civil citizenship. Thus, women still could not bring suit against their husbands for assault and battery, nor could they have citizenship in a different state than their husband. Women's supposed domestic obligations also continued to trump their obligations as citizens. As late as 1965, twenty-nine states either excluded women from jury duty or granted special exemptions based on their domestic responsibilities (Freeman 1995, 372).

As to other racialized minorities, before the 1882 Chinese Exclusion Act there were no race or ethnic barriers to immigration, nor before 1924 any nationality-based quotas. Although the 1790 Naturalization Act was used to bar Japanese and Chinese immigrants from being naturalized from the 1880s on, not until the 1910s did states, courts, and Congress invent a new category to classify Asian immigrants—"aliens ineligible for citizenship." This category of noncitizen was subject to special restrictions not placed on other noncitizens. Eleven states passed alien land acts prohibiting "aliens ineligible for citizenship" from owning land. Restrictions on Chinese, Japanese, and Filipinos kept male immigrants in the status of long-term "sojourners" and barred the entry of Asian wives. Thus, Asian men and women were denied the right to establish families, and the birth of a second generation entitled to citizenship was retarded or forestalled. Not until 1953 did Asian immigrants become eligible for naturalization, and not until 1965 was immigration from Asia again allowed (Lopez 1996, 128–29). As late as 2001, several states still had alien land acts on their books.

EXPLAINING EXCLUSION

How are we to account for this extensive and multifarious history of exclusion? Until recently, many American historians and social scientists viewed ascriptive exclusions from citizenship as deviations from otherwise dominant principles of universal equality. Rogers Smith (1997, 17) traces the origins of this belief to Alexis de Tocqueville. As a European, Tocqueville was struck most by the revolutionaries' rejection of aristocratic privilege, which he attributed to the liberal egalitarianism of American thought. Tocqueville also spent most of his time reflecting on the political activities of a small segment of American society, namely, middle- and upper-class white men. Tocqueville and those who followed more or less took for granted gender and race hierarchies or relegated them to the margins, so that inequality was not seen as central to the American political system.

Over one hundred years later, the Swedish sociologist Gunnar Myrdal (1944, 1–25, 1021–22) focused specifically on the subordination of African Americans as a central "dilemma" in American society. Myrdal subscribed to the Tocquevillian myth of an overarching American Creed—a belief in universal equality. He interpreted the widespread racial segregation and discrimination against blacks that he documented as contradictory to Americans' professed beliefs. The challenge that he posed to (white) Americans was whether they would live up to their highest ideals by accepting blacks as equal citizens. Speaking from the perspective of the early 1940s, a period of democratic ferment, Myrdal (1944, xix) concluded: "[Not] since reconstruction has there been more reason to anticipate fundamental changes in American race relations, change which will involve a development toward the American ideals."

In this respect, Myrdal was more optimistic than the vast majority of American social scientists. James McKee (1993, 2, 6–9) found that prior to the 1960s race scholars were locked into an assimilationist framework. Many sociologists and social anthropologists viewed blacks as a "folk" people who would have to go through a long process of education and acculturation to become integrated into American society. Full citizenship for blacks would occur only when white Americans were ready to accept blacks as equals, a process that would take many generations. They discounted the possibility of black agency, overlooking evidence of black discontent and political activism. Race relations "experts" thus were taken by surprise by the civil rights revolution of the 1950s and 1960s. In fact, their accumulated wisdom suggested its impossibility.

More critical perspectives on liberal citizenship have been offered by Marxist and feminist writers. Marx himself was somewhat equivocal about the relationship between liberal democracy and capitalist rule. On the one hand, he saw the universalistic elements of democracy as incompatible with class divisions in capitalist society. On the other hand, his general claims about the liberal state were to the effect that it was a means for organizing and reproducing class rule. According to Anthony Giddens (1996, 66), Marx preserved the primacy of class by treating democratic rights as "narrow and partial." Workers in a liberal democratic regime might be allowed to participate in elections every few years, but they lacked any real power to control their own lives or to affect the distribution of material resources. Thus, such rights as they had were largely hollow (Michael Buroway, personal communication, 1999).

Feminist theorists have also been critical of liberal citizenship, arguing that exclusion of women is inherent in liberal assumptions. For example, some political theorists have pointed out that the rights-bearing subject in liberalism is a discrete and disembodied individual who can act according to abstract principles. Women are viewed as held in thrall by bodily demands (pregnancy and childbirth). As the ultimate embodied subjects, they cannot be accommodated within the liberal concept of citizen. Still, despite their criticism of particular liberal writings, many feminist critics have acknowledged that classic liberal contract theory, which is premised on natural rights, has the potential for challenging all forms of hierarchical authority. Moreover, because liberal rights doctrine has been the most effective rhetorical device for subordinated groups to claim rights, many feminists, including critical race theorists such as Angela Harris (1994, 744), have emphasized the importance of retaining a commitment to universalistic principles such as truth, justice, and objectivity, even while recognizing their insufficiency.

Other writers have concluded that race and gender exclusion is indeed a central and continuing theme in American citizenship, but argue that it stems from distinctly nonliberal roots. Benjamin Ringer, in *"We the People" and Others* (1983), focuses solely on race, arguing that exclusion of racial minorities has been an inherent feature of the U.S. political system from its inception as a white settler society. The founders set up a dual legal and political system based on colonial and colonialist principles. The "people's domain" consisted of those included as part of the national community, among whom "universalistic, egalitarian, achievement-oriented, and democratic norms and values were to be ideals." Existing alongside the people's domain was a second level of those who were excluded from the national community and, based on colonialist principles, were "treated as conquered subjects or property" (Ringer 1983, 8).

In a more recent study, *Civic Ideals,* Rogers Smith (1997, 35–39) documents the history of exclusion of women, as well as blacks and Native Americans, from American citizenship. Smith, like Ringer, argues that exclusionary tendencies cannot be explained as deviations from an otherwise dominant liberal egalitarianism or as inherent in liberalism. He instead hypothesizes that U.S. concepts of citizenship have been shaped by three ideological strands, some of which are consensual and egalitarian and some of which are ascriptive and inegalitarian: *liberalism* (which emphasizes limited government, personal freedom, and protection of individual rights); *republicanism* (which emphasizes self-government, political participation, civic virtue, and regulation of the economy to ensure the public good); and *ascriptive Americanism* (which emphasizes the notion of Americans as a special people endowed with superior moral and intellectual traits associated with certain ascriptive categories of race, religion, gender, and sexual orientation). Smith argues that all three strands have been used in different combinations by political leaders to achieve their dual goals of creating a sense of peoplehood in their followers and persuading them of the rightness of their vision and the need for their leadership. In his view, liberalism and republicanism have been effective in creating a sense of progress, prosperity, and personal freedom, but not in convincing people that "we" are a special people and that they should care about "us." For this task, ascriptive Americanism has been effective in that it has offered civic myths about our specialness as a people.

These two studies are extremely important both because of their thoroughness and because they view ascriptive exclusion and stratification as central and not peripheral to the story of American citizenship. However, while I build on these works, my focus and approach differ in at least two major ways. Both Ringer (1983) and Smith (1997) concentrate on the national level and on formal definitions and doctrines as decreed in official documents, laws, and court decisions. Second, their analyses center on debates and arguments among key political actors (for example, political leaders, reformers, judges and lawyers). Although they consider conflict, their focus keeps them looking primarily at discursive conflict among competing elites rather than at "hidden transcripts" of resistance by excluded groups (Scott 1990).

In my view, important aspects of the story of American citizenship are thereby overlooked. Citizenship is not just a matter of formal legal status; it is a matter of belonging, including recognition by other members of the community. Formal laws and legal rulings do matter, of course: they create a structure that legitimates the granting or denial of recognition. However, the maintenance of boundaries relies on "enforcement," not only by designated officials but also by so-called members of the public. During the Jim Crow era, segregation was maintained on a daily basis by ordinary people. For example, on segregated streetcars whites rode at the front and blacks at the rear. However, there was no fixed physical line. Rather, whites boarded and paid at the front, while blacks paid at the front and reboarded at the rear. The line marking the white section was established by how far back whites chose to sit. Thus, the segregation of public conveyances was carried out and enforced not only by white drivers and conductors but also importantly by white passengers, who imposed sanctions on blacks whom they perceived as violating boundaries (Delaney 1998, 101; Meier and Rudwick 1969, 761; Kuhn, Joye, and West 1990, 80).

Contrarily, men and women may act on the basis of schemas of race, gender, and citizenship that differ from those in formal law or policy. For example, when the Southwest was taken over by the United States, the U.S. government agreed under the Treaty of Guadalupe Hidalgo in 1848 that all Mexican citizens residing in the territory would be recognized as U.S. citizens unless they elected to remain citizens of Mexico. In an era when full citizenship rested on white racial status, Mexicans by implication were "white." Indeed, the explicit policy of the federal government was that Mexicans were white. For this reason, Mexicans were not enumerated separately from whites in the census prior to 1930. However, Anglos in the Southwest increasingly did not recognize the official whiteness of Mexicans and often refused to view them as "Americans" entitled to political and civil rights (Lopez 1996, 61–62; Reisler 1976, 136).

As a result, even though the segregation of Mexicans was technically illegal, de facto segregation was rampant. Consequential public sites—hospitals, municipal buildings, banks, stores, and movie theaters—were Anglo territory. When Mexicans entered Anglo territory, they were confined to certain restricted times or sections. Mexican women "were only supposed to shop on the Anglo side of town on Saturdays, preferably during the early hours when Anglos were not shopping." Municipal swimming pools barred "colored" patrons except on the day before the pool was cleaned. In Anglo-run cafés, Mexicans were allowed only to eat at the counter or order carryout, and theaters relegated Mexicans to the balcony (Montejano 1987, 168; Taylor 1930; Foley 1997, 42–44; Haas 1995, 185). In short, de facto segregation in the Southwest was "maintained through the actions of government officials, the voters who supported them, agricultural, industrial, and business interests, the residents of white neighborhoods, Parent-Teacher Association members—in short, all those who constituted the self-identified white public" (Haas 1995, 106).

Similarly, challenges to exclusion have been made not just through formal legislative and legal channels. Because excluded groups by definition have often lacked access to courts and other formal venues, much of their opposition has taken place in more informal or "disguised" ways and in informal sites. Returning to the example of streetcar segregation, black men and women challenged segregation not only when they brought legal suits and organized boycotts but also when individuals refused to "move to the back of the streetcar." Historical records suggest that enforcement of streetcar segregation was one of the most frequent sparks for spontaneous black resistance. North Carolinian Mary Mebane recounted several instances of blacks in Durham refusing to move and told of one incident in which a black woman came to the defense of a fellow passenger who refused to move when ordered, shouting, "These are nigger seats! The government plainly says these are nigger seats!" Mebane noted with satisfaction that the driver backed down (Janiewski 1985, 141).

Excluded groups have also acted on concepts of citizenship that differed from those of the dominant society. Elsa Barkley Brown (1994) found that in post-Reconstruction Richmond and other parts of the South, African Americans operated in two separate political arenas, internal and external. Within the external political realm, black women were disfranchised and the vote was considered an individual act. In the internal realm, black women were enfranchised and participated in all public forums, rallies, meetings, and conventions, and the vote was considered a collective resource. In the 1876 election, for example, women as well as men took off from work to show up en masse at polling sites, often arriving the night before and camping out. Women's presence at the polls was meant not only to forestall attempts by whites to intimidate black voters and deter poll officials from turning them away but also to remind black men that their votes should be cast in the interests of the entire community. A Sea Island, South Carolina, woman reported that a Republican speaker had counseled women to refuse to marry men who voted a Democratic ticket, or if already married, "don't service them in bed" (Holt 1977, 35; Brown 1994, 122–24; Sterling 1984, 370).

Attention to how the boundaries and meanings of citizenship are reinforced, enacted, and contested in raced and gendered ways at the local level and in everyday interaction is useful in three major ways.

First, it clarifies the distinction between formal and substantive citizenship. I view formal citizenship—defined by national, state, and local laws and policies—as setting certain parameters within which individuals and groups maneuver, strategize, and construct meaning. But what happens when people go about their daily lives? Are they allowed to live and work where they want, to vote, to go to school, and to enter public facilities? In general are they recognized as members of the community and as competent adults? The answers to these questions constitute substantive citizenship. This notion of ongoing relationships and interactions as constituting substantive citizenship is an important addition to understanding inequalities in American citizenship.

Second, a focus on the local avoids an overly monolithic view of oppression by revealing the "state of play"—the variability and unevenness—in the race-gender regime of citizenship. The similarities and differences in the ways national laws and policies were interpreted at the local level and in day-to-day relations can be compared in the experiences of particular groups in different regions of the country. For example, regional variation in ethnic concentration and economic competition might lead us to expect regional differences in the degree of exclusion experienced by particular groups. An older Japanese American who grew up in Los Angeles and then studied and worked in New York and Boston in the midtwentieth century found that his co-ethnics were less likely to be subjected to segregation and denial of access to public accommodations in eastern cities than in California and other parts of the West (Scott Miyakawa, personal communication, 1977). Within each region, we can also view variability in the enforcement of boundaries of inclusion or exclusion and changes over time in the drawing of these boundaries. Tomas Almaguer (1994, 212) describes his surprise upon studying the history of the racialization of Mexicans in California to learn that in the nineteenth century not all Mexicans were considered "brown" and that European-identified Californios claimed and were accorded recognition and rights as full citizens. By the midtwentieth century, he notes, "to be Mexican in the Southern California agricultural world that I grew up in meant that one was unambiguously *not* white."

Third, a focus on everyday interaction highlights the role of human agency, including that of the excluded. For example, historians have begun to argue that black agency was in fact one of the impetuses for the imposition of Jim Crow segregation after 1900. Black literacy rates had climbed from 10 percent at Emancipation to over 50 percent; the percentage of black farmers owning land had risen from 3 to 8 percent in 1880 to 25 percent by 1900; and a visible black middle class of small entrepreneurs, professionals, and educators had grown during the same period. Harold Rabinowitz (1978, 336) points to increasing assertiveness in black "insistence on voting independently, protesting unequal justice, and calling for control of their own education." Another example was the tendency for blacks to clash with urban police, particularly to prevent the arrest of other blacks. As custom and informal controls seemed no longer effective enough to keep blacks in their "place," whites turned to legal measures to buttress white domination. One suggestive piece of evidence to confirm the role of black assertiveness in motivating segregation laws is that Mississippi, where whites attained the greatest degree of domination through violence and state repression, actually had fewer such laws than other states (Fredrickson 1995, 99; Rabinowitz 1978, 336; Meier and Rudwick 1966; McMillen 1989, 9).

What I am suggesting is that we develop a more sociological conception of citizenship, one that brings it closer to core theoretical and methodological themes in sociology. I suggest conceiving of citizenship as a product of rhetorical and material practices that include the everyday interactions through which the boundaries of the community are enforced and contested.

This approach makes citizenship amenable to some of the same methods that are used to study other kinds of social categories that involve boundary maintenance and enactment, and it therefore allows citizenship to be studied in relation to these other categories. We can ask such questions as, how do race, gender, and class intersect in the creation and maintenance of citizenship, and how does citizenship shape whiteness, manhood, and middle-class status?

By tracing the material and ideological roots of American citizenship, I have tried to expose the extent to which race and gender have been central organizing principles of the ideals and assumptions underlying American democracy. Ironically, however, the very tenets of republican and democratic ideology that proclaim universal equality have helped to obscure the existence of institutionalized systems of inequality. To the extent that Americans subscribe to beliefs in independence and free choice and the separation of public and private realms, they deny interdependence between groups (such that privilege for some rests on the subordination and exploitation of others) and are blind to institutional constraints on choice. There is thus an overwhelming tendency among Americans to view racism and sexism as products of individual beliefs and attitudes. According to this view, if individual bias and prejudice can be eliminated, racism and sexism will no longer serve to divide the society and hobble efforts to achieve social justice. Since twenty-first-century Americans are less likely than ever before to express overtly negative views of minorities and women, one likely conclusion is that sexism and racism are disappearing and thus women and minorities increasingly play on a level field.

Unfortunately, such conclusions ignore the fact that the various forms of exclusion and discrimination that Native Americans, African Americans, Mexican Americans, and Asian Americans were subjected to in earlier periods are still clearly operative in the contemporary United States. Sometimes they are directed at the same groups and sometimes at new groups. The cruel sweatshops of New York and Los Angeles, filled with Chinese and Southeast Asian immigrant women, mirror the lack of rights of plantation laborers in the earlier period. Central American and Mexican women employed as live-in nannies and housekeepers in private households in California perform gendered caring labor under conditions akin to those of indentured servants: they are on call twenty-four hours a day, with room and board counted as part of their pay, even though living-in is a requirement of the job. Mexican and Mexican American agricultural workers are still subjected to inhuman labor conditions as well as being poisoned by pesticides, threatened with deportation if they protest, and often denied access to schooling and health care. And as was dramatically revealed in the national presidential election of 2000, blacks, particularly black men, continue to be systematically disfranchised, as well as subjected to grossly disproportionate rates of imprisonment and permanent loss in many states of the franchise after serving time. Proposals by some members of Congress to end birthright citizenship for children of undocumented immigrants and to deny welfare rights to naturalized citizens mirror earlier attempts to exclude those deemed to be "nonwhite" from full membership in the community. All of these examples testify to the continued centrality of citizenship as a site for maintaining and challenging race and gender inequality in American society.

This chapter draws on portions of my book *Unequal Freedom: How Race and Gender Shaped American Citizenship and Labor* (Glenn 2002).

REFERENCES

Almaguer, Tomas. 1994. *Racial Faultlines: The Historical Origins of White Supremacy in California.* Berkeley, Calif.: University of California Press.
Anderson, Benedict. 1991. *Imagined Communities.* Rev. ed. London: Verso.
Brown, Elsa Barkley. 1994. "Negotiating and Transforming the Public Sphere: African American Political Life in the Transition from Slavery to Freedom." *Public Culture* 7: 122–24.
Cheng, Lucie, and Edna Bonacich. 1984. *Labor Immigration Under Capitalism: Asian Workers in the United States Before World War II.* Berkeley: University of California Press.
Delaney, David. 1998. *Race, Place, and the Law, 1836–1948.* Austin: University of Texas Press.
Foley, Neil. 1997. *The White Scourge: Mexicans, Blacks, and Poor Whites in Texas Cotton Culture.* Berkeley, Calif.: University of California Press.
Fraser, Nancy, and Linda Gordon. 1994. "A Genealogy of Dependency: Tracing a Keyword of the U.S. Welfare State." *Signs* 19: 313.
Fredrickson, George M. 1995. *Black Liberation: A Comparative History of Black Ideologies in the United States and South Africa.* New York: Oxford University Press.

Freeman, Jo. 1995. "The Revolution for Women in Law and Public Policy." In *Women: A Feminist Perspective,* 4th ed. Mountain View, Calif.: Mayfield.

Giddens, Anthony. 1996. "T. H. Marshall, the State, and Democracy." In *Citizenship Today: The Contemporary Relevance of T. H. Marshall,* edited by Martin Bulmer and Anthony M. Rees. London: UCL Press.

Glenn, Evelyn Nakano. 2002. *Unequal Freedom: How Race and Gender Shaped American Citizenship and Labor.* Cambridge, Mass.: Harvard University Press.

Gunderson, Joan R. 1987. "Independence, Citizenship, and the American Revolution." *Signs* 12(1): 60.

Haas, Lisbeth. 1995. *Conquests and Historical Identities in California, 1769–1936.* Berkeley: University of California Press.

Hall, Stuart, and David Held. 1989. "Citizens and Citizenship." In *New Times: The Changing Face of Politics in the 1990s,* edited by Stuart Hall and David Held. London: Lawrence and Wishart.

Harris, Angela P. 1994. "Foreword: The Jurisprudence of Reconstruction." *California Law Review* 82: 741–85.

Holt, Thomas. 1977. *Black over White: Negro Political Leadership in South Carolina During Reconstruction.* Urbana: University of Illinois Press.

Horsman, Reginald. 1981. *Race and Manifest Destiny.* Cambridge, Mass.: Harvard University Press.

Janiewski, Delores E. 1985. *Sisterhood Denied: Race, Gender, and Class in a New South Community.* Philadelphia: Temple University Press.

Jordan, Winthrop. 1968. *White over Black: American Attitudes Toward the Negro, 1550–1812.* Chapel Hill: University of North Carolina Press.

Kerber, Linda. 1998. *No Constitutional Right to Be Ladies: Women and the Obligations of Citizenship.* New York: Hill and Wang.

Kettner, James H. 1978. *The Development of American Citizenship, 1608–1870.* Chapel Hill: University of North Carolina Press.

Kuhn, Cliff, Harlon E. Joye, and E. Bernard West, eds. 1990. *Living Atlanta: An Oral History of the City, 1914–1948.* Athens: University of Georgia Press.

Lopez, Ian Haney. 1996. *White by Law: The Legal Construction of Race.* New York: New York University Press.

Marshall, Thomas Humphrey. 1964. "Citizenship and Social Class." In *Class, Citizenship, and Social Development.* New York: Doubleday.

McKee, James B. 1993. *Sociology and the Race Problem: The Failure of a Perspective.* Urbana: University of Illinois Press.

McMillen, Neil R. 1989. *Dark Journey: Black Mississippians in the Age of Jim Crow.* Urbana: University of Illinois Press.

Mehta, Uday S. 1990. "Liberal Strategies of Exclusion." *Politics and Society* 18: 436–37.

Meier, August, and Ernest Rudwick. 1966. "Negro Retaliatory Violence in the Twentieth Century." *New Politics* 5: 41–51.

———. 1969. "The Boycott Movement Against Jim Crow Streetcars in the South, 1900–1906." *Journal of American History* 55(4): 756–75.

Melendy, Brett H. 1977. *Asians in America: Filipinos, Koreans, and East Indians.* Boston: Twayne.

Montejano, David. 1987. *Anglos and Mexicans in the Making of Texas, 1836–1986.* Austin: University of Texas Press.

Myrdal, Gunnar. 1944. *The American Dilemma: The Negro Problem and Modern Democracy.* 2 vols. New York: Harper.

Okin, Susan Moller. 1979. *Women in Western Political Thought.* Princeton, N.J.: Princeton University Press.

Pateman, Carole. 1988. *The Sexual Contract.* Stanford, Calif.: Stanford University Press.

———. 1989. *The Disorder of Women.* Cambridge: Polity.

Pocock, John Greville Agard. 1995. "The Ideal of Citizenship Since Classical Times." In *Theorizing Citizenship,* edited by Ronald Beiner. Albany: State University of New York.

Rabinowitz, Harold N. 1978. *Race Relations in the Urban South, 1865–1890.* New York: Oxford University Press.

Reisler, Mark. 1976. *By the Sweat of Their Brow: Mexican Immigrant Labor in the United States, 1900–1940.* Westport, Conn.: Greenwood Press.

Ringer, Benjamin. 1983. *"We the People" and Others: Duality and America's Treatment of Its Racial Minorities.* New York: Tavistock Publications.

Roediger, David. 1991. *The Wages of Whiteness: Race and the Making of the American Working Class.* London: Verso.

Salyer, Lucy E. 1995. *Laws as Harsh as Tigers: Chinese Immigrants and the Shaping of American Immigration Law.* Chapel Hill: University of North Carolina Press.

Scott, James C. 1990. *Domination and the Arts of Resistance: Hidden Transcripts.* New Haven, Conn.: Yale University Press.

Shklar, Judith N. 1991. *American Citizenship: The Quest for Inclusion.* Cambridge, Mass.: Harvard University Press.

Smith, Rogers M. 1989. " 'One United People': Second-Class Female Citizenship and the American Quest for Community." *Yale Journal of Law and the Humanities* 1: 229–93.

———. 1997. *Civic Ideals: Conflicting Visions of Citizenship in U.S. History.* New Haven, Conn.: Yale University Press.

Sterling, Dorothy, ed. 1984. *We Are Your Sisters: Black Women in the Nineteenth Century.* New York: W. W. Norton.

Taylor, Paul S. 1930. "Mexican Labor in the United States: Dimmit County, Winter Garden District, South Texas." *University of California Publications in Economics* 6(5): 293–464.

Young, Iris Marion. 1995. "Polity and Group Differences: A Critique of the Ideal of Universal Citizenship." In *Theorizing Citizenship,* edited by Ronald Beiner. Albany: State University of New York Press.

8

TOWARD AN INTEGRATED THEORY OF
SYSTEMIC RACISM

஛

Joe R. Feagin

IN THE UNITED STATES, theories about racial and ethnic matters often take the form of theories of assimilation and ethnicity (seen as an umbrella category including nationality and "race"), theories dealing with "race" and stratification issues (for example, middleman minorities theory), and theories dealing with the social or ideological construction of "race" (for example, racial formation theory).

Although these are often useful frameworks, each has its own problems. Those who use a racial-formation approach place too much emphasis on the ideological construction of racial meanings and identities. Whether in the past or the present, racism is not just about the construction of images and identities; it is centrally about the creation, development, and maintenance of white privilege, material wealth, and institutional power at the expense of racialized "others." In U.S. history, systemic racism has emerged out of the *material exploitation* of particular groups, such as the theft of Native American lands and African American labor by generations of European Americans. Today systemic racism significantly shapes which socioracial groups have the best income, the best educational and economic opportunities, the best health, and even the longest lives. Not only has racism stereotyped people and created racial identities, but most significantly, it has damaged many lives and killed many people (see Feagin 2000; Feagin and McKinney 2003).

Major theories of assimilation (for example, Gordon 1964), as well as other mainstream scholarship on "race" and ethnicity, often view the racial or ethnic "problem" as less than fundamental to the historical development and current condition of U.S. society. From such perspectives, the problem is, to use a common metaphor, a temporary "disease" in an otherwise healthy society. One variant of this assimilation perspective portrays the U.S. racial-ethnic problem as one of groups of white bigots betraying fundamentally egalitarian institutions—the theme developed well by Gunnar Myrdal (1944/1964) and his many contemporary followers. A related approach speaks of vague "race relations," with whites seen as just one racial-ethnic group among many such groups contending for critical socioeconomic positions.

Indeed, phrases like "race relations" and "ethnic relations" are sometimes used euphemistically by social analysts who prefer to view all racial groups as more or less responsible for the U.S. "race problem" (for examples, see McKee 1993). The underlying metaphor for many such analysts seems to be one of a roughly level playing field on which all racial-ethnic groups jockey for status or power (see Sollors 1989). Others use the metaphor of a social organism whose diseased parts are not functioning well, but which over time can be made to function properly because the organism itself is healthy. The impersonal terminology associated with these metaphors allows the spotlight to be taken off the many white actors, especially powerful white men, who have created and maintained the system of white racism and its long-term wealth-generating features, which still privilege most whites. These impersonal metaphors for social reality—the playing field, a diseased body, the functioning organism, geological strata—are *much more* than figures of speech. Powerful metaphors often hide critical social realities and constrain people's understandings, and thus people's lives. Commonplace metaphors like the playing field, the organism, or the "free market" are commonly used to rationalize oppressive socioeconomic systems. Such metaphorical images frequently collude in human oppression by papering over oppressive underlying realities.

Moreover, these traditional metaphors are generally inappropriate for describing the racist realities of U.S. society. From the 1600s to the 2000s this country's major institutions have been racially hierarchical, white-supremacist, and inegalitarian. A better metaphor is a hierarchical *ladder of exploitation and oppression*. Also suggestive and powerful is the *vampire* metaphor. Analyzing class exploitation in capitalist economic systems, Karl Marx (1867/1977, 342) used the metaphor of the blood-sucking vampire: "Capital is dead labor which, vampire-like, lives only by sucking living labor, and lives the more, the more labor it sucks." More recently, Eduardo Galeano (1973/1997, 2) has used a variant of this metaphor in assessing Latin America's relationship to outsiders: "Latin America is the region of open veins. Everything, from the discovery until our times, has always been transmuted into European—or later United States—capital, and as such has accumulated in distant centers of power. Everything: the soil, its fruits and its mineral-rich depths, the people and their capacity to work and to consume, natural resources and human resources." Similarly, the "open veins" of Native Americans, African Americans, and Mexican Americans, among other non-European groups, have been intensively exploited by European Americans for nearly four centuries. The metaphor of vampires sucking blood from many victims, while rather harsh, does strongly suggest the continuing *process* of extraction of resources from one group to the great benefit of another.

SYSTEMIC RACISM: DIMENSIONS OF A HARSH REALITY

What is lacking in most contemporary analyses of racial-ethnic stratification and conflict is a broader theoretical framework that encompasses the issues raised in the aforementioned theories, yet goes beyond them to emphasize the material, social, educational, and political dimensions of racism. I suggest that we need a clear term for this tradition that parallels terms like Marxism (for class oppression) and feminism (for sexist oppression). I suggest the phrases "antiracist theory" and "antiracist strategies" for this developing anti-oppression tradition.

In developing a broader antiracist framework, I have emphasized elsewhere (Feagin 2000; Feagin and Feagin 2003) the political-economic realities of *racial exploitation* and suggested a number of concepts that are useful for understanding the development and maintenance of racial oppression in North America. These general concepts include: systemic racism, racial exploitation, unjust enrichment and impoverishment and the social reproduction of enrichment and impoverishment; rationalization of oppression in racist ideology; and resistance to racism. Here I focus mainly on examples of racial oppression from the history and current situations of black men, women, and children in the United States, although much of this analysis can be applied to the situations of other people of color here and overseas. Also, because of space limitations, I can touch only briefly on the important issues of the critical intersections and overlapping of racism, sexism, and classism that I have analyzed in much earlier as well as more recent work (Feagin and Feagin 1978; Feagin 1982; Ronai, Zsembik, and Feagin 1997).

DEFINITION OF SYSTEMIC RACISM

From its coinage in the 1930s by Magnus Hirschfeld (1938) as a term to describe anti-Semitic ideas and actions directed against European Jews, the term "racism" has meant more than scattered acts of bigotry—the watered-down meaning emphasized by many white Americans (including many scholars) today. From the beginning, the term "racism" has meant an institutionalized oppression that is rationalized in a strong racist ideology. In my view, an integrated and invigorated theory of racism should use the term "racism" in this original systemic sense for which it was created.

In the history of African Americans and other Americans of color, systemic racism has included: (1) the many exploitative and discriminatory practices of whites; (2) unjustly gained resources and power for whites; and (3) the maintenance of major resource inequalities by white-controlled ideological and institutional mechanisms. In this chapter, I discuss these three features in more detail. Given more space, I would discuss other important dimensions of systemic racism in more detail: (4) the prejudices and stereotyping covered by the umbrella racist ideology; (5) the racialized emotions accompanying prejudice and discrimination; and (6) the multiple and costly impacts of racism on targets and perpetrators (for more on this, see Feagin 2000; see also Feagin and Vera 1995). In the conclusion, I touch briefly on yet another central aspect of systemic racism, past and present: the broad range of resistance strategies developed by those, such as African Americans, who are routine targets of racial oppression. These strategies have periodically altered the character of systemic racism.

Here I explore two major arguments underlying this theoretical framework: that systemic racism is a material, social, and ideological reality, and that racism has been part of this society's *foundation* since at least the seventeenth century.

By "systemic racism" I mean that core racist realities are manifested in each of society's major parts. One useful analogy is the hologram: if one breaks a three-dimensional hologram into separate parts and shines a laser through any part, the whole three-dimensional image is projected from within one part. Like a hologram, each part of U.S. society—the economy, politics, education, religion, the family—reflects the fundamental reality of systemic racism.

THEORIZING RACIAL EXPLOITATION

Interestingly, the word "exploit," in the sense of taking advantage of another for one's personal gain, appeared in the English language in the 1840s during the zenith of slavery in the United States. The idea of *material exploitation institutionalized in society* is central in the thinking about racism in the black radical and anticolonialist tradition that has inspired my analysis. Perceptive analysts like Frederick Douglass, Ida B. Wells-Barnett, W. E. B. DuBois, Oliver C. Cox, Kwame Ture, Charles Hamilton, Angela Davis, and Philomena Essed, to name just a few, have long led the way to deeper understandings of how fundamental racism is to Western societies.[1] The nineteenth-century abolitionist Frederick Douglass was perhaps the first to feature systemic socioeconomic exploitation in his conceptual analysis of racial oppression. To take one example, in one assessment of the discrimination faced by black Americans, Douglass (1881/1968, 446–47, emphasis in original) argued: "In nearly every department of American life they are confronted by this insidious influence. It fills the air. It meets them at the workshop and factory, when they apply for work. It meets them at the church, at the hotel, at the ballot-box, and worst of all, it meets them in the jury-box. . . . [The black American] has ceased to be a *slave of an individual,* but has in some sense become *the slave of society.*" This early analysis highlights the reality that African Americans faced a totally racist society that held them firmly as a group in well-institutionalized bondage.

Working against racial oppression around the turn of the twentieth century, Ida B. Wells-Barnett (1895) developed key sociological ideas about how white oppression is grounded not only in the material reality of economic exploitation but also in the brutal gendering (and related violence and lynching) of black men and women. She accented the *institutionalization* and overlapping of racism and sexism. Working about the same time, W. E. B. DuBois (1920/1996) developed fully a point of view that understood Western societies like the United States as pervaded by well-institutionalized racism. Perhaps the first social scientist to analyze the globalizing white-supremacist order in detail, DuBois analyzed how the worldwide *exploitation* of the land and labor of Africans and other indigenous peoples has long been critical in generating great resources and wealth for both Europeans and European Americans. From the fifteenth century to the twentieth, the great expansion of resources and wealth for whites, including those in the working class, was made possible by the worldwide colonialism and imperialism of European countries and the United States.

By the 1940s, Oliver C. Cox (1948, 332–33, emphasis in original) was developing an extended analysis of the United States as *materially* exploitative: the sustained exploitation of black Americans had created a hierarchical structure of "racial classes," with whites firmly at the top. Seizing the labor of non-Europeans in overseas colonialism and in North America "is the beginning of modern race relations. It was not an abstract, natural, immemorial feeling of mutual antipathy between groups, but rather a *practical exploitative relationship* with its socio-attitudinal facilitation—at that time only nascent race prejudice. . . . As it developed, and took definite capitalist form, we could follow the white man around the world and see him repeat the process among practically every people of color." Thus, exploitative racism is well institutionalized and encompasses far more than racialized beliefs and hostile feelings. During the 1960s and 1970s, moreover, this institutional-racism perspective was honed by several sociological analysts, including Kwame Ture (Stokely Carmichael) and Charles Hamilton (1967) in *Black Power*. Empirically and theoretically, their investigations established the magnitude of the recurring patterns of racist practices inculcated in all major U.S. institutions—practices that entailed more than the discriminatory actions of scattered bigots.

By the 1970s black women scholars were developing the earlier insights of Ida B. Wells-Barnett, Anna Julia Cooper, and Fannie Barrier Williams in examining institutionalized racism in relation to gender and class exploitation. For example, Angela Davis (1971) showed how slavery encompassed both black men and women. An early analyst of the intersection of racism, classism, and sexism, Davis underscored the point that enslaved black women were exploited for their productive labor as workers and their reproductive labor as breeders of new slaves. More recently, drawing on interviews with black women in Europe and the United States, Philomena Essed (1991) has developed the concept of *gendered racism* and shown that black women, facing racial exploitation that is gendered, developed systems of knowledge critical for fighting that gendered racism.

Today *material exploitation* remains an important concept for the analysis of racial-ethnic matters across the globe. Exploitation means taking advantage of a person or group of people for individual or group gain. Long ago, Karl Marx showed that exploitation of the labor of subordinated groups is possible because a small powerful group (the users of labor) has full and ongoing control over the major means of economic production. Thus, in a slavery system, labor is coerced into giving its service for less than its value, but under capitalism the full value of one's labor is given up more or less voluntarily as part of an apparently "free" market exchange. Workers are therefore the central source of wealth creation in a capitalist country. Marx developed the idea of "surplus value"—the value created by productive workers that is not returned to them (see Roemer 1982). Wage labor is exploitative because workers do not receive the full value of the work they do in wages (Honderich 1995). Indeed, Marx uses terms like "robbery" and "embezzlement" for what happens to the value of the work done by workers in capitalistic economies (see Marx 1867/1977).

In addition to the exploitation of workers because of their subordinated class position, an added degree of exploitation is possible in a racist system when employers exploit the labor of workers of color. Black workers and other workers of color can be *super-exploited*. Thus, within a system of racism "racial surplus value" can be extracted from workers of color in addition to the surplus value that is typically taken from proletarian workers. In such social frameworks, African Americans and other workers of color are paid substantially lower wages (directly or indirectly through job typing or channeling) than white workers, with women of color facing yet more exploitation in its gendered-racist forms (Feagin 1982; for more discussion of the ways in which women, and especially women of color, are super-exploited, see Benokraitis and Feagin 1986; St. Jean and Feagin 1998).

ONGOING REALITIES: UNJUST IMPOVERISHMENT AND ENRICHMENT

Historically, the North American colonies, and later U.S. society, were centered economically in the impoverishment of some social groups to the enrichment of others. Early narratives of enslavement, such as that of Frederick Douglass (1855/2002, 135), make this point eloquently: on slave plantations the labor of many men "supports a single family in easy idleness and sin. . . . it is here that we shall find the height of luxury which is the opposite of that depth of poverty [of the enslaved]." The idea of unjust enrichment in Anglo-American law can be used to assess this reality of institutional racism today (see Cross 1984; Ayres and Vars 1998; Delgado 1996). The term "unjust enrichment" is usually associated with exploitative relationships between individuals. In U.S. court decisions, for example, some defendants have been required to give up their unjust enrichment at the expense of other individuals (Kull 1995). As a general rule, U.S. law does not permit a thief's child to knowingly benefit from her or his father's theft. Those who are enriched unjustly by a relative must return ill-gotten gains to those impoverished in the process. We can extend this idea of requiring remedies for the unjust impoverishment of an individual to requiring remedies for the *socially created* impoverishment arising from racial exploitation and oppression, such as that faced by African Americans and other Americans of color over several centuries. It makes much moral sense in a putatively democratic society to compensate those groups that are victims of large-scale and long-term unjust impoverishment, and this view might conceivably be the basis for new legal concepts aimed at reparations for the unjust impoverishment and enrichment stemming from such "crimes against humanity" as three centuries of slavery, apartheidlike segregation, and anti-Indian genocide.

Central here is the idea of *unjust impoverishment,* which I suggest to describe the conditions of those who have suffered greatly at the hands of those who have unfairly enriched themselves (current white Americans or their ancestors). In *The World and Africa,* DuBois (1946/1965, 37) suggested that large-scale impoverishment in the former European colonies of Africa was "a main cause of wealth and luxury in Europe." Many contemporary Western commentators who discuss poverty and immiseration in Africa today conveniently overlook the fact that Europeans violently took much of the wealth of Africa for their own development. This expropriation of great African mineral and human wealth for Western prosperity continues today under the auspices of multinational corporations. One can also link the long-term, across-the-board impoverishment of African Americans and other Americans of color to the growing prosperity of many white Americans over many generations across several centuries. Unjust enrichment for one group is often intimately connected to unjust impoverishment for another.

THE REPRODUCTION OF RACISM OVER TIME: SOME CRITICAL PROCESSES

Research on racial oppression in the United States and elsewhere remains underdeveloped in regard to some important questions. For example, how are the wealth and privilege unjustly secured by one generation perpetuated to later generations? How are wealth and privileges socially reproduced and transmitted? More generally, how is the whole societal system of exploitation and inequality reproduced over the generations? How is this cross-generational enrichment and exploitation rationalized and legitimated by those who benefit? There is remarkably little discussion of such important issues in the mainstream media and social science literatures. Denial of the foundational realities of racial oppression in the United States and other Western societies seems essential for their reproduction over long periods of time.

INTERGENERATIONAL MECHANISMS

An intertemporal perspective on racial oppression is decisive for a profound understanding of the development and structure of a racialized society like the United States. For institutionalized racism to persist across successive generations, it must reproduce all the necessary socioeconomic and ideological conditions, not only across numerous generations of individuals and families but also across succeeding incarnations of particular communities and social institutions. Among the essential conditions is a greatly disproportionate control by whites of major socioeconomic resources. These conditions also include control over major political, police, and ideology-generating organizations. These powers, and the societal structures and processes in which they are imbedded, are central to sustaining a racist system. For both oppressors and oppressed, each succeeding generation inherits from their ancestors and predecessors the organizational structures that work to maintain, if not enhance, unjust enrichment and impoverishment. Essential as well to this social reproduction over time of resources and other inequalities is a racist ideology that legitimates the racial oppression and its continuing reproduction.

EXPLOITATION, RESOURCE EXTRACTION,
AND SYSTEM MAINTENANCE

Social theft lies at the heart of American colonial, and later U.S., socioeconomic development. Valuable lands of Native American societies were taken by (often genocidal) force by European colonists. These white invaders could not secure enough European or Indian labor to develop this stolen land, so some sought enslaved African labor. By the 1700s the colonial system of slavery was well entrenched and profitable for many whites, including not only slaveholders and their families but also the many whites in various classes who policed, serviced, or traded with plantations. Black Americans as a group were proletarianized to *build up prosperity and wealth for whites as individuals and for the white-dominated society.* After the initiation of slavery, the next step was its cross-generational perpetuation and regular maintenance, not only to meet the internal requirements of the system but also to deal with resistance to it from those oppressed. From 1790 onward, numerous antiblack laws were passed in the United States in order to buttress the racist system. Most legislatures, state and federal courts, and chief executives (state and federal) worked to extend or maintain slavery and the subsequent system of legal segregation.

Significantly, most white Americans do not now realize the extent to which the unjustly gained resources and privileges of their ancestors have been passed down over the generations to the present day. Not surprisingly, perhaps, societal inheritance mechanisms are well masked by an ideological rationale (including the heralded work ethic, thought to be greatest among whites), making them appear fair to most white analysts. One generation after another of European Americans has inherited an array of oft-hidden racial advantages. The majority of whites today have received from their immediate or distant ancestors some form of economic or cultural (for example, educational) capital that has enabled them to do better socioeconomically in the society, on average, than otherwise comparable African Americans. Yet African Americans, ironically, are likely to have ancestors going back many more generations in U.S. history than the average white American whose ancestors came in the late nineteenth or early twentieth century. Once developed and institutionally imbedded, the unjustly derived assets and advantages take on a life of their own—and are thus often misrepresented in the typical white mind as individual or immediate family achievements disconnected from the past history of racialized exploitation.

Which white Americans are indeed the privileged ones? I frequently encounter this question from callers to talk shows on which I am a guest or from audience members when I lecture. Many white Americans do not feel they are privileged, especially those who are the descendants of the millions of Southern and Eastern European immigrants who came to the United States in the decades around the turn of the twentieth century. They often say, and often emotionally, that their grandparents also faced discrimination yet made it in U.S. society, mainly by dint of hard work. They often claim that African Americans and other Americans of color could easily do the same. Yet many such Americans do not know their history. While Southern and Eastern European immigrants did face some initial discrimination at the hands of British Americans, these immigrants and their descendants have benefited greatly over time from the fact that within a generation or so they came to be accepted as "white." Therefore, they benefited, often quite substantially, from the far more extensive discrimination (such as in housing, unions, and skilled blue-collar job opportunities) that has long targeted African Americans, up to the present day. Within a few decades the majority in these white ethnic groups were able to prosper economically and politically. Much social science research indicates that socioeconomic conditions at the time of immigrants' entry into the United States and the level of racially discriminatory barriers made the employment, housing, and other life experiences of African Americans *far more* oppressive than those of the New European immigrants. Group mobility was possible for these immigrant groups, and for their children and grandchildren, because most arrived when U.S. capitalism was expanding and jobs were more abundant, they faced far less severe discrimination than African Americans, and they found housing reasonably near their workplaces (Hershberg et al. 1981). Their economic opportunities, and those of their children and grandchildren, were also far better over ensuing decades, to the present day. The typically substantial economic and educational benefits gained in previous generations have usually been passed down to later generations. Whites today, including those descended from relatively recent immigrant groups, continue to benefit from the contemporary discrimination that widely targets African Americans and other Americans of color.

Consider the long-term impact of racial oppression. It is quite possible that without the enslavement of Africans, and the great wealth and development generated by the slavery-centered Atlantic economy, there would have been no United States and no Industrial Revolution in Europe—at least not at the relatively early times they actually developed in Western history. Much of the wealth of the European countries and of the new United States came off the lands stolen from Native Americans and off the laboring backs of those African and African American women, men, and children who were enslaved—for considerably more than two centuries. This prosperity and wealth was generated not only by the slave trade but by the trade in slave-produced products (for example, rice, cotton, sugar, and tobacco), by the direct commercial trade with plantations (for example, British textiles), and by the spin-off commercial trade (for example, banking and insurance) generated as the result of the large-scale, slavery-related trade. The importance of black labor was generally recognized by white European and American elites in the eighteenth and nineteenth centuries, as this eighteenth-century pamphleteer indicated in comments on Britain's rapidly increasing wealth:

> It is also allowed on all Hands, that the trade to Africa is the Branch which renders our American Colonies and Plantations so advantageous to Great Britain: that Traffic only affording our Planters a constant supply of Negro Servants for the Culture of their Lands in the Produce of Sugars, Tobacco, Rice, Rum, Cotton, . . . all other our Plantation Produce: so that the extensive Employment of our Shipping in, to, and from America, the great Brood of Seamen consequent thereupon, and the daily Bread of the most considerable Part of our British Manufactures, are owing primarily to the Labour of Negroes; who, as they were the first happy instruments of raising our Plantations: so their Labour only can support and preserve them, and render them still more and more profitable to their Mother-Kingdom. The Negro-Trade therefore, and the natural consequences resulting from it, may be justly esteemed an inexhaustible Fund of Wealth and Naval Power to this Nation. (Parry and Sherlock 1971, 110–11).

The 1700s and first half of the 1800s constituted an era of great Atlantic economic expansion: a booming trade in enslaved workers and slave-produced products provided much capital for the commercial and industrial revolutions in Europe and North America. For example, between the seventeenth century and the nineteenth century, the *majority* of the major agricultural exports in world trade were produced by enslaved Africans (Williams 1944/1994; Bailey 1994).

Millions of enslaved Africans and African Americans paid the price for this expansion with their labor and lives. They were followed by millions more whose labor under legalized segregation and European colonialism in Africa created yet more wealth for whites, including whites at most class levels. The sum total of the worth of all the labor stolen through slavery, segregation, and contemporary discrimination is indeed staggering. The great amount of labor lost also meant capital lost for immediate and later African and African American generations. For about *fifteen* generations the exploitation of black Americans has redistributed the wealth earned by their labor to white Americans, leaving the former relatively impoverished and the latter relatively privileged. Consider just the monetary value of the labor expropriated. One scholar has estimated that the contemporary worth of the slave labor taken by whites from about 1620 to 1865 is at least $1 trillion, and perhaps much more depending on calculations of interest forgone (Swinton 1990). In addition, very large amounts of labor were stolen during the period of legal segregation—from about 1890 to the 1960s—in the form of greatly discriminatory wage rates, some of which continue to exact losses from black workers. Writing about the transition from slavery to segregation, Gunnar Myrdal (1944/1964, 209) noted: "In the beginning the Negroes were owned as property. When slavery disappeared, caste remained. Within this framework of adverse tradition the average Negro in every generation has had a most disadvantageous start. Discrimination against Negroes is thus rooted in this tradition of economic exploitation." Historically, then, there is a direct and continuing line of exploitation and unjust enrichment from slavery to legal segregation to informal discrimination today. The major manifestations of systemic racism are connected and reinforcing across this long period, and in this way they accumulate to further accentuate advantages for white Americans and disadvantages for African Americans.

Let us examine one major example of wealth-generating resources that were provided for many ancestors of today's white families, including immigrant families, but were largely denied to the ancestors of today's black families. After the Civil War, most black families never got access to the land promised by President Abraham Lincoln and Republican members of Congress, and the resulting racial inequality in wealth-generating agricultural land has been a major cause of persisting racial inequality. Pressed through Congress during the Civil War, the Homestead Act allowed the federal government to provide much farmland, an important wealth-generating asset, to many white homesteading families. From the 1860s to the 1930s and beyond, about 246 million acres were provided by the U.S. government, often at little cost, for about 1.5 million homesteads. Research by Trina Williams (2000) estimates that, depending on calculations of multiple ownership, mortality, marriage, and childbearing patterns, somewhere between 20 million and 93 million Americans are *currently* the beneficiaries of this large wealth-generating program, which operated over several generations.

Williams suggests a middle-range estimate of about 46 million current beneficiaries, the overwhelming majority of whom are white. Moreover, economic modeling of the impact of this initial gap in farmland access has shown that it has produced *most of the long-term racial gap in income between white and black Americans*, even without considering other aspects of racial discrimination and segregation that have been very destructive for black Americans seeking to build up families and communities (DeCanio 1981), including thousands of lynchings, much other violence against African Americans, a lack of schooling opportunities, and widespread employment discrimination.

Calculating the further costs of antiblack oppression from the end of slavery in 1865 to the year 1969, the end of legal segregation, and on into the present day increases the economic-loss estimate to a multitrillion-dollar figure. And there are many discriminatory mechanisms at work in recent decades that have added to the damage of discrimination in the past. For example, discrimination in home sales and insurance has limited the ability of black Americans to build up equities that they could have used to start businesses or help their children get a college education (Oliver and Shapiro 1995). Discrimination in securing mortgages for homes as well as for businesses has cost African Americans an estimated $100 billion over just the current generation, as compared to otherwise similar whites (Darity and Myers 1998). Private foundation and governmental reports regularly repeat the grim statistics: an average black family earns about 60 percent of the income of an average white family and has only 10 percent of the economic wealth of an average white family. We should also note that the costs of slavery, segregation, and contemporary discrimination are far more than economic, for there are many human and community costs as well. For example, African Americans have significantly shorter life spans (about six years less) than whites. This is one more lasting legacy, in the contemporary era, of systemic racism. It costs now—and has cost in the past—a great deal in human and economic terms to be black in North America. Indeed, for all their comments to the contrary, few whites would trade places today with an African American, for most know at some level the terrible cost of racism. The political scientist Andrew Hacker (1992) has asked his white students how much compensation they would want if they were suddenly changed from white to black. Most would want about $50 million for this reversal of racial fortunes.

Once a group is far ahead in terms of socioeconomic resources, it is very difficult for another group that does not have similar access to those critical resources—or even one that has access to modest new resources—to catch up, even over a substantial period of time. With entry to employment, education, and business blocked by slavery, legal segregation, and widespread informal discrimination for nearly four hundred years, African Americans have high entry and continuing costs and barriers for doing well in such institutional arenas. Moreover, even with the relatively recent removal of some major barriers, black Americans entering traditionally white arenas are likely to enter with much greater resource problems than whites who have been privileged for centuries. Over time the "bloodsucking vampires" get stronger as their prey get weaker. That is, without major societal changes, such as large-scale government intervention, U.S. society will always be characterized by racial inequality. This is one rationale that lies behind recent calls and organized movements among African Americans for government and private reparations for the past and present damages of racial oppression.

MAINTAINING INEQUALITY:
WIDESPREAD DISCRIMINATION TODAY

Carried out by whites at all class levels, racial discrimination and exclusion persist dramatically in the United States today and play a role in keeping African Americans and other Americans of color from being able to catch up socioeconomically with white Americans. Recall Myrdal's (1944/1964, 209) comment that racial discrimination is "rooted in this tradition of economic exploitation." Numerous studies show *large-scale* antiblack discrimination in employment, education, housing, and other settings (see Feagin and Feagin 2003). To demonstrate the high level of contemporary antiblack (and anti-Latino) discrimination, we can examine housing audit studies. For example, one federally funded project conducted 3,800 test audits in numerous cities. Estimates from the study indicated that black renters faced discrimination half the time, while black Americans trying to buy a home faced discrimination 59 percent of the time (Turner, Struyk, and Yinger 1991). More recent housing studies conducted in various cities have found higher rates. Compared to white testers paired with them, black renters faced discrimination about 60 to 80 percent of time, depending on the city. Studies using Latino renter-testers have also found high rates of discrimination (see Fair Housing Council of Fresno County 1997; Central Alabama Fair Housing Center 1996; Fair Housing Action Center, 1996; San Antonio Fair Housing Council 1997). Similarly high levels of discrimination have been found for employment. Thus, one Los Angeles study found that about 60 percent of more than one thousand black workers reported discriminatory barriers in their workplaces (Bobo and Suh 2000). In addition, a survey of forty thousand military personnel found that half or nearly half of the black personnel reported racist jokes, offensive discussions of race, or racial condescension during the previous year. Many also reported discrimination in career-related matters (Scarville et al. 1999; U.S. Department of Defense 1999).

RACIST IDEOLOGY: THE RATIONALIZATION OF
RACISM AND THE REPRODUCTION OF RACIAL CONSCIOUSNESS

Systemic racism is rooted in the material exploitation of African Americans and other Americans of color, but it involves considerably more than just material exploitation. Over time exploitative racism comes to encompass a wide range of racist symbols, interpretations, and ideologies as well. Over nearly four centuries, white Americans, especially those in the ruling elite, have developed a racialized perspective and ideologies that rationalize white exploitation and material privileges. For centuries now, whites have argued that their unjust enrichment is legitimate and the result, entirely or mainly, of their own (and their ancestors') meritorious efforts. A *racist ideology* is "a socially imbedded set of beliefs that is widely accepted and critical to maintaining the subordination of Black Americans and other people of color" (Feagin 2000, 32). Such an ideology, in the European and American contexts, has rationalized the ongoing racist hierarchy as one that places "superior" racial groups above racially "inferior" ones. Recall DuBois's (1946/1965, 37) comment about the connections between the point of view of the former European colonies in Africa and the wealth and luxury in contemporary Europe. He adds in this connection that the problems of poverty "had to be represented as natural characteristics of backward peoples." This is also true for the United States, where a racist ideology accenting biological differences and a racist ideology accenting cultural differences (for example, the "culture of poverty") between "superior" and "inferior" racial groups still vie for the racist white mind's attention. It is also the case that, once racist ideologies are well developed in children's minds, they become concrete and powerful over the long term (see Van Ausdale and Feagin 2001).

In the United States, white elites, almost entirely male, have been central in creating racist ideologies for centuries, yet most ordinary whites have also bought into these racist ideologies, as we see in the continuing racial prejudice and stereotyping that targets Americans of color today. Over centuries, most whites have accepted the hierarchy of racial groups because they benefit from it. Most have accepted the "public and psychological wage" of whiteness (DuBois 1935/1992, 700). Thus, for many decades most white workers have rejected organizing with black workers to improve working conditions for all. From the 1830s to the early 1900s, European immigrant groups, including those not initially considered to be "white" by native-born whites, pressed hard to be viewed as white, thereby making elimination of the longstanding racist system difficult. Today there are still new immigrants—such as *some* (but by no means all) Cuban and Middle Eastern immigrants—who press to be considered white. White racial identity has "generally determined the social world and loyalties, the life world, of whites—whether as citizens of the colonizing mother country, settlers, nonslaves, or beneficiaries of the 'color bar' and the 'color line' " (Mills 1997, 138). Early in this process of creating a white racial identity, systemic racism became much more than a matter of economic exploitation and worker competition. It became a societywide system designed to reproduce in all its major aspects, especially in institutions, the generally privileged position of white Americans and generally disadvantaged position of African Americans and many other Americans of color.

RACIST ATTITUDES TODAY

This long-standing racist ideology is an umbrella for many racist prejudices and stereotypes. Racist ideas become imbedded in the white mind, for individual minds are largely social minds. We learn notions about the world substantially from interaction with other human beings, beginning as very young children. Thus, today most whites still hold negative views of African Americans, and probably of other Americans of color as well. Note the national survey by the Anti-Defamation League in which three-quarters of white respondents accepted as true one or more eight racist statements about African Americans (Anti-Defamation League 1993). Recent research by Eduardo Bonilla-Silva and Tyrone Forman (2000) and by Kristen Myers and Passion Williamson (2001) strongly suggests that the level of racist thought in the white population remains high, though often hidden by the adeptness most whites have at keeping these views backstage.

Significantly, the collective memory (social mind) of white Americans, those unjustly enriched with resources and privileges, is not the same as the collective memory of those who are unjustly impoverished.[2] In this context, collective memory can be seen as how people understand and experience the present in terms of their group's collective past, which is "what is left of the past in the lived experiences of groups, or what groups make of their past" (Nora 1988, 170). Many relatives and friends are carriers of this collective memory into the present. For whites, there is a positive memory of individual and family achievements over generations, of hard work that made possible the achievements of recent generations, unmarred by memories of contemporary racial discrimination. However, for black men, women, and children, strong memories of family, community, and positive achievements are accompanied by strong negative memories of past *and* recent racism (St. Jean and Feagin 1998).

THE RACIAL EXPLOITATION OF
OTHER PEOPLE OF COLOR

In U.S. history, racial exploitation has not been limited to African Americans. Many other Americans of color have suffered from white oppression. Interestingly, in recent years numerous U.S. analysts have criticized what they call the dominant "black-white paradigm" in the analysis of racial-ethnic issues in the United States (see Perea 1997). For the most part, these analysts are not actually referring to a theoretical paradigm but rather to the fact that much U.S. discourse about racial-ethnic relations centers on "black-white" issues. Although these analysts make very important points about the discrimination faced by other Americans of color, in these commentaries they focus too little on who controls both the public discourse and the underlying racist system. Too seldom do these analysts note that it is powerful *whites* (not blacks) who are in control of most of the public racial-ethnic discourse, and it is whites, often elite whites, who are more or less obsessed with issues of black and white Americans. Moreover, the central reality often being tiptoed around in these analyses is "white-on-black" or "white-on-nonwhite" (not "black-white") *oppression* (Feagin 2002; see also Feagin and Vera 1995; Feagin 2000). As I showed earlier, white-on-black oppression is the archetypical case of white racism in U.S. history. At the time when Africans were enslaved in large numbers in the American colonies, the only other non-Europeans present, Native Americans, were mostly driven away from white areas (to the West) or targeted for extermination. For the most part, it was African Americans who were centrally integrated as laborers into the new white-controlled economy of the colonies, and later the United States. Indeed, African Americans are the only group of color in U.S. history to have been chattel slaves on a large scale—and for more than two centuries. They were also the main group of color targeted for socioeconomic and political oppression in the U.S. Constitution, whose construction was substantially in the hands of slaveholders. For centuries the dominant white group has maintained a racialized ladder of oppression—running from whites at the top to blacks and Native Americans at the bottom. They have incorporated into this ladderlike framework each new non-European group brought into the sphere of white control. Each new group is placed *by dominant whites* somewhere in the white-to-black hierarchy of resources and power (see Feagin 2000, 205–20; Feagin and Feagin 2003, passim).

Of course, the character of the racial oppression faced by an entering group varies depending on the timing of its entry, its region of entry, and its size, economic resources, cultural characteristics, and physical characteristics. Thus, whites particularly accent the cultural "alienness" and "foreignness" of Latino and Asian immigrants. Indeed, viewing Americans of color as alien goes back to white views of enslaved Africans, who were early on considered to be uncivilized, strange, and foreign. Asian and Latino immigrants and their descendants have usually been positioned, and initially and principally by powerful whites, somewhere on the racialized ladder of oppression and given social status somewhere between whites and blacks—with a negative evaluation on both axes of alienated social relations, that of superior-inferior and that of insider-foreigner (Kim 1999; Feagin 2002).

More recent non-European immigrant groups do not share exactly the same fate, but in all cases it is the dominant white group that mostly determines the character of the societal treatment (mistreatment) and incorporation into various socioeconomic sectors, as well as the prevailing interpretation of that group incorporation. For example, some immigrant groups, such as Taiwanese, Vietnamese, Cuban, and Korean immigrants, have come to the United States as a result of U.S. involvement in imperialistic or neocolonial operations and wars overseas, while others have been brought in to meet continuing demand by capitalists for low-wage labor (see Feagin and Feagin 2003, passim). For example, Juan Gonzalez (2000, xiv) notes that "the Latino migrant flows were directly connected to the growth of a U.S. empire, and they responded closely to that empire's needs, whether it was a political need to stabilize a neighboring country or to accept its refugees as a means of accomplishing a broader foreign policy objective (Cubans, Dominicans, Salvadorans, Nicaraguans), or whether it was an economic need, such as satisfying the labor demands of particular U.S. industries (Mexicans, Puerto Ricans, Panamanians)." Once again we see the central role of material exploitation in the history of U.S. *racist* relations.

CONCLUSION

Assessing the coming Civil War, President Abraham Lincoln made the prediction that a "house divided against itself cannot stand." As we look across the twenty-first century, we can see a great need for the "house" that is U.S. society to be substantially rebuilt along more democratic and egalitarian lines. The foundation of this great house is still one of systemic racism. "We the people"— a term originally created by white men with property for themselves—have never replaced the underlying racist foundation of this society. We have remodeled this racist house two times, during the abolitionist and Civil War periods and again during the civil rights revolution of the 1950s and 1960s, yet the household's racist foundation today is still substantially in place.

Analyzing workers' exploitation under capitalism, Karl Marx had two objections. One was that such labor exploitation was *unjust,* an objection rooted in traditional egalitarian political theory. Yet Marx had a second objection to exploitation that goes deeper. Exploitation is objectionable not just because of distributive inequality but also "because it involves social relations in which agents view the needs of others as levers manipulated for their own private advantage. Each agent views his or her own capacities as powers to be used to take advantage of others, rather than as powers either to be developed for their own sake or as powers to be used for the common good" (quoted in Warren 2001, n.p.). It is not just the unjust extraction of resources from the other that is troubling, but also the reality and quality of the *alienated* social relationships, which under capitalism are grounded in individualistic concerns and selfishness (Marx 1959; Ollman 1976). This is also true for other exploitative systems, including modern racism and sexism. These racist and sexist systems radically divide human beings from each other, thereby creating alienated human relations and severely impeding the development of a common consciousness and solidarity. This is not a healthy situation for any Americans, whatever their racial and ethnic background. It is certainly not healthy for the future of a multiracial society trying to become a truly operational and fully developed democracy.

If we are to generate a complete and useful theory of systemic racism, we must also focus on how to generate greater sociopolitical resistance to racial oppression. The course of U.S. history shows that racial and other social oppressions have periodically generated major resistance movements involving Americans of many socioeconomic backgrounds. I do not have the space here to develop some ideas on the great and ongoing importance of people's resistance, which I have sketched out elsewhere (see Feagin 1982, 2000). Various scholars have shown how African Americans, other people of color, and white women have played a central role in loosening their own chains of oppression. We have previously noted the abolitionist movements of the nineteenth century and the civil rights movements of the twentieth century. This important history shows that when human beings build up knowledge about structures of oppression and knowledge of how to destroy structures of oppression, they can, and eventually will, rebel. The great inequality of socioeconomic resources across the color line has often led to subtle or overt resistance by black Americans and other Americans of color. Human beings have a unique ability to reflect on their own circumstances and to create, in association with others, a collective consciousness leading to major societal change in the direction of greater democracy.

NOTES

1. In portions of this chapter, I summarize and expand on arguments made in Feagin 2000 and Feagin and Feagin 2003.
2. I am indebted to Bernice McNair Barnett for suggesting this point and for comments on an early draft of this paper; I am also indebted to Danielle Dirks for copyediting assistance.

REFERENCES

Anti-Defamation League. 1993. *Highlights from an Anti-Defamation League Survey on Racial Attitudes in America.* New York: ADL.

Ayres, Ian, and Fredrick E. Vars. 1998. "When Does Private Discrimination Justify Public Affirmative Action?" *Columbia Law Review* (November): 1598–1610.

Bailey, Ronald. 1994. "The Other Side of Slavery." *Agricultural History* 68(Spring): 40.

Benokraitis, Nijole, and Joe R. Feagin. 1986. *Modern Sexism: Blatant, Subtle, and Covert Discrimination.* Englewood Cliffs, N.J.: Prentice-Hall.

Bobo, Lawrence D., and Susan A. Suh. 2000. "Surveying Racial Discrimination: Analyses from a Multiethnic Labor Market." In *Prismatic Metropolis: Inequality in Los Angeles,* edited by Lawrence D. Bobo, Melvin L. Oliver, James H. Johnson Jr., and Abel Valenzuela Jr. New York: Russell Sage Foundation.

Bonilla-Silva, Eduardo, and Tyrone A. Forman. 2000. " 'I Am Not a Racist but . . .': Mapping White College Students' Racial Ideology in the U.S.A." *Discourse and Society* 11: 50–85.

Carmichael, Stokely (Kwame Ture), and Charles V. Hamilton. 1967. *Black Power: The Politics of Liberation in America.* New York: Vintage.

Central Alabama Fair Housing Center. 1996. "Discrimination in the Rental Housing Market: A Study of Montgomery, Alabama, 1995–1996." Montgomery: Central Alabama Fair Housing Center.

Cox, Oliver C. 1948. *Caste, Class, and Race.* Garden City, N.Y.: Doubleday.

Cross, Theodore. 1984. *Black Power Imperative: Racial Inequality and the Politics of Nonviolence.* New York: Faulkner.

Davis, Angela. 1971. "Reflections on the Black Woman's Role in the Community of Slaves." *Black Scholar* 3: 2–15.

Darity, William A., Jr., and Samuel L. Myers. 1998. *Persistent Disparity: Race and Economic Inequality in the United States Since 1945.* Northampton, Mass.: Edward Elgar.

DeCanio, Stephen J. 1981. "Accumulation and Discrimination in the Postbellum South." In *Market Institutions and Economic Progress in the New South 1865–1900,* edited by Gary Walton and James Shepherd. New York: Academic Press.

Delgado, Richard. 1996. *The Coming Race War?* New York: New York University Press.

Douglass, Frederick. 1855/2002. *My Bondage and My Freedom.* New York: Humanity Books.

———. 1968. "The Color Line." *North American Review* (June 1881), as excerpted in *Jones et ux. v. Alfred H. Mayer Co.* 392 U.S. 409, 446–47.

DuBois, W. E. B. 1920/1996. "Darkwater." In *The Oxford W. E. B. DuBois Reader,* edited by Eric J. Sundquist. New York: Oxford University Press.

———. 1946/1965. *The World and Africa.* New York: International Publishers.

———. 1935/1992. *Black Reconstruction in America 1860–1880.* New York: Atheneum.

Essed, Philomena. 1991. *Understanding Everyday Racism.* Newbury Park, Calif.: Sage Publications.

Fair Housing Action Center. 1996. "Greater New Orleans Rental Audit." New Orleans, La.: Fair Housing Action Center.

Fair Housing Council of Fresno County. 1997. "Audit Uncovers Blatant Discrimination Against Hispanics, African Americans, and Families with Children in Fresno County." Fresno, Calif.: Fair Housing Council of Fresno County.

Feagin, Joe R. 1982. *Social Problems: A Critical Power-Conflict Perspective.* Englewood Cliffs, N.J.: Prentice-Hall.

———. 2000. *Racist America: Roots, Current Realities, and Future Reparations.* New York: Routledge.

———. 2002. "White Supremacy and Mexican Americans: Rethinking the Black-White Paradigm." *Rutgers Law Review* 54(4): 959–87.

Feagin, Joe R., and Clairece B. Feagin. 1978. *Discrimination American Style: Institutional Racism and Sexism.* Englewood Cliffs, N.J.: Prentice-Hall.

————. 2003. *Racial and Ethnic Relations.* 7th ed. Upper Saddle River, N.J.: Prentice-Hall.

Feagin, Joe R., and Karyn D. McKinney. 2003. *The Many Costs of Racism.* Lanham, Md.: Rowman & Littlefield.

Feagin, Joe R., and Hernan Vera. 1995. *White Racism: The Basics.* New York: Routledge.

Galeano, Eduardo. 1973/1997. *Open Veins of Latin America.* New York: Monthly Review Press.

Gonzalez, Juan. 2000. *Harvest of Empire: A History of Latinos in America.* New York: Penguin Books.

Gordon, Milton M. 1964. *Assimilation in American Life.* New York: Oxford University Press.

Hacker, Andrew. 1992. *Two Nations: Black and White, Separate, Hostile, Unequal.* New York: Scribner's.

Hershberg, Theodore, with the Philadelphia Social History Project. 1981. "A Tale of Three Cities: Blacks, Immigrants, and Opportunity in Philadelphia: 1850–1880, 1930, 1970." In *Philadelphia,* edited by Theodore Hershberg. New York: Oxford University Press.

Hirschfeld, Magnus. 1938. *Racism.* London: Gollancz.

Honderich, Ted, ed. 1995. "Exploitation." In *The Oxford Companion to Philosophy.* Oxford: Oxford University Press.

Kim, Claire Jean. 1999. "The Racial Triangulation of Asian Americans." *Politics and Society* 27(March): 105–38.

Kull, Andrew. 1995. "Rationalizing Restitution." *California Law Review* 83: 1191–1242.

Marx, Karl. 1959. *Economic and Philosophical Manuscripts.* Moscow: Progress Publishers.

————. 1867/1977. *Capital: A Critique of Political Economy.* New York: Vintage Books.

McKee, James. 1993. *Sociology and the Race Problem.* Urbana: University of Illinois Press.

Mills, Charles W. 1997. *The Racial Contract.* Ithaca, N.Y.: Cornell University Press.

Myers, Kristen A., and Passion Williamson. 2001. "Race Talk: The Perpetuation of Racism Through Private Discourse." Unpublished paper. Northern Illinois University, De Kalb.

Myrdal, Gunnar. 1944/1964. *An American Dilemma.* New York: McGraw-Hill.

Nora, Pierre. 1988. *Histoire et Mémoire,* edited by Jacques Le Goff. Paris: Édition Gallimard.

Oliver, Melvin L., and Thomas M. Shapiro. 1995. *Black Wealth/White Wealth: A New Perspective on Racial Equality.* New York: Routledge.

Ollman, Bertell. 1976. *Alienation: Marx's Conception of Man in Capitalist Society*. 2nd ed. Cambridge: Cambridge University Press.

Parry, John H., and Philip M. Sherlock. 1971. *A Short History of the West Indies*. 3rd ed. New York: St. Martin's Press.

Perea, Juan F. 1997. "The Black-White Binary Paradigm of Race: The 'Normal Science' of American Racial Thought." *California Law Review* 85(October): 1219–21.

Roemer, John E. 1982. *A General Theory of Exploitation and Class*. Cambridge, Mass.: Harvard University Press.

Ronai, Carol R., Barbara Zsembik, and Joe R. Feagin, eds. 1997. *Everyday Sexism in the Third Millennium*. New York: Routledge.

St. Jean, Yanick, and Joe R. Feagin. 1998. *Double Burden: Black Women and Everyday Racism*. New York: M. E. Sharpe.

San Antonio Fair Housing Council. 1997. "San Antonio Metropolitan Area Rental Audit 1997." San Antonio, Tex.: San Antonio Fair Housing Council.

Scarville, Jacquelyn, Scott B. Button, Jack E. Edwards, Anita R. Lancaster, and Timothy W. Elig. 1999. "Armed Forces Equal Opportunity Survey." Arlington, Va.: Defense Manpower Data Center.

Sollors, Werner. 1989. *The Invention of Ethnicity*. New York: Oxford University Press.

Swinton, David H. 1990. "Racial Inequality and Reparations." In *The Wealth of Races: The Present Value of Benefits from Past Injustices*, edited by Richard F. America. New York: Greenwood Press.

Turner, Margery Austin, Raymond J. Struyk, and John Yinger. 1991. *Housing Discrimination Study: Synthesis*. Washington: U.S. Government Printing Office, 1991.

U.S. Department of Defense. Office of the Undersecretary of Defense Personnel and Readiness. 1999. *Career Progression of Minority and Women Officers*. Washington: U.S. Department of Defense.

Van Ausdale, Debra, and Joe R. Feagin. 2001. *The First R: How Children Learn Race and Racism*. Lanham, Md.: Rowman & Littlefield.

Warren, Paul. 2001. "Two Marxist Objections to Exploitation." Boston: Boston University, The Paideia Project. Available at: http://www.bu.edu/wcp/Papers/Soci/SociWarr.htm (accessed June 14, 2004).

Wells-Barnett, Ida B. 1895. *A Red Record*. Chicago: Donahue and Henneberry.

Williams, Eric. 1944/1994. *Capitalism and Slavery*. Chapel Hill: University of North Carolina Press.

Williams, Trina. 2000. "The Homestead Act—Our Earliest National Asset Policy." Paper presented to the Center for Social Development symposium "Inclusion in Asset Building." St. Louis (September 21–23).

9

THE POLITICAL AND THEORETICAL CONTEXTS
OF THE CHANGING RACIAL TERRAIN

✺

Manning Marable

AT THE FIRST Pan-African Conference held in London in August 1900, the great African American scholar W. E. B. DuBois (1970, 125) predicted that "the problem of the twentieth century is the problem of the color line, the question as to how far differences of race . . . will hereafter be made the basis of denying to over half the world the right of sharing . . . the opportunities and privileges of modern civilization." Today, with the both tragic and triumphant racial experiences of the twentieth century behind us, we may say from the vantage point of universal culture that the problem of the twenty-first century is the problem of "global apartheid"—the construction of new racialized ethnic hierarchies, discourses, and processes of domination and subordination in the context of economic globalization and neoliberal public policies. Within the more narrow context of the United States, the fundamental problem of the twenty-first century is the problem of "structural racism": the deeply entrenched patterns of socioeconomic and political inequality and accumulated disadvantage that are coded by race and color and constantly justified in both public and private discourses by racist stereotypes, white indifference, and the prison-industrial complex.

The African political scientist and anthropologist Mahmood Mamdani (1996) has observed that beginning with the imposition of European colonial rule in Africa, the institution of race was central to the development of the modern state. Mamdani's insight about the racialized construction of the modern state holds true for the U.S. state as well. Racial categories and racial identities in the United States are politically constructed. That is, racial identities continue to be legally sanctioned categories, supported by the weight of the courts, political institutions, organized religion, and custom and reinforced by both deliberate as well as random acts of violence. The African American has become the permanent reference point for the racialized other within political and civil society. To be "black" is to be excluded from the social contract that links all other citizens to the state through sets of rights and responsibilities.

Even prior to the American Revolution against the British and the consolidation of the new federal system of the United States in 1787, race was firmly set as the organizing principle of power in the early American colonies, after more than a century of black civic and political exclusion. One outcome of the institutionalization of the system of racial hierarchy was the evolution, as the United States grew and matured, of two very distinct political narratives about the nature of U.S. democracy, how the American nation-state was founded, and the character of the social contract between the American people and the state. For most white Americans, U.S. democracy is best represented by values such as personal liberty, individualism, and the ownership of private property. For most African Americans, the central goals of the black freedom movement have always been equality—the eradication of all structural barriers to full citizenship and full participation in all aspects of public life and in economic relations—and self-determination—the ability to decide, on their own collective terms, what their future as a community with a unique history and culture might be. "Freedom" for black Americans has always been perceived in collective terms as something achievable by group action and capacity building. "Equality" means the elimination of all social deficits between blacks and whites and the eradication of the cultural and social stereotypes and patterns of social isolation and group exclusion generated by white structural racism over several centuries.

Historically, the United States has witnessed two great struggles to achieve a truly multicultural democracy, both of which have focused on the status of African Americans. The First Reconstruction (1865 to 1877) ended slavery and briefly gave black men voting rights, but it failed to provide meaningful compensation for two centuries of unpaid labor. The promise of "forty acres and a mule" was for most blacks a dream deferred. The Second Reconstruction (1954 to 1968), or the modern civil rights movement, outlawed legal segregation in public accommodations and achieved major legislative victories such as voting rights. But these successes paradoxically obscured the tremendous human costs of historically accumulated disadvantage. Those costs remain central to black Americans' lives today.

MANIFESTATIONS OF STRUCTURAL RACISM

The disproportionate wealth that most white Americans enjoy today was first constructed from centuries of unpaid black labor. Many white institutions, including Ivy League universities, insurance companies, and banks, profited from slavery. This pattern of white privilege and black inequality continues today, even though legal segregation has ended. As the legal scholar Cheryl Harris

(1993) observed over a decade ago, in a racialized social hierarchy "whiteness" is essentially a form of private property. The state is organized around the processes of what can be termed "racial accumulation." The racial benefits accrued by whites include higher salaries, superior working conditions, lower rates of unemployment, higher rates of homeownership, greater access to professional and managerial positions, and average life expectancies that are seven years longer than those of black Americans. White Americans have benefited from nearly four hundred years of accumulated white privilege, which is reflected in vast disparities in material resources and property between racial groups. Here are just a few examples of the historical consequences of America's structural racism:

- *Wealth:* One-third of all black households actually have a negative net wealth. In 1998 the typical black family's net wealth was $16,400, less than one-fifth that of white families. Black families are denied home loans at twice the rate of whites. Blacks are frequently forced to turn to "predatory lenders" who charge outrageously high home mortgage rates.

- *Labor market:* Blacks remain the last hired and first fired during recessions. For example, during the 1990 to 1991 recession, African Americans suffered disproportionately. At Coca-Cola, 42 percent of employees losing their jobs were black. At Sears, 54 percent were black. Black workers usually have less job seniority and are less able to be hired through informal networks of friends and relatives.

- *Health:* Blacks have significantly shorter life expectancies. Part of the reason is racism in the health establishment. Blacks are statistically less likely than whites to be referred for kidney transplants or early-stage cancer surgery. The percentage of blacks without health insurance is about twice that for whites.

- *Criminal justice:* African Americans constitute only one-seventh of all drug users. Yet we are 35 percent of all drug arrests, 55 percent of drug convictions, and 75 percent of prison admissions for drug offenses. For juveniles arrested and charged with a crime, black youths are six times more likely than whites to be sentenced to prison.

HISTORICAL RESPONSES TO STRUCTURAL RACISM

How have African Americans responded to the evolving domains of structural racism? In terms of racial counterhegemonic approaches, the black American community over the course of 150 years has developed three overlapping protest strategies: integration or racial assimilation, black nationalism or black separatism, and what the feminist anthropologist Leith Mullings and I have termed "transformation" (Marable and Mullings 2003). Integrationist movements sought full democratic rights and interracial assimilation within the existing institutions of society. Integration called for the desegregation of public accommodations, schools, and residential patterns, as well as more equitable black representation throughout the class structure. Black nationalism was premised on the pessimistic (or realistic) notion that most white Americans' prejudices were relatively fixed and meaningful racial reforms were impossible in the long run. What was required was the construction of strong black-owned institutions, businesses, and schools, an emphasis on black cultural awareness and group consciousness, and frequently a strong identification with Africa. Transformationists, or black radicalists, focused on the link between racial oppression and class exploitation, calling for a redistribution of wealth as a key strategy in dismantling racism. Transformationists attempted to construct strategic coalitions across racial boundaries, focusing on issues of socioeconomic inequality and the day-to-day violence perpetuated by poverty.

Each of these three strategies had certain strengths and weaknesses. Integrationists placed too much faith in the American capitalist class's commitment to liberal democracy and social fairness, and they tended to believe that racism was rooted in ignorance rather than cold, deliberate exploitation. Black nationalists perhaps underestimated the "American-ness" of black Americans, a people who share many of the same economic values, political aspirations, and cultural practices as white Americans. Strategies of black entrepreneurial capitalism in segregated racialized markets cannot work in a period of global markets and transnational corporations. Transformationists possibly gave too much emphasis to class conflict as the driving force in social history and underestimated the psychological and cultural factors that justified and perpetuated white power and privilege.

THE FUTURE: THE NEXT STEPS IN CHALLENGING STRUCTURAL RACISM

First, as scholars who study ethnicity and race, especially as they relate to modes of state power, we should contribute to a richer theoretical and historically grounded understanding of diversity. Instead of just celebrating diversity, we must theorize it, interrogate it, and actively seek the parallels and connections between people of various communities. Instead of talking about race, we should popularize the public's understanding of the social processes of "racialization," that is, how certain groups in U.S. society have been relegated to an oppressed status by the weight of law, social policy, and economic exploitation. This has never been solely a black-white paradigm. Although slavery and Jim Crow segregation were decisive in framing the U.S. social hierarchy, with whiteness defined at the top and blackness at the bottom, people of African descent have never experienced racialization by themselves. As the historian Gary

Okihiro (2001a, 2001b) has observed, the 1790 Naturalization Act defined citizenship only for immigrants who were "free white persons." Asian immigrants who were born outside the United States were largely excluded from citizenship until 1952. U.S. courts constantly redefined the rules determining who was "white" and who was not. For example, as Okihiro observes, Armenians were originally classed as "Asians" and thus were nonwhite, but they legally became "whites" through a 1909 court decision. Syrians were "white" in court decisions in 1909 and 1910; they became "nonwhite" in 1913, then "white" again in 1915. Asian Indians were legally white in 1910, but nonwhite after 1923. Historians like David Roediger (1991), Noel Ignatiev (1995), and Tom Guglielmo (2003) illustrate how a series of ethnic minorities, such as the Irish and Jews, experienced racialization but scaled the hierarchy of whiteness.

Historically, all too frequently, the oppressed have defined themselves largely, and often unthinkingly, by the boundaries of identities that were superimposed on them. Louis Althusser once referred to this social dynamic as "overdetermination." Oppressed people living at the bottom of any social hierarchy are constantly reinforced to see themselves as "others," as individuals who dwell outside of society's social contract, as subordinated categories of marginalized, fixed minorities. Frequently, oppressed people have utilized these categories and even terms of insult and stigmatization, such as "nigger" or "queer," as a site for resistance and counterhegemonic struggle.

The difficulty inherent in this kind of oppositional politics is twofold. First, it tends to anchor individuals to narrowly defined, one-dimensional identities that can essentially be the inventions of others. For example, how did African people become known as "black," or in Spanish, "Negro"? Europeans launching the slave trade across the Atlantic four hundred years ago created the terminology as a way of categorizing the people of an entire continent with tremendous variations in language, religion, ethnicity, kinship patterns, and cultural traditions. "Blackness," or the state of being black, was completely artificial; *no people* in Africa called themselves "black." Blackness exists only as a social construct in relation to something else. That "something else" became known as "whiteness." Blackness as a totalizing category relegates other identities—ethnicity, sexual orientation, gender, class affiliation, religious traditions, kinship affiliations—to a secondary or even nonexistent status. In other words, those who control or dominate hierarchies—whether they own the means of production or dominate the state—have a vested interest in manufacturing and reproducing categories of difference.

An excellent recent example of this occurred in the United States in 1971 when the U.S. Census Bureau "invented" the category "Hispanic." The census category "Hispanic" was then imposed on a population of nearly 20 million people who reflected widely divergent and often contradictory nationalities, racialized ethnic identities, cultural traditions, and political affinities: black Panamanians of Jamaican or Trinidadian descent who spoke Spanish;

Argentines of Italian or German descent; anti-Castro, white, upper-class Cubans in Miami's Dade County; impoverished Mexican American farm-workers in California's Central Valley; and black Dominican working-class people in New York City's Washington Heights. Yet when states or hierarchies name the "other," the act of naming creates its own materiality for the oppressed. Government resources, economic empowerment zones, and affirmative action scholarships are in part determined by who is classified as Hispanic and who is not. Identities may be situational, but when the power and resources of the state are used to categorize groups under a one-size-fits-all designation, the life chances of individuals who are defined within these categories are largely set and determined by others.

A second issue we need to consider is the question: how do we begin to rebuild the protest capacity of and resistance organizations within black, Latino, Asian-Pacific Island, and other racialized immigrant communities? Part of this effort must be frankly defensive: the construction of racialized minority-based institutions to provide goods and services, educational and child care resources, and health clinics, frequently with little or no government funding. Nongovernmental organizations, such as neighborhood associations and comprehensive community initiatives, may enhance the ability of disadvantaged groups to realize their specific, objective interests. We need new approaches to combat what Angela Davis (2003, forthcoming) describes as "civic death"—the legal marginalization and civic disempowerment that have become so widespread that they threaten not only to negate the Voting Rights Act of 1965 but also, in many respects, to void the Fifteenth Amendment of the U.S. Constitution, which granted black males the right to vote.

To revitalize the African American social protest movement, we must also break with the idea that "politics" is something that takes place in the electoral arena alone. Voter registration and mobilization are, of course, crucial tools in the struggle for black empowerment. But electoralism by itself cannot transform the actual power relations between racialized, oppressed minorities and the white majority. New tactical protest approaches, which employ creative political confrontations by mass constituencies of African Americans, must be initiated.

Black political history provides several successful models of mass collective mobilizations around issues of public policy. One excellent example is A. Philip Randolph's Negro March on Washington Movement of 1941. The first March on Washington mobilization was established outside of the formal organizational structures of civil rights groups like the NAACP. Like Marcus Garvey's Universal Negro Improvement Association (UNIA), it was largely if not exclusively an all-Negro movement. It advanced a specific set of public policy objectives that pointed toward the ultimate elimination of legal Jim Crow segregation. The Negro March on Washington focused its energies not on persuading white liberals to support racial reforms but instead on action by the black masses, through town hall–style meetings and protest demonstrations. It linked the issues of the most oppressed sectors of the black community to the organized efforts of black unions and more progressive black middle-class organizations.

Randolph's intervention forced President Franklin Roosevelt to issue Executive Order 8802, declaring that "there shall be no discrimination in the employment of workers in defense industries or government because of race, creed, color or national origin." Roosevelt also established the Fair Employment Practices Committee. Because of Executive Order 8802, more than one-quarter million African Americans would be hired in defense industries during World War II. The Negro March on Washington created a new political environment of black militancy that directly contributed to the creation of the Congress of Racial Equality (CORE) in 1941 and the unprecedented growth of the NAACP, increasing its membership from 50,000 in 1940 to over 200,000 by 1945.

The demand for black reparations may have the same potential for transforming the national public policy discourse on race relations as the Negro March on Washington Movement did sixty years ago. Randolph's 1941 movement brought together young leftist intellectuals like Ralph Bunche with black trade unionists, constructing a multiclass, black-identified coalition that espoused both a long-term vision—the complete dismantling of Jim Crow segregation and the democratic access of Negroes to all levels of American society and public life—and short-term objectives, such as the end of racial exclusion in hiring in wartime industries and the outlawing of racially segregated units in the U.S. military. The reparations campaign must approach the challenge of breaking apart the leviathan of American structural racism in a similar way. We must clearly set out the long-term objective—the realization of a truly multicultural, pluralistic democracy without the barriers of race, class, and gender—while focusing specifically on the immediate, realizable reforms that are necessary to achieve as part of a broad counterhegemonic democratic movement.

A third critical area for both theory and practice is critical and concrete engagement with the intersectionalities of race with gender, sexuality, and class. Black feminists for decades have made the effective theoretical observation that racism does not exist in a gender vacuum and that structures of domination and social hierarchy reinforce each other across the boundaries of identity. In practical political terms, from day-to-day experiences working with multiethnic communities, we can observe how the intersectionalities of gender, sexuality, and class combine with structural racism. A plethora of contemporary and historical examples illustrate the particular ways in which race and gender, for example, have intersected to shape the lives of women of color. In one example, Andrea Smith (2001) details the nonconsensual sterilization of Latina and Native American women during the 1970s—a practice deeply connected to the women's racialized sexuality, which constructed them as hyperfertile and thus dangerous to national stability. In a different example, Smith cites statistics showing that women of color are far overrepresented in the prison population and tend to serve longer sentences for the same crime than do white women or men of color. Moreover, women of color are much more likely to be poor than their white peers.

A fourth area of concern for the future politics of racialized ethnicity is the need to incorporate understandings of transnational contexts into our analysis. The black freedom movement in the United States must reorient itself in a period of globalization and transnational corporations toward the antiracist struggles being waged across international communities. White supremacy in the United States has always endeavored to reinforce political parochialism among the African American people, encouraging them to perceive themselves in isolation from the rest of the racialized nonwhite world. Those black revolutionary activists and progressive social reformers, such as W. E. B. DuBois, Paul Robeson, Dr. Martin Luther King Jr., Angela Y. Davis, and Malcolm X, who advocated internationalist perspectives on black liberation were invariably defined as subversive and as most threatening to the established order. Yet in the age of globalization, there can be no "national" solution to the problem of structural racism. As the power of nation-states declines relative to the growth of transnational capital, individual counterhegemonic political projects confined to one narrow geographical area will lack the theoretical and organizational tools to transform their societies.

The twenty-first century truly began—politically, socially, and psychologically—with two epochal events: the World Conference Against Racism, held in Durban, South Africa, and the terrorist attacks of September 11, 2001, which destroyed the World Trade Center towers and part of the Pentagon. These events were directly linked to the political economy of global apartheid and to the crystallization of new transnational hierarchies of racialized "otherness" and new modes of power and powerlessness.

At Durban, the Third World, led primarily by African Americans and African people, attempted to renegotiate its historically unequal and subordinate relationships with Western imperialism and globalized capitalism through the processes of diplomacy. Reparations were seen by black delegates at Durban as a necessary precondition for the socioeconomic development of the black community in the United States, as well as for African and Caribbean nation-states. September 11 was another type of renegotiation, but through terror, a violent statement by fundamentalist Muslims demanding an end to American imperialism's economic and political domination throughout the Arab world. Both events symbolized a challenge to America's almost completely uncritical support for Israel and were to some extent expressions of solidarity with the Palestinians' struggle for self-determination. The aftermath of both events left the U.S. government more politically isolated from the African and Islamic worlds than ever before.

Although the traumatic events of September 11 have pushed the black reparations issue temporarily into the background in the United States, the reality is that U.S. and Western European imperialism ultimately will be forced to acknowledge the legitimacy and necessity of at least a limited reparations agreement. U.S. policymakers will undoubtedly attempt to solidify their problematic relationships with African and Caribbean countries and separate them from any possible strategic coalition with more radical Islamic states. The price for their diplomatic cooperation may be debt forgiveness and some kind of financial aid package to assist in development projects. If African countries are successful in renegotiating their debt payments, based in part on the history of colonial exploitation and slavery, the granting of some program of black reparations in the United States also becomes more likely.

The official U.S. delegation at Durban rejected the definition of slavery as "a crime against humanity." It refused to acknowledge the historic and contemporary effects of colonialism, racial segregation, and apartheid on the underdevelopment and oppression of the non-European world. It dishonestly manipulated charges of anti-Semitism to evade serious discussions concerning the right of self-determination for the Palestinian people. The world's subaltern masses represented at Durban sought to advance a new political discussion about the political economy of global apartheid—and the United States insulted the entire international community.

The majority of dark humanity is saying to the United States that racism and militarism are not the solutions to the world's major problems. Transnational capitalism and the repressive neoliberal policies of structural adjustment represent a dead end for the developing world. We can end the threat of terrorism only by addressing constructively the routine violence of poverty, hunger, and exploitation that characterizes the daily existence of several billion people on this planet. Racism is, in the final analysis, only another structural manifestation of violence. To stop the violence of terrorism, we must stop the violence of xenophobia, racialization, and class inequality. To struggle for peace and find new paths toward reconciliation across the international boundaries of religion, culture, and color is the only way to protect our cities, our country, and ourselves from the violence of terrorism.

The World Conference Against Racism of August and September 2001 may be judged by history to have represented a dramatic turning point toward the construction of a global antiracism. But to create practical, democratic instruments of social advocacy and capacity building and community-centered institutions that can make real changes in the material conditions and contexts of the lives of people of color, we must acknowledge two different orientations or ideological tendencies within this antiracist counterhegemonic current: a liberal, democratic, and populist tendency and a radical, egalitarian tendency. Both tendencies were present throughout the Durban conference and made their presence felt in the deliberations of the nongovernmental organization panels and in the final conference report. They reflect two very different political strategies and tactical approaches in deconstructing processes of racialization.

The liberal democratic tendency focuses on a discourse of rights, calling for civic participation, political enfranchisement, and capacity building of institutions for the purposes of civic empowerment and multicultural diversity. The liberal democratic impulse seeks to reduce societal conflict by sponsoring public conversations and multicultural dialogues. It seeks not a rejection of economic globalization but its constructive engagement, with the goal of building political cultures of human rights. The most attractive quality of the liberal perspective is its commitment to multicultural social change without resorting to violence.

The radical egalitarian tendency of global antiracists speaks a discourse about inequality and power. It seeks the abolition of poverty and the realization of universal housing, health care, and educational guarantees across the non-Western world. It is less concerned about abstract rights and more concerned about concrete results. It seeks not political assimilation in an old world order but the construction of a new world from the bottom up.

Both of these tendencies exist in varying degrees in the United States, as well as throughout the world, and now define the ideological spectrum within the global anti-apartheid struggle. Scholars and activists alike must contribute to the construction of a broad front bringing together both the multicultural liberal democratic and radical egalitarian currents representing globalization from below. New innovations in social protest movements will also require the development of new social theory and new ways of thinking about the relationship between structural racism and state power.

In its original form, this chapter was presented as a paper under the title "Structural Racism and U.S. Democracy" at the research conference "Racism and Public Policy," sponsored by the United Nations Research Institute for Social Development at the United Nations World Conference Against Racism, Durban, Kwazulu-Natal, South Africa, September 4, 2001. Revised and expanded versions of the paper were presented at the conference "Changing Terrain of Race and Ethnicity: Theory, Methods, and Public Policy," sponsored by the Institute for Research on Race and Public Policy and the Department of Sociology at the University of Illinois, Chicago, October 26, 2001; and at the conference "Race and Globalization," sponsored by the Institute for Research in African American Studies, Columbia University, October 31, 2001. I would like to thank the Aspen Institute for its support in the development of several concepts expressed here as part of its Structural Racism Project.

REFERENCES

Davis, Angela. 2003. *Are Prisons Obsolete?* New York: Seven Stories Press.
————. Forthcoming. *Punishment and Democracy: Essays on the Prison Industrial Complex.* New York: Pantheon Press.
DuBois, W. E. B. 1970. *W. E. B. DuBois Speaks: Speeches and Addresses, 1890–1919,* edited by Philip S. Foner. New York: Pathfinder Press.
Guglielmo, Thomas. 2003. *White on Arrival.* New York: Oxford University Press.
Harris, Cheryl I. 1993. "Whiteness as Property." *Harvard Law Review* 106(8): 1710–91.
Ignatiev, Noel. 1995. *How the Irish Became White.* New York: Routledge.
Mamdani, Mahmood. 1996. *Citizen and Subject: Contemporary Africa and the Legacy of Late Colonialism.* Princeton, N.J.: Princeton University Press.
Marable, Manning, and Leith Mullings. 2003. *African-American Thought: Social and Political Perspectives from Slavery to the Present.* Lanham, Md.: Rowman & Littlefield.
Okihiro, Gary. 2001a. *The Columbia Guide to Asian American History.* New York: Columbia University Press.
————. 2001b. *Common Ground: Reimagining American History.* Princeton, N.J.: Princeton University Press.
Roediger, David. 1991. *Wages of Whiteness.* London: Verso.
Smith, Andrea. 2001. "The Color of Violence." *ColorLines* 3(4): 14.

10

RACIAL EXPLOITATION AND THE
WAGES OF WHITENESS

෯

Charles W. Mills

DISCUSSIONS IN THE academy in general, and in philosophy in particular, of racial injustice have come a long way over the past decade or two. More senior African American philosophers in normative theory, such as Bernard Boxill (1984/1992) and Howard McGary (1999), can testify far better than I can how little interest there was in these matters only a few years ago, and how the torch was kept burning by a few figures, mostly blacks such as themselves, but with a scattering of white progressives. From being a strictly fringe concern, the issue of reparations has become sufficiently mainstream for city councils across the country to take a position on the question and for "white" universities to debate the matter. Unfortunately, very little of the credit for this development can go to mainstream white philosophy, despite the fact that philosophers are by their calling supposed to be the group professionally concerned about justice as a concept and an ideal, and indeed the book regarded by many as the fountainhead of the Western tradition, Plato's *Republic*, is focused single-mindedly on that very subject. Instead, it is black intellectuals, black activists such as Randall Robinson, and community groups such as N'COBRA, the National Coalition of Blacks for Reparations in America, who deserve the credit. Yet there is certainly enough blame to go around—one would not want to pick just on one's own profession. The indictment for (relative) historic silence on the question of racial justice can be extended to American social and political theory in general, not merely social and political philosophy, but mainstream American sociology and mainstream American political science. (Depending on how one defines "mainstream"—and from the racial margins, pretty well everything else looks mainstream—this judgment also holds true for a lot of orthodox left theory in these fields, not just liberalism, since Marxists have tended to dissolve the specificities of these racial problems into the general oppression of capital, with socialism then being plugged as the universal panacea.)

How do we correct this situation? In this chapter, extrapolating the line of argument I have articulated elsewhere in my work, I want to make some suggestions toward the development of a possible long-term theoretical strategy for remedying this deficiency. My recommendation is that we (1) retrieve and elaborate, as an alternative, more accurate global sociopolitical paradigm, the concept of *white supremacy;* (2) develop an analysis of a specifically *racial* form of exploitation, in its manifold dimensions; (3) uncover and follow the trail of the W. E. B. DuBois–inspired concept of the "wages of whiteness"; and then (4) locate normative demands for racial justice within this improved descriptive conceptual framework.

"WHITE SUPREMACY" AS AN ALTERNATIVE PARADIGM

At least since Marx's time, if not long before, it has been a cliché that major political battles are ideological battles also, struggles over rival understandings of the sociopolitical order and conflicting framings of the crucial issues. Normative debates about right and wrong, justice and injustice, typically involve not merely axiological clashes but rival pictures of the factual: competing narratives of what has happened in the past and what is happening right now, alternate descriptive frameworks and interpretations. The ignoring of race as a global issue in American sociopolitical theory—I distinguish "global" from, say, "local" discussions of race in subsections of a field such as the sociology of race relations, urban politics, or affirmative action debates in applied ethics—is made possible by a certain conception of the American polity and social order. With appropriate disciplinary adjustments for the particular subject in question (whether sociology or political science or political philosophy), this picture provides the common overarching framework of debate in the field: the United States is conceptualized as basically an egalitarian (if a bit flawed) liberal democracy free of the hierarchical social structures of the Old World. This profoundly misleading picture is Eurocentric in at least two interesting ways: (1) it focuses on the Euro-American population, those we call "whites," and takes their experience as representative, as the raw material from which to construct theoretical generalizations; (2) it draws on a set of theoretical paradigms drawn *from* European sociopolitical theory—the classic writings of the great figures in European sociology and modern political thought, centered on class as the primary social division, and either not recognizing race as an emergent structure in its own right or biologizing it. The New World is being intellectually grasped with the tools of the Old World, and with reference to the Old World's transplanted population, an operation thus doubly blinded to the possibility that the experience of expropriated reds, enslaved blacks, annexed browns, and excluded yellows may be sufficiently different as to warrant the development of a new tool kit and, accordingly, a new paradigm. To the extent that race is not ignored altogether, it is naturalized or marginalized, and the nonwhite non-nation is assimilated in theory to the white nation. The results can be seen in the typical silences and evasions of these disciplines. In an article giving a historical overview of American sociology, for example, Stanford Lyman (1993, 370–71, 397) argues that from the very start the discipline has had a "resistance to a civil rights orientation":

> Race relations has been conceived of as a social problem within the domain of sociology ever since that discipline gained prominence in the United States; however, the self-proclaimed science of society did not focus its attention on the problem of how the civil rights of racial minorities might be recognized, legitimated, and enforced. . . . Indeed, tracing the history of the race problem in sociology is tantamount to tracing the history and the central problem of the discipline itself— namely, its avoidance of the issue of the significance of civil rights for a democratic society. . . . The reformist solution to social problems . . . rests upon a rational approach to modifying the structures of a society that is regarded *a priori* as fundamentally sound with respect to its basic values and norms. . . . Sociology, in this respect, has been part of the problem and not part of the solution.

In political science, similarly, Rogers Smith's (1997, 15, 17, 27) recent important and prizewinning book *Civic Ideals* outlines the various ways in which the most important theorists of American political culture, Alexis de Tocqueville, Gunnar Myrdal, and Louis Hartz, have managed to represent racism as an "anomaly" within a polity conceived of as basically egalitarian:

> When restrictions on voting rights, naturalization, and immigration are taken into account, it turns out that for over 80 percent of U.S. history, American laws declared most people in the world legally ineligible to become full U.S. citizens solely because of their race, original nationality, or gender. For at least two-thirds of American history, the majority of the domestic adult population was also ineligible for full citizenship for the same reasons. . . . Although such facts are hardly unknown, they have been ignored, minimized, or dismissed in several major interpretations of American civic identity that have massively influenced modern scholarship. . . . All these Tocquevillian accounts falter because they center on relationships among a minority of Americans—white men, largely of northern European ancestry—analyzed in terms of categories derived from the hierarchy of political and economic status such men held in Europe. . . . [Writers in the Tocquevillian tradition] believe . . . that the cause of human equality is best served by reading egalitarian principles as America's true principles, while treating the massive inequalities in American life as products of prejudice, not rival principles.

Finally, in my own discipline, philosophy, it is notorious—at least among black philosophers—that racial justice has been a major theme or subtheme of hardly *a single one* of the numerous books on justice by white philosophers written in the three decades since the revival of political philosophy following John Rawls's (1971) work. One must conclude either that racial justice is of no concern to them or that they think it has already been achieved.

How are such evasions possible in a country built on Native American expropriation and hundreds of years of African slavery, followed by 140 years of first de jure, and now de facto, segregation? An interesting essay, or even a whole book, in the sociology of belief (or here, more accurately, the sociology of ignorance) could certainly be written on this question. But briefly, one would need to highlight the role of historical amnesia (the suppression, or the downplaying of the significance, of certain facts), the group interests and nonrepresentative experience of the privileged race (what cognitive psychologists would identify, respectively, as hot and cold factors of cognitive distortion), and, crucially, a conceptual apparatus inherited, as I said, from European sociopolitical theory, for which race is marginal. So the problem is by no means confined to philosophy but is much broader, though in philosophy (for home-team reasons, I want to make sure that we get the credit for something) it is worst of all, because of the much greater possibilities for abstracting away from reality provided by the non-empirical nature of the subject.

Consider my own discipline, then. In philosophy it becomes possible for what some see as the most important work in Anglo-American political philosophy of the twentieth century, or even the most important work in twentieth-century political theory period, *A Theory of Justice,* to be written by an American, John Rawls, and yet make next to no mention of the centrality of racial *injustice* to the American polity. Defenders will, of course, tell me—I have had these debates before—that that is because Rawls expressly set out to do a book in *ideal* theory. My response would be to ask why he chose to do this, considering that the role of normative inquiry is presumably ultimately to intervene in our own, manifestly *non*-ideal world. I would also suggest, though I suppose this verges on the ad hominem, that it is only those whose experience is one of privilege who would find it so natural to deal purely with "ideal" theory in the first place. After all, having mapped out the ideal theory, shouldn't the natural next move be to *apply* this theory to social reality so as to generate concrete prescriptions for making it more just? Moreover, in the three decades since the publication of Rawls's book, why have so many white philosophers followed his lead? As my colleague Tony Laden has pointed out to me, having done an *Ethics* review essay on a five-volume collection of articles on Rawls's work that includes no less than eighty-eight papers from the past three decades, only *one* of these essays—by the African American philosopher Laurence Thomas—deals with race (see Laden 2003; Richardson and Weithman 1999). Why has nobody done for race what Susan Moller Okin (1989) did with Rawls's apparatus for gender, and imagined what kind of social structure you would prescribe from behind the veil if you knew how people of color were disadvantaged by white supremacy? For that matter, why are European imperialism, African slavery, Native American expropriation, Jim Crow, and so on, not part of the "general facts" about society and history knowledge of which you take with you behind the veil? How is it that in a book that appeared in 1971, whose chapters were being written and circulated in the 1960s, during a time of national civil rights protest, from the mainstream NAACP to the more radical Black Panthers, we get no whiff of these struggles, no consideration—over the span of six hundred pages—of what the implications might be if the "basic structure" is itself unjust?

And from a black point of view, of course, Rawls's (1993) later work is even less helpful, in that the focus has shifted from the distributive concerns, which at least provided some opening for philosophers of color, to what I think most of us feel to be a largely irrelevant, profoundly *non*-urgent, and sleep-inducing debate about whether a just and stable society is possible when citizens are divided by their adherence to reasonable but incompatible doctrines. In a post–Cold War United States where liberalism (in the broad, antifeudal sense) is obviously hegemonic, this is hardly a pressing matter. Of far greater importance from the point of view of justice, one would think, are the growing divisions between rich and poor of all colors and the decades-long retreat from whatever weak corrective measures had been implemented in the 1970s and 1980s to address the legacy of de jure racial domination, which many black intellectuals have seen as the betrayal of the "Second Reconstruction."

So there has been a debilitating "whiteness" to mainstream political philosophy, in terms of the crucial assumptions, the issues typically taken up, and the mapping of what is deemed to be the appropriate and important subject matter. And my claim is that the transdisciplinary framing of the United States as an if-not-quite-ideal-then-pretty-damn-close-to-it liberal democracy, particularly in the exacerbatedly idealistic and abstract form typical of philosophy, has facilitated and underwritten these massive evasions on the issue of racial injustice. Accordingly, I have suggested in my own work that to counter this framing we need to revive "white supremacy" (which is already being used by many people in critical race theory and critical white studies) as a descriptive concept (Mills 2003). Normative questions, as pointed out earlier, hinge not merely on clashes of values but on rival factual claims, both with respect to specific incidents and events and with respect to determining and constraining social structures. And particularly when challenges are coming from the perspective of *radical* political theory (for example, Marxism, feminism, critical race theory), it may well be the case that most or all of the work in claims about injustice is being done by the divergent factual picture put forward rather than different values. Marxism is famously associated with anti-moralism, but for those Marxists who *have* sought to make a normative case for the superiority of socialism, the appeal has often been made with reference to standard liberal norms of equality and well-being. (Indeed, some Marxist theorists have argued that there are *no* distinctively socialist values—that insofar as Marxism has a normative critique of capitalism, it is basically parasitic on liberal-democratic norms.) And while there are numerous varieties of feminism, the most important kind historically has obviously been mainstream liberal feminism, which has simply sought to extend liberal values across the gender divide. So the point is that one can utilize mainstream values to advance quite radical demands: the key thing is to contest the factual picture with which mainstream theorists are operating. With the feminist concept of *patriarchy* and the Marxist concept of *class society,* women and the left have been better able to intervene in mainstream discussions of justice, because they have also contested the factual picture that has framed these discussions.

My claim, then, is that African American philosophers and others working on race, and critical race theorists more generally, should make a comparable theoretical move: challenge the mainstream liberal "anomaly" framing of race by developing the concept of white supremacy. Doing so would have several advantages.

To begin with, just on the level of words, this is the term that *was* traditionally used to denote white domination, so one would be drawing on a vocabulary already established and familiar (see Fredrickson 1981). Feminists had to appropriate a term ("patriarchy") with a somewhat different sense and shift its meaning; Marx had to provide an analysis of class society not merely in terms of rich and poor but, more rigorously, in terms of ownership of the means of production. So both are being employed as terms of art. But in the case of race in the United States, "white supremacy" was the term standardly used. What would now be necessary, of course, would be to give it a more detailed theoretical specification than it has hitherto had, to map in detail its various dimensions, and to try to work out its typical dynamic.

Second, and more importantly, the term carries with it the connotation of systematicity. Unlike the current, more fashionable "white privilege," "white supremacy" implies the existence of a system that does not just privilege whites but is also run by whites, for white benefit. As such, it is a global conception, including not just the socioeconomic but also the juridical, political, cultural, and ideational realms. Thus, it contests—paradigm versus paradigm—the liberal individualist framework of analysis that has played, and continues to play, such an important and pernicious role in obfuscating the real centrality of race and racial subordination to the polity's history.

Finally, by shifting the focus from the individual and attitudinal (the discourse of "racism") to the realm of structures and power, the concept of white supremacy facilitates the highlighting of the most important thing from the perspective of justice, which is how the white population benefits illicitly from their social location. Current debates about "racism" are hindered by the fact that the term is now used in such a confusingly diverse range of ways that it is difficult to find a stable semantic core. Moreover, the dominant interpretation of white racism in the white population is probably individual beliefs about innate nonwhite (particularly black) inferiority and individual hostility toward people of color (especially blacks). Given this conception, most whites think of themselves as nonracist—one positive thing about the present period is that nobody wants to be a racist, though this has also motivated a shift in how the term is defined—while still continuing to hold antiblack stereotypes. But in any case, with the decline in overt racism in the white population, the real issue for a long time has not been individual racism but, far more important, the reproduction of white advantage and black disadvantage through the workings of racialized social structures. The idea of white supremacy is intended, in part, to capture the crucial reality that the *normal* workings of the social system continue to disadvantage blacks in large measure *independently* of racist feeling. Insofar as, since Rawls, our attention as philosophers concerned about justice is supposed to be on the "basic structure" of society and its functioning, the concept of white supremacy then forces us to confront the possibility that the basic structure is itself systemically unjust. Corrective measures to end racial injustice would thus need to begin here.

However, the term also has one major and, some might argue, insuperable disadvantage. Apart from sounding "extremist" to white, and perhaps some black, audiences, it will just seem flagrantly inaccurate, a description that (if this much is conceded) may once have been true but is no longer so. White supremacy for most people will be identified with slavery, the hoods of the Ku Klux Klan, "White" and "Colored" signs, legal segregation and discrimination, police dogs attacking black demonstrators, and so on. So considerable spade-work will have to be done in arguing that the key referent of the term is white domination and in demonstrating that white domination can persist in the absence of overt nonwhite subordination, white terrorism, and legal persecution. But there is a sense in which such spadework would have to be done regardless of the term chosen, inasmuch as individualist analyses of the sociopolitical order, which deny the existence of structures of domination (not just for race but in general), are hegemonic in the popular mind. So this would be an ideological obstacle to be overcome no matter what term is chosen. And in the case of race, by contrast with class and gender, one should in theory at least face a somewhat easier task in convincing people, since although the society is routinely thought of as classless (or—the same thing—middle-class) and gender domination is seen as natural, it cannot (one would think) be denied that people of color were long legally suppressed. So even if whites are reluctant to concede the *continuing* existence of white supremacy, the concession that it *once* existed provides at least some theoretical foothold, since one can then make an argument (if no more than this) that it would have to have left some legacy.

Finally, I would claim that philosophers have a distinctive role to play in analyzing white supremacy (see Mills 2003). Obviously, crucial work would have to be done at the empirical level, in sociology and political science. But investigations and formulations at a higher level of abstraction would be invaluable also. My model here, of course, is Marx's analysis of capitalism, which, as we recall, moved back and forth between the empirical and the philosophical. Think of all the articles and books there have been in Marxist theory over the past hundred years, looking at such issues as philosophical anthropology, class exploitation, the role of class ideology, the influence on cognition of class division, fetishism, naturalistic mystification, and so on. My belief is that white supremacy has been sufficiently important as a social reality over the past few hundred years, and has been sufficiently influential in shaping human beings, that a parallel abstract philosophical investigation on race will turn out to be equally fruitful. The loftily meta-theoretical vantage point of philosophy could then provide the insights about human existence, value, and cognition that are peculiar to the discipline, but informed (unlike the ostensibly colorless "view from nowhere") by the realities of white domination.

RACIAL EXPLOITATION

I now want to turn specifically to the idea of racial exploitation and draw a comparison between racial and class exploitation, since it will be illuminating for us to consider both their similarities and their differences. Exploitation is, of course, central to Marxist theory, since what distinguishes his analysis of capitalism from that of liberal theorists is that for him it is necessarily an exploitative system. Exploitation is not a matter of low wages or poor working conditions, though these will, of course, make it worse. Rather, exploitation has to do with the transfer of surplus value from the workers to the capitalists. To the extent that there is a normative critique in Marxism, then, it relies centrally on the claim that this relation is an exploitative one. Moreover, it is not just capitalism but class society in general that is exploitative, which is why we need to move toward a classless society. Finally, the exploitative nature of the system does not reside in class prejudice, in hostile views of the workers, but rather in their systemic disadvantaging by this transfer of surplus value through the wage relation. If Marx is right, class exploitation is *normal,* not requiring extraordinary measures, but flowing out of the routine functioning of the system.

The claim that capitalism is necessarily exploitative historically rested on the labor theory of value, and with the discrediting of this theory, it has become harder to defend. The left-wing economist John Roemer (1982) has for many years been developing a revisionist view of exploitation, but his development of the notion is quite far from traditional conceptions. For Marx, exploitation was a real relationship, not merely an artifact of mathematical manipulation, and was linked with proletarian agency: it was in part precisely because of their exploitation that the workers were supposed to develop class consciousness, form trade unions, and ultimately participate in a movement to overthrow capitalism. So exploitation provides both an explanation for the logic of domination and a potential basis for its political overcoming. Marxism's pretensions to being a social science hinge in part on claims about the centrality of exploitation and how it organizes bourgeois and proletarian interests, thus generating behavioral uniformities that Marx thought could be expressed in social laws. And his theory is not merely a holistic, social-systemic one that opposes the "Robinsonades" of liberal theory, but famously a *materialist,* and thus a realist, one. Note that (1) analyses of a social-systemic kind need not be materialist, since they can be idealist—for example, seeing everything in terms of language or discourses—and (2) materialism is a species of realism rather than coextensive with it, since while political realists claim that determination by group interests is crucial, they do not necessarily identify those interests as material ones. For Marx, though, what are supposed to make the sociopolitical wheels go round are class interests of a material kind, tied to economic advantage.

The case I want to make is that racial exploitation can provide a parallel, even superior, illumination and that it is greatly advantaged over the Marxist concept by not being tied to a dubious economic theory. Comparatively little work has been done on the concept of racial exploitation. I think this is because it has fallen between theoretical and political stools in an interesting way. In his recent book on "mutually advantageous and consensual exploitation," Alan Wertheimer (1996) points out that though the term "exploitation" is routinely tossed around, mainstream liberal theorists have had surprisingly little to say about it: "Exploitation has not been a central concern for contemporary political and moral philosophy." He suggests that there are at least three reasons for this silence: the concept's guilt-by-association with Marxism; the aforementioned post-Rawlsian focus on ideal theory; and the fact that whereas exploitation is typically a "micro-level wrong" characterizing individual transactions, "much of the best contemporary political philosophy tends to focus on macro-level questions, such as the just distribution of resources and basic liberties and rights" (Wertheimer 1996, ix, 8). (The presumptive contrast in this last point arguably vindicates my earlier claim about the racially sanitized picture of the United States dominant in mainstream normative political theory. Do not *macro*-level questions about the unjust "distribution of resources and basic liberties and rights" arise from the history of American white supremacy? Can it not be argued that racial exploitation has been national and structural?)

On the other hand, where Marxists have looked at race, as another author, Gary Dymski (1997, 335), points out in a left-wing anthology on exploitation, they have typically reduced it to a variant of class exploitation: "Race has been virtually ignored in Marxian theorizing about exploitation. Race is assumed to enter in only at a level of abstraction lower than exploitation; and anyway, since minorities are disproportionately workers, racial inequality is simply a special case readily accounted for by a racially neutral exploitation theory." And this, of course, is part of a larger problematic pattern of Marxist theory: its failure to recognize race as a system of domination in itself (see Robinson 1983/2000; Mills 2003). Indeed, this is well illustrated by one of the classic texts of Marxism, Lenin's (1916/1996) *Imperialism: The Highest Stage of Capitalism*. Someone from the Third World (someone like me!) who had never read this pamphlet might come to it thinking from its title that Lenin is going to talk about the role of race and racism in First World imperialist exploitation of its colonies. But in fact Lenin barely refers to race at all. For him, the populations in the colonial world suffer the exploitation of finance capital, which is merely an exacerbated variant of the exploitation typical of wage labor. So what one has is a "quantitative" change—it is the same thing, but worse. The idea that racial exploitation could have qualitatively distinct dimensions, that racial exploitation could crucially involve the active participation of white workers both in the metropole and in the colonies, is not envisaged by Lenin. Racial domination is subsumed under capitalist domination, and no separate theorization of its distinctive features is recognized as necessary. If we utilize the orthodox base-superstructure taxonomy, then the materialist region of society, which is the most important, "determining" part, is the base—the relations of production that encapsulate class relations of domination. Insofar as race is recognized, then, race would be at best part of the superstructure, a set of ideological relations. Even when race is cashed out in terms of superexploitation, the process is still assimilated to class exploitation in that the "race" in question is thought of as a differentially subordinated section of the working class and the exploitative relation involves getting extra value for the bourgeoisie.

So neither in mainstream liberal theory nor in oppositional Marxist theory has racial exploitation been properly recognized and theorized. And I am suggesting that we redress this theoretical deficiency and follow up on the insight expressed by W. E. B. DuBois (1935/1998) seventy years ago, in his now-classic *Black Reconstruction in America,* when he spoke of the "public and psychological wage" enjoyed by white workers. The idea represents a conceptual breakthrough, since at a time (even more than now) when Marxist theories effectively monopolized accounts of exploitation—and of course long before what we now know as "critical white studies" had come into existence—DuBois was tentatively raising the possibility of whiteness as a system of exploitation in itself: that *whiteness paid* (see also DuBois 1920/1995). In keeping with the shift in the radical academy over the past two decades from Marxism to poststructuralism, much of the recent literature on whiteness, as Ashley Doane (2003) and Margaret Andersen (2003) complain in their introductory essays in *White Out: The Continuing Significance of Racism* (Doane and Bonilla-Silva 2003), focuses on the discursive, the cultural, and the personal testimonial. This is not to deny, of course, that whiteness has numerous aspects and that the orthodox left of the past was deficient (following Marx's own footsteps) in its handling of what were dismissed as "superstructural" issues. But DuBois's own insight was in terms of political economy, and the discussion arguably needs to be brought back to these fundamentals. The concept of "white privilege," Cheryl Harris's (1993) notion (following Derrick Bell) of whiteness as "property," and George Lipsitz's (1998) idea of a "possessive investment" in whiteness can all be seen as indebted to DuBois's original insight. Yet though this subsection of the field is well established, comparatively little has been done, so far as I know, to develop and articulate the conceptual mapping of the structure they presuppose. And within the African American scholarly community, DuBois's (1903/1996) concept of "double consciousness," from *The Souls of Black Folk,* has received far more attention than the wages of whiteness. So I am arguing that we need to redress this imbalance.

Before getting into the analysis, though, we have to deal with some preliminary objections.

It might be objected, to begin with, that racial exploitation cannot exist because races do not exist. If, as the growing scholarly consensus in anthropology on the question agrees, races have no biological existence, then how can they be involved in relations of exploitation, or for that matter any other relations? And here, of course, the standard answer from critical race theorists is that races can have a reality that, though social rather than biological, is nonetheless causally efficacious within our racialized world. From the fact that race is socially constructed, it does not follow that it is unreal (see Haslanger 1995; Mills 1998; Sundstrom 2002).

Secondly, however, it might be claimed that insofar as race *is* socially constructed, then it is to the constructing agent that causality and agency really have to be attributed. In historical materialist versions of this claim, for example, it might be insisted that class forces, and ultimately the ruling class, the bourgeoisie, are the real actors. (So we could think of these as two Marxist reasons—though they come in other theoretical varieties also—apart from simple myopia, to deny racial exploitation: races do not exist in the first place, or if their social reality is grudgingly conceded, then, as a fallback position, this reality is reduced to an underlying class reality.) But even if Y is created by X, so that there is generating causation, it does not follow that Y continues to be moved, either wholly or at all, by X, so that there may not be sustaining and ongoing causation. In other words, even if we concede (and an argument would be necessary to prove this) that race is originally created by a class dynamic, this does not mean that race cannot attain what used to be called, in Marxist theory, at least a "relative autonomy" (if not more), an intrinsic dynamic, of its own. One of the key books in initiating the current flood of "whiteness" literature was David Roediger's (1991/1999) study of white American workers, *The Wages of Whiteness,* and the significance of his paying tribute to DuBois in his title was precisely because his conclusion was that these workers' whiteness *was* a real social fact about them, one that played a crucial role in their motivations and actions. So social "whiteness"—the belief that one is a member of the privileged race—and the institutional reflections of this belief are causally efficacious.

Finally, it might be objected that "whites" come in all classes, different genders, and divergent nationalities, that there are power relations and great power differences among them, and that they also are exploited. But the claim that racial exploitation exists does not commit one to the claim that its benefits are all necessarily distributed *equally,* so if some whites get more than others, this is still consistent with the thesis. Nor does it require that all whites be equally active in the processes of racial exploitation—some may be both actors and beneficiaries, while others are just beneficiaries. Finally, as should be obvious, claiming that racial exploitation exists does not imply that it is the *only* form of exploitation. All of us will have different hats, and so it will be not merely possible but *routinely* the case that people are simultaneously the beneficiaries of one system of exploitation while being the victims of another, as with white women, for example. Society can be thought of as a complex of interlocking and overlapping systems of domination and exploitation, and I am by no means asserting that race is the only one. My claim rather is that it is an undertheorized one and that it has repercussions for holding the overall system together that are not generally recognized.

Let us contrast race and class exploitation, then. To begin with, assuming that the dominant position on the origins of race is correct, race is a product of the modern period, so that racial exploitation is limited to the last few hundred years and is much younger than class exploitation, and even more so by comparison with gender exploitation. Moreover, it is a historically contingent form of exploitation: while it is almost impossible to imagine the development of human society having taken place without class and gender hierarchy and exploitation, the fact that race might never have existed in the first place implies that racial exploitation might never have existed.

Suppose we use the terms R1 and R2 for the races involved, respectively dominant and subordinate. (Obviously, it is possible to have more than two races involved—think of apartheid South Africa and the role of "Coloreds"— but we will make this simplifying assumption.) Now, to begin with, it needs to be pointed out that the mere fact that two races are involved in relations of exploitation does not mean it is a relationship of *racial* exploitation. Racial exploitation is, as emphasized, just one variety of exploitation, and if it is a necessary condition that races be involved in the transaction, it is not a sufficient one. For it could be that the relations between R1 and R2 are simply standard capitalist relations. Imagine, say, that a group of capitalists from one racial group hires a group of workers from another racial group, but race plays no role in the establishment or particular character or reproduction of the relations of exploitation. What is also required is that the relations of race play a role in the nature and degree of the exploitation itself. What makes racial exploitation *racial* exploitation, then, is not merely that the parties to the transaction are races, but that race determines, or significantly modifies, the nature of the relation between them. (Note also that it is not necessary for racial exploitation that the parties in every transaction be of *different* races, for it could be that the overall structure of R2 subordination allows for a few R2s to participate in the exploitation of their fellow R2s, for example, the small number of black slaveholders in the South.)

In what does this determination or modification consist? We are a bit handicapped here by the fact that the transaction has to be described in suitably general terms, encompassing (as I will soon argue) such a wide range of possibilities. But I suggest that the paradigm case of racial exploitation is one in which the moral/ontological/civic status of the subordinate race makes possible the transaction in the first place (that is, the transaction would have been morally or legally prohibited had the R2s been R1s) or makes the terms significantly worse than they would have been (the R2s get a much poorer deal than if they had been R1s). And the term "transactions" is being used broadly to encompass not merely cases in which R2s are directly involved but also (and this is another significant difference from classic class exploitation) cases in which they are *excluded.* In Marx's vision of class exploitation, surplus value is extracted through the expenditure of the labor power of the working class, so obviously the workers have to be actually working for this transfer to take place. But I want to include scenarios in which R2s are kept out of the transaction but are nonetheless exploited, because R1s benefit from their exclusion (for example, in the case of racial restrictions on hiring). For me, then, racial exploitation is being conceptualized so as to accommodate both differential and inferior treatment of R2s (for example, lower wages) and their exclusion where they should legitimately have been included (for example, the denial of the job in the first place).

Now, it needs to be noted that the role of R2 normative inequality is in sharp contrast to Marx's vision of class exploitation under capitalism. In the class systems of antiquity and the Middle Ages, the subordinate classes did indeed have a lower normative status. But capitalism, as the class system of modernity, is distinguished by the fact that these distinctions of ascriptive hierarchy are leveled. So in Marx's discussion of capitalism, the whole point of his analysis— what made capitalism different from slave and feudal modes of production— was that the workers nominally had *equal* moral status. Hence his sarcasm in *Capital* about the freedom and equality that obtain on the level of the relations of exchange being undercut at the level of the relations of production. But at least juridically, that freedom and equality are real. So it is not that the subordinated are overtly forced to labor for the capitalist class (as with the slave or the serf), since such coercion would be inconsistent with liberal capitalism. Rather, it is the economic structure that (according to Marx anyway) coerces them, reduces their options, and forces them to sell their labor power.

But in what I suggest is the paradigm case of racial exploitation, the R2s do *not* have equal status, which implies that bourgeois-democratic norms either do not apply to them at all or do not apply fully. In both liberal and many Marxist theories of racism, this has usually been represented as a return to the *premodern*. But as various theorists, including myself, have argued, it is better thought of in terms *of* the modern, but within the framework of a revised narrative and conceptual framework that deny that egalitarianism is in fact the universal norm of modernity (Mills 1999). In other words, to represent racism as a throwback to previous class systems accepts the mystificatory representation of the modern as the epoch when equality becomes the globally hegemonic norm, when in fact we need to reject this characterization and see the modern as bringing about white (male) equality while establishing nonwhite inequality as an accompanying norm. In Rogers Smith's (1997) language, racism is not an "anomaly" in the global system but a norm in its own right. What justifies African slavery and colonial forced labor, for example, is the lesser moral status of the people involved—they are not seen as full humans in the first place. If in the colonies blacks, browns, and yellows are coerced by the colonial state to work, while in the metropole, according to Marxist theory, white workers are compelled by the market to work, this is not a minor but a major and qualitative difference.

Now, one of the straightforward implications of this is that, by contrast with class exploitation, racial exploitation in its paradigm form is straightforwardly unjust by deracialized liberal democratic standards. By contrast, in the Marxist tradition, as is well known, there has been a general leeriness about appealing to morality and a specific leeriness about appealing to justice, because of the dominant meta-ethical interpretation of Marx as a theorist disdainful of ethical norms and hostile to justice in particular as a putatively transhistorical value. So some Marxists have repudiated moral argument in principle as a return to a supposedly discredited "ethical" (as against "scientific") socialism. But if one does want to make a moral case for socialism, some theorists have argued, one has to appeal to freedom rather than justice, or to social welfare, or to Aristotelian self-realization. A discourse of rights is not amenable to prosecuting the proletarian case insofar as bourgeois rights *are* being respected. (One can, of course, appeal to positive "welfare" rights, but these are far more controversial in the liberal tradition.) And such an argument would have to rely on factual and conceptual claims that were obviously highly controversial even then—and far more so now in a post-Marxist world—about capitalist economic constraint undermining substantive freedoms, or people as a whole doing better under socialism. By contrast, the striking feature of demands for racial justice in the paradigm cases of racial injustice is that they can be straightforwardly made in terms of the dominant discourse, since the whole point of racial exploitation is that (at least in its paradigm form) it trades on the differential status of the R2s to legitimate its relations. For example, contrast the proletarian struggle with the black struggle in the United States. The banner under which the latter has been organized has typically been the banner of equal rights: for civil rights—indeed for human rights—and for first-class rather than second-class citizenship. But it would be far more difficult to represent the struggle for socialism as a struggle for equal rights, since it would, of course, be denied that capitalist wage relations *are* a violation of workers' rights.

So in the first instance (in the period of overt white supremacy), what justifies racial exploitation is that the R2s are seen of lesser human worth, or zero worth. They have fewer rights, or no rights. A certain normative characterization of the R2s is central to racial exploitation in a way that it is not to class exploitation in the modern period.

But apart from this paradigm form, there is also a secondary derivative form, which becomes more important over time (so there is a periodization of varieties of racial exploitation, with the different salience of different kinds shifting over time) and which arises from the legacy of the first kind. Here the inequity does not arise from the R2s' being still stigmatized as of inferior status, or at least such stigmatization is not essential to the process. White supremacy is no longer overt, and the statuses of R1s and R2s have been formally equalized (for example, through legislative change). Of course, the perception of R2s as inferior, as not quite of equal standing, may continue to play a role in tacitly underwriting their differential treatment. But it is no longer essential to it. Rather, what obtains here is that the R2s inherit a disadvantaged material position that handicaps them—by comparison with what, counterfactually, would have been the case if they had been R1s—in the bargaining process or the competition in question. At this stage, then, it *is* possible for them to be treated "fairly," by the same norms that apply to the R1 population. Nonetheless, it is still appropriate to speak of racial exploitation, because they bring to the table a thinner package of assets than they otherwise would have had, and so they will be in a weaker bargaining position than they otherwise would have been. Whites are differentially benefited by this history insofar as they have a competitive advantage that is not the result—or not completely the result—of innate ability and effort, but the inheritance of the legacy of the past. So unfairness here is manifest in the failure to redress this legacy, which makes the perpetuation of domination the most likely outcome.

I would also claim (and will elaborate in the next section) that another crucial difference between class and racial exploitation is that the latter takes place much more broadly than at the point of production. (Here, of course, I am referring to Marx's classic conceptualization; in Roemer's revisionist view, this contrast will no longer be as sharp.) For insofar as racial exploitation in its paradigm form requires only that the R2s receive differential and inferior treatment, this can be manifested in a much wider variety of transactions than proletarian wage labor. Society is characterized by economic transactions of all kinds, and if race becomes a normative dividing line running through all or most of these transactions, then racial exploitation can pervade the whole economic order. Moreover, it is not just the market that is involved, but the active role of the state, not merely in writing the laws and fostering the moral economy that makes racial exploitation normatively and juridically acceptable, but in creating opportunities for the R1s not extended to the R2s and making transfer payments on a racially differentiated basis.

Another important difference is that whereas Marx's analysis of class exploitation was focused on economic benefit, the transfer of surplus value from worker to capitalist, I would claim that racial exploitation has crucial additional dimensions beyond the economic. Indeed, this is encapsulated in DuBois's phrase itself, since the whole point he was making was that whiteness garners wages other than the straightforwardly economic. The peculiar character of race as a social structure and its perceived intimate link with what one essentially and biologically *is* make possible a variety of benefits greater than those typical of class exploitation.

Finally, whereas it is, of course, Marx's famous claim that capitalism needs to be abolished to achieve the end of class exploitation (since a capitalism that did not extract surplus value would liquidate itself), racial exploitation is at least in theory eliminable within a capitalist framework. That is, it is possible to have a nonracial capitalism, either because races do not exist as social entities within the system or because, though they do exist, there is no additional racial exploitation on top of class exploitation. Since we live in a postcommunist world in which Marx's vision seems increasingly unrealizable, with no attractive socialist models to point to, this conclusion is welcome because it implies that the struggle for racial justice need not be anticapitalist. Particularly in the United States, of course, such an ideological designation has historically been a heavy handicap—see Seymour Lipset and Gary Marks's *It Didn't Happen Here: Why Socialism Failed in the United States* (2000)—and in the present time period more so than ever before. The long-entrenched hostility to black demands need not, then, be compounded and redoubled (or some far greater multiple) by the additional antipathy to communism, to black and red together. One simple formulation of the political project would be as the demand for a nonracial—or non-white-supremacist—capitalism. (Representing white supremacy as a system in its own right, with its distinctive modes of exploitation, has the virtue of clarifying what the real target is.)

However, I qualified the term "eliminable" with "in theory." The counterargument that needs to be borne in mind, coming from the left in particular, is that while a nonracial capitalism could certainly have developed in another world, the fact that the capitalism in *our* world has been so thoroughly racialized from its inception means that racial inequality has long been crucial to its reproduction *as* a particular kind of capitalist formation. Logical distinctions in theory between U.S. capitalism and white supremacy are all very well, but their fusion in reality into the composite entity of white-supremacist capitalism makes any political project of attempting to separate the two a nonstarter, in part because of the reciprocal imbrication of class and race, class being racialized, race being classed. I will not say anything more about this counterargument, but it should be noted as an important objection to the whole project.

To summarize then. By comparison with class exploitation, racial exploitation (1) benefits R1s generally, not just the capitalist class of the R1s; (2) disadvantages R2s generally, not just the working class of the R2s; (3) involves the causality and agency (albeit to different extents) of R1s besides the capitalist class; (4) is in its paradigmatic form straightforwardly wrong by (deracialized) liberal norms; (5) includes economic transactions other than labor; (6) typically involves the intervention and/or collusion of the state; (7) extends to other spheres of society besides the economic; and (8) could in theory be eliminated within a capitalist framework.

THE WAGES OF WHITENESS

The discussion so far has been very abstract. Let us now move to the level of the concrete.

In the United States members of the privileged race, the R1s, are, of course, whites. There will be a core whiteness that is relatively clear-cut and a penumbral whiteness that is fuzzier. A significant part of the burden of the whiteness literature over the past decade has, of course, been the emphasis on the historically variant character of whiteness, and various books—most famously Noel Ignatiev's *How the Irish Became White* (1995) but also Karen Brodkin's *How Jews Became White Folks* (1998) and Matthew Frye Jacobson's *Whiteness of a Different Color* (1998)—have tracked the shifting boundaries of the white population. And part of the motivation for aspiring to and becoming white is precisely so that one can benefit from this exploitation.

Now, Roediger's phrase is a bit misleading insofar as it is limited, if taken literally, to "wages" and the white working class. But one could also speak illuminatingly, focusing on different kinds of relationships, of whiteness as property, whiteness as a joint-stock company, the interest on whiteness, the rent on whiteness, the profit on whiteness, the residuals on whiteness, the returns on whiteness, and so on. The point is that racial exploitation is manifest in many more economic relations than just that of wage labor. So if we retain the phrase for the sake of convenience and its historic resonances, we must remind ourselves that we are not talking just about wages.

Let us now go through some concrete examples to put some flesh on these abstractions (see Oliver and Shapiro 1995; Lipsitz 1998).

- Native Americans are cheated out of their land. They are not given a fair price in the first place, or the original deal is reneged upon, or their understanding of what they were signing away was mistaken because of deliberate deceit, and so on.

- Africans are enslaved at a time when slavery is dead or dying out in the West. (Obviously, if Africans were enslaved in the ancient world, as they were, there was nothing *racial* about this, since race played no role in their enslavement—indeed, at the time they did not even have a race.)

- Blacks freed from slavery are conscripted into "debt servitude" as share-croppers, from which they can never get free, since the plantation owner forces them to buy goods he provides, at higher prices, and weighs the cotton they produce himself, so that at the end of each year they owe more than before.

- Blacks are not permitted, or only permitted to a far lesser extent, to stake their claim on lands opened up by the settling of the West. (This illustrates the complexities of racial exploitation, since had they been allowed to do so, they would, of course, have been participating in the exploitation of Native Americans.)

- Male Chinese immigrants are forced to pay a head-tax for admission into the United States, at a time when no such tax is imposed on white immigrants.

- Black children are given an inferior education by state governments, with most of the resources going to white children.

- Blacks are given higher sentences than whites for comparable crimes so that they can supply a population of convict lease labor in the South.

- Black enterprises are not permitted access to white markets.

- Black enterprises are burned down or otherwise illicitly driven out of business by white competitors.

- Blacks pay higher rent in the ghettos for housing.

- Blacks pay more for inferior goods in the ghettos.

- White workers refuse to admit blacks into their unions.

- Blacks, Mexican Americans, and Asian immigrants hired in jobs are paid less than white workers would be.

- Blacks, Mexican Americans, and Asian immigrants hired in jobs are not promoted or are promoted at differential rates and to lower levels than whites with comparable credentials.

- Black candidates with superior credentials are turned down in favor of white candidates.

- Black candidates with inferior credentials are turned down in favor of white candidates, and the reason their credentials are inferior is that they have had poorer schooling and poorer opportunities at every step of the way than they would have had if they were white.

- Black performers are forced to sign contracts on worse terms than white performers because they have no alternative company to give them a better deal.

- Black performers sign contracts with worse terms because they are not sufficiently educated to know better, and racism explains their inferior knowledge.

- Blacks and Latinos do not get a chance to compete for certain jobs in the first place because racially exclusionary word-of-mouth networks restrict notice of these jobs to white candidates.

- Federal money earmarked for Native Americans ends up in white hands instead.

- Transfer payments from the state (for example, unemployment benefits, welfare) are not extended equally to the black population, either through overt racial exclusion or because the terms are carefully designed to exclude certain jobs in which blacks are differentially concentrated. The Federal Housing Agency (FHA), established under the New Deal, discriminates against would-be black homeowners, thereby denying them access to the main route to wealth accumulation by the middle class. The Wagner Act and the Social Security Act "excluded farm workers and domestics from coverage, effectively denying those disproportionately minority sectors of the work force protections and benefits routinely afforded to whites" (Lipsitz 1998, 5).

Now, there are several things about this (very short) list that should be striking.

One is the diversity of examples of racial exploitation. Even focusing just on the economic aspect, we can see how many ways there are for racial exploitation to manifest itself. Thus, there is a sense in which, far from being a theoretical appendage or minor codicil to Marxism's view of class exploitation, racial exploitation is *much broader* and should long ago have received the theoretical attention it deserves. Marx's focus was on just one relation because he was working within a framework in which it was assumed (since he was really talking about the white population) that normative status differentials had been eliminated, so that exploitation had to take place in a framework of the transaction of equals. Once one rejects this assumption, one comes to recognize that the relation can manifest itself in *any* economic transaction, or any transaction with economic effects, and thus is ubiquitous. And this is one of the very important ways in which Marxism is Eurocentric: in its failure to conceptualize how broadly exploitation as a concept can be shown to apply once one takes the focus off the white population.

Secondly, notice the cumulative and negatively synergistic effect of these transactions. It is not merely that blacks (for example) are exploited serially in different transactions, but that the different forms of exploitation interact with one another, exacerbating the situation. For example, blacks receive inferior education, thereby losing an equal opportunity to build human capital, thereby losing out in competition with white job candidates, thereby having to take inferior jobs, thereby having less money, thereby being disadvantaged in dealings with banks that are already following patterns of discrimination, thereby being forced to live in inferior neighborhoods, thereby having homes of lesser value, thereby providing a lower tax base for schooling, thereby being unable to pass on to their children advantages comparable to those of whites, and so on. It is not a matter of a single transaction, or even a series, but a *multiply interacting* set, with the repercussions continually compounding and feeding back in a destructive way.

But what has been negative for blacks has been very beneficial for whites. The point of utilizing the political economy category of "exploitation," as against just talking with a liberal vocabulary about the "unfairness" of discrimination against nonwhites, is, as emphasized at the start, to shift the discussion from the personal to the social-structural, so that we can start seeing white supremacy as itself a *system* for which this "wage" is the motivation. Melvin Oliver and Thomas Shapiro's prizewinning *Black Wealth/White Wealth* (1995), judged by many to be one of the most important books on race of the last two decades, argues that to understand racial inequality, its origins, and its reproduction, wealth is a far better investigative tool than income. As they point out:

> Whites in general, but well-off whites in particular, were able to amass assets and use their secure economic status to pass their wealth from generation to generation. What is often not acknowledged is that the accumulation of wealth for some whites is intimately tied to the poverty of wealth for most blacks. Just as blacks have had "cumulative disadvantages," whites have had "cumulative advantages." Practically, every circumstance of bias and discrimination against blacks has produced a circumstance and opportunity of positive gain for whites. When black workers were paid less than white workers, white workers gained a benefit; when black businesses were confined to the segregated black market, white businesses received the benefit of diminished competition; when FHA policies denied loans to blacks, whites were the beneficiaries of the spectacular growth of good housing and housing equity in the suburbs. The cumulative effect of such a process has been to sediment blacks at the bottom of the social hierarchy and to artificially raise the relative position of some whites in society. (Oliver and Shapiro 1995, 51)

And if one were to go back to slavery and Native American expropriation and track the financial consequences of these institutions and processes for the respectively racialized populations, the size and ubiquity of the white wage would be even greater. Whites will sometimes receive the wage directly, by themselves participating in these transactions, but far more often they receive it indirectly—from their parents, from the state and federal governments, from the general advantage of being the privileged race in a system of racial subordination. The transparency of the connection between race and social advantage or disadvantage also has implications for social consciousness. Marx famously claimed that capitalism was differentiated from slave and feudal modes of production by the seemingly egalitarian nature of the transactions involved: the "fair exchange" between worker and capitalist requires conceptual labor to be revealed as (allegedly) inequitable. As a result, the subordinated workers often do not recognize their subordination—capitalism is the classless class society. By contrast, the transparency of racial exploitation, certainly in its paradigm form, means that the R2s will usually have little difficulty in seeing the unfairness of their situation. If Marxist "class consciousness" has been more often dreamed of by the left than found in actual workers, "racial consciousness" in the subordinated has been far more evident historically.

Finally, I should also say something briefly about non-economic varieties of racial exploitation. One will be cultural. What I am thinking of here is the representation of some important cultural innovation or breakthrough as owing to the R1s when it really comes from the R2s. In other words, I do not just mean that the R1s differentially and unfairly profit from such innovations in material terms, but that, in addition, R1s *claim them as their own.* Native Americans, for example, often point out that many agricultural products that have now become worldwide staples were originally developed through their farming techniques, but that they are not given credit for them. The controversy over the relation between ancient Egypt and ancient Greece remains unresolved, and Martin Bernal's (1987) claims that a "black Athena" (in a black tradition long predating him, indeed going back to the nineteenth century) was written out of the record by racist scholarship has been subjected to fierce and unyielding criticisms by the scholarly establishment in classical studies (see Lefkowitz and MacLean 1996; Bernal 2001). The payoff from cultural exploitation is, of course, the positioning of one's race as superior for being differentially endowed with talents and abilities.

There are also specific gendered dimensions to racial exploitation where racism intersects with sexism. The sexual exploitation of black women under slavery and into the post-Emancipation period is well known. Black women were differentially forced into prostitution because of the lack of respectable economic opportunities for them. Some feminists, such as my colleague Sandra Bartky, have argued for a distinct form of exploitation of the affective labor of women. Insofar as generations of white children in the South were raised with black "mammies," one could see this as a peculiarly racialized form of affective labor exploitation.

Finally, I would like to suggest, admittedly more fancifully (but what else is philosophy for?), that we could also talk about "ontological" exploitation. In Marx's *1844 Manuscripts,* he represents the relation between worker and capitalist not merely in terms of the growing wealth of the latter and the growing poverty of the former, but also in terms of their respective "beings": "So much does labor's realization appear as loss of realization that the worker loses realization to the point of starving to death. . . . Whatever the product of his labor is, he is not. Therefore the greater this product, the less is he himself . . . the more values he creates, the more valueless, the more unworthy he becomes" (Marx and Engels 1975, 272–73). I would claim that this exploitative transfer of being moves from the metaphorical to the (almost) literal in the case of paradigmatic racial exploitation, since in this period nonwhites, particularly blacks, were seen as of lesser, or close to zero, human worth. They were, in the vocabulary I have used elsewhere, "subpersons" rather than persons (Mills 1997). And this subpersonhood, as a result of racial exploitation, increasingly becomes *materially grounded*—that is, it is a matter not merely of stigmatized representations of blacks but of the literal destruction of black being by slavery and colonial forced labor, regimes under which people were often worked to death and were at all times reduced to a condition beneath the human. Thus, it is not only that whites are depicted as the superior race, beings of a higher order, but that this depiction begins to seem *true* in a world in which they dominate the planet and become the exemplars of the human.

RACIAL JUSTICE

The articulation of such a framework would, I claim, greatly facilitate discussions about racial justice. Instead of focusing exclusively on "racism," our attention would shift to *illicit white benefit.* The ideal for racial justice would, quite simply, be the end to current racial exploitation and the equitable redistribution of the benefits of past racial exploitation. Obviously, working out the details would be hugely complicated, and in fine points impossible, but at least on the level of an ideal to be simply stated, and by which present-day society could be measured, it would give us something to shoot at. In dialoguing with the white majority, the imperative task has usually been to convince them that, independently of whether or not they are "racist" (however that term is to be understood), they are the beneficiaries of a system of racial domination and that *this* is the real issue, not whether they have goodwill toward people of color or whether they owned any slaves. The concept of racial exploitation is designed to bring out this central reality. Relying not on dubious claims about surplus value, it derives its legitimacy from the simple appeal to the very normative values (albeit in their inclusive, race-neutral incarnation) to which the white majority already nominally subscribes. And because it encompasses a derivative as well as a primary form (exploitation inhering not in the assumption of unequal normative status but in the continuing impact of the unfair distribution of assets resulting from that original normative inequality), it can handle transactions seemingly just but actually inequitable because of the legacy of the past. That is not to say that it will not be very controversial; obviously it *will* be very controversial and will be militantly and furiously opposed. But such hostility goes with the territory and will greet *all* attempts to prosecute the struggle for racial justice, no matter what conceptual banner is chosen to fly over it. At least the advantage of selecting this framework is that it appeals to norms central to the American tradition (if not normally extended to blacks) and a factual picture for which massive documentation, at least in broad outline, can be provided. In addition, the macro, big-picture, social-systemic analysis—the emphasis on the structural dynamic—locates it in the same conceptual space as the famous "basic structure" that, since Rawls, has been the central focus of discussions of social justice. Thus, we would be better positioned, as I emphasized at the start, to pose the simple and crucial challenge to mainstream white theorists: what if the basic structure is itself unjust because it is predicated on racial exploitation? Both from the mainstream liberal perspective, then—the normative focus on the justice of foundational institutions—and from the nonmainstream left perspective—the political economy of a system of exploitation and how it shapes political, juridical, and ideological realms—we are considerably advantaged by developing the concept of white supremacy as a theoretical framework intended to compete with (most importantly) liberal individualism and (less importantly) orthodox Marxist class theory.

Moreover, another signal virtue of approaching things this way is that it would provide a more realistic sense of the *obstacles* to achieving racial justice. It is a standard criticism of normative political philosophy, especially from nonphilosophers, that the authors of these inspiring works give us no indication at all as to how these admirable ideals are to be realized, of how we are to get from A to Z. By contrast, in the left tradition—at least the non-amoralist strain of it—the claim has always been that the strength of a materialist approach is that it not only articulates ideals but shows how they can be made real, that it unites description and prescription by identifying both the barriers to a more just social order and the possible vehicles for overcoming those barriers. If race and racism are thought of in the standard individualistic terms of irrational prejudice, lack of education, and so on, then their endurance over so many years becomes puzzling. Once one understands that they are tied to benefit, on the other hand, the mystery evaporates: racial discrimination is, in one uncontroversial sense of the word, "rational," linked to interest. Studies have shown that the major determinant of both white and black attitudes on issues related to race is their respective perceptions of their *collective group interests*—of how, in other words, their group will be affected by whatever public policy matter is up for debate (see Kinder and Sanders 1996). (To repeat an earlier point of comparison with class: the role of group interests in determining consciousness, which was Marx's hoped-for engine of proletarian revolution, is *far more* convincingly borne out, at least in the United States, for race than it is for class.) Rational white perception of their vested group interest in the established racial status quo can then be understood as the primary reason for their resistance to change.

But, as with orthodox left theory, a materialist, or at least realist, privileging of group interests as the engine of the social dynamic also opens up the possibility of progressive social change. The natural constituency is, of course, the population of color, who would be the obvious beneficiaries of the end or considerable diminution of white supremacy. But given their minority status both in straightforward quantitative terms and, more important, the qualitative dimension of access to social sources of power, they will clearly not be able to do it on their own. I suggest there are two main political strategies for recruiting a smaller or larger section of the white population to the struggle. The left strategy, which comes in a classic Marxist version as well as a milder, left-liberal and social-democratic version, would seek to split off those whites who benefit less from white supremacy and try to persuade them that they—or perhaps they and their children (the appeal might be more convincing in terms of long-term outcomes)—would be better off in an alternative nonracial social order, socialism for Marx, social-democratic redistributivist capitalism for liberals. The strategy would be to appeal to group interests as well as justice, the latter, alas, not having historically proven itself to be that efficacious as a social prime mover. White workers, for example, would be asked to compare their present situation not to that of blacks in this actual system, RS, but to what their situation would be in a counterfactual nonracial system, ~RS, the presumption being that a convincing case can be made that though they do gain in this present order, they lose by comparison to an alternative one. Indeed, with the massive upward transfer of wealth in the booming 1990s, followed by the collapse of the last few years, some theorists might argue for increasing interracial class convergence (see Wilson 1999). The other, more centrist political strategy would try to appeal to the white population as a *whole,* the argument this time being that in a sense racism hurts everybody, given the costs of racial exclusion (the expenses of incarcerating the huge prison population, the untapped resources of marginalized racial groups), and that from an efficiency point of view the overall GDP would be greater in a nonracist United States.

It might be felt, understandably enough, that there is something ignoble, perhaps even demeaning, about such arguments and that the case for racial justice should be made on moral grounds alone. I am in sympathy with such a feeling, but I want to differentiate two ways of presenting these arguments: (1) the demand for racial justice cannot be justified on purely moral grounds, and (2) the motivation for the white majority to implement racial justice cannot be activated on purely moral grounds. Endorsing the second does not commit one to endorsing the first. The struggle for racial justice is indeed a noble struggle, and on moral grounds alone its completion is indeed justifiable. But unfortunately—whether as a general truth about human beings or as a more contingent truth about human beings socialized by racial privilege—I do not think the historical evidence supports the view that many whites will be effectively motivated purely by such considerations. Philip Klinkner and Rogers Smith's (1999) important recent book, *The Unsteady March,* for example, makes what is to my mind a convincing historical case that major racial progress in the United States has depended, whether in the Revolutionary War, the Civil War, or the Cold War, on the contingent convergence of a white elite or white majoritarian agenda with black interests, and in the present time period, absent such convergence, we are in for more rollback.

I want to conclude by pointing out a possible obstacle to interest-based theoretical optimism about the possibilities for the realization of a nonracial social order—that is, an obstacle apart from the obvious ones (familiar from the 1980s discussions of proletarian rationality) of transition costs as a factor in one's calculations, the temptations of free-riding, and the simple preference for the comfortable familiar rather than the dangerous unknown. The multidimensionality of the wages of whiteness means that it is possible for the benefits to come apart and be in opposition to one another in a way not found in straightforward working-class computations of gain under socialism. Material benefit does not necessarily include any relational aspect to others, but benefits of a political or status or cultural or "ontological" kind do. In other words, if it has become important to whites that they be politically dominant, have higher racial social status, enjoy the hegemonic culture, and be positioned "ontologically" as the superior race, then the threatened loss of these perks of whiteness may well outweigh for them the gains they will be able to make in straight financial terms in a deracialized system. One can only be white in relation to nonwhites. So some or many whites may calculate, consciously or unconsciously, that by this particular metric of value they gain more by retaining the present system than by trying to alter it, even if by conventional measures they would be better off in the alternative one. It may well be, then, that apart from all the other problems to be overcome, this simple fact alone is powerful enough to derail the whole project.

Nonetheless, the important thing is obviously to get the debate going, so that discussion of these issues in an increasingly nonwhite United States can move from the margins to the mainstream. Facing up to the historically white-supremacist character of the polity and the society will be an important conceptual move in facilitating this debate, and philosophy, committed by its disciplinary pretensions to both Truth (getting it right) and Justice (making it right), can and should play an important role in bringing about this paradigm shift, even if—or rather especially since—it has been culpably absent so far.

This chapter was originally presented as a paper at a conference, "The Moral Legacy of Slavery: Repairing Injustice," sponsored by the Department of Philosophy, Bowling Green State University, October 18–19, 2002. It was subsequently published in Martin and Yaquinto (2003) and is reprinted here with permission.

REFERENCES

Andersen, Margaret L. 2003. "Whitewashing Race: A Critical Perspective on Whiteness." In *White Out: The Continuing Significance of Racism,* edited by Ashley W. Doane and Eduardo Bonilla-Silva. New York: Routledge.

Bernal, Martin. 1987. *Black Athena: The Afroasiatic Roots of Classical Civilization.* Vol. 1. New Brunswick, N.J.: Rutgers University Press.

———. 2001. *Black Athena Writes Back: Martin Bernal Responds to His Critics,* edited by David Chioni Moore. Durham, N.C.: Duke University Press.

Boxill, Bernard. 1984/1992. *Blacks and Social Justice.* Rev. ed. Lanham, Md.: Rowman & Littlefield.

Brodkin, Karen. 1998. *How Jews Became White Folks and What That Says About Race in America.* New Brunswick, N.J.: Rutgers University Press.

Doane, Ashley W. 2003. "Rethinking Whiteness Studies." In *White Out: The Continuing Significance of Racism,* edited by Ashley W. Doane and Eduardo Bonilla-Silva. New York: Routledge.

DuBois, William E. B. 1920/1995. "The Souls of White Folk." In *W. E. B. DuBois: A Reader,* edited by David Levering Lewis. New York: Henry Holt.

———. 1903/1996. *The Souls of Black Folk.* New York: Penguin.

———. 1935/1998. *Black Reconstruction in America, 1860–1880.* New York: Free Press.

Dymski, Gary A. 1997. "Racial Inequality and Capitalist Exploitation." In *Exploitation,* edited by Kai Nielsen and Robert Ware. Atlantic Highlands, N.J.: Humanities Press.

Fredrickson, George. 1981. *White Supremacy: A Comparative Study in American and South African History.* New York: Oxford University Press.

Harris, Cheryl. 1993. "Whiteness as Property." *Harvard Law Review* 106(8): 1709–91.

Haslanger, Sally A. 1995. "Ontology and Social Construction." *Philosophical Topics* 23(2): 95–125.

Ignatiev, Noel. 1995. *How the Irish Became White.* New York: Routledge.

Jacobson, Matthew Frye. 1998. *Whiteness of a Different Color: European Immigrants and the Alchemy of Race.* Cambridge, Mass.: Harvard University Press.

Kinder, Donald R., and Lynn M. Sanders. 1996. *Divided by Color: Racial Politics and Democratic Ideals.* Chicago: University of Chicago Press.

Klinkner, Philip A., and Rogers M. Smith. 1999. *The Unsteady March: The Rise and Decline of Racial Equality in America.* Chicago: University of Chicago Press.

Laden, Anthony Simon. 2003. "The House That Jack Built: Thirty Years of Reading Rawls." *Ethics* 113(2): 367–90.

Lefkowitz, Mary R., and Guy MacLean. 1996. *Black Athena Revisited.* Chapel Hill: University of North Carolina Press.

Lenin, Vladimir I. 1916/1996. *Imperialism: The Highest Stage of Capitalism.* Chicago: Pluto Press.

Lipset, Seymour Martin, and Gary Marks. 2000. *It Didn't Happen Here: Why Socialism Failed in the United States.* New York: W. W. Norton.

Lipsitz, George. 1998. *The Possessive Investment in Whiteness: How White People Profit from Identity Politics.* Philadelphia: Temple University Press.

Lyman, Stanford M. 1993. "Race Relations as Social Process: Sociology's Resistance to a Civil Rights Orientation." In *Race in America: The Struggle for Equality,* edited by Herbert Hill and James E. Jones Jr. Madison: University of Wisconsin Press.

Martin, Michael T., and Marilyn Yaquinto, eds. 2003. *America's Unpaid Debt: Slavery and Racial Justice.* Working Papers Series on Historical Systems, Peoples, and Cultures 14–16. Bowling Green, Ohio: Bowling Green State University, Department of Ethnic Studies (May).

Marx, Karl, and Frederick Engels. 1975. *Collected Works.* Vol. 3. New York: International Publishers.

McGary, Howard. 1999. *Race and Social Justice.* Malden, Mass.: Blackwell.

Mills, Charles W. 1997. *The Racial Contract.* Ithaca, N.Y.: Cornell University Press.

———. 1998. " 'But What Are You *Really?'* The Metaphysics of Race." In Charles W. Mills, *Blackness Visible: Essays on Philosophy and Race.* Ithaca, N.Y.: Cornell University Press.

———. 1999. "European Spectres." *Journal of Ethics* (special issue on Marx and Marxism) 3(2): 133–55.

———. 2003. *From Class to Race: Essays in White Marxism and Black Radicalism.* Lanham, Md.: Rowman & Littlefield.

Okin, Susan Moller. 1989. *Justice, Gender, and the Family.* New York: Basic Books.

Oliver, Melvin L., and Thomas M. Shapiro. 1995. *Black Wealth/White Wealth: A New Perspective on Racial Inequality.* New York: Routledge.

Rawls, John. 1971. *A Theory of Justice.* Cambridge, Mass.: Harvard University Press.

———. 1993. *Political Liberalism.* New York: Columbia University Press.

Richardson, Henry, and Paul Weithman, eds. 1999. *The Philosophy of Rawls: A Collection of Essays.* 5 vols. New York: Garland.

Robinson, Cedric. 1983/2000. *Black Marxism: The Making of the Black Radical Tradition.* Chapel Hill: University of North Carolina Press.

Roediger, David. 1991/1999. *The Wages of Whiteness: Race and the Making of the American Working Class.* Rev. ed. New York: Verso.

Roemer, John. 1982. *A General Theory of Exploitation and Class.* Cambridge, Mass.: Harvard University Press.

Smith, Rogers M. 1997. *Civic Ideals: Conflicting Visions of Citizenship in U.S. History.* New Haven, Conn.: Yale University Press.

Sundstrom, Ronald R. 2002. " 'Racial' Nominalism." *Journal of Social Philosophy* 33(2): 193–210.

Wertheimer, Alan. 1996. *Exploitation.* Princeton, N.J.: Princeton University Press.

Wilson, William Julius. 1999. *The Bridge over the Racial Divide: Rising Inequality and Coalition Politics.* Berkeley, Calif.: University of California Press.

INDEX

Boldface numbers refer to figures and tables.